PARTY AND MANAGEMENT IN
PARLIAMENT, 1660–1784

Party and Management in Parliament, 1660-1784

edited by Clyve Jones

1984

LEICESTER UNIVERSITY PRESS

ST. MARTIN'S PRESS, NEW YORK

First published in 1984 by Leicester University Press
Copyright © Leicester University Press
All rights reserved. No part of this publication may be
reproduced, stored in a retrieval system, or transmitted,
in any form or by any means, electronic, mechanical,
photocopying, recording or otherwise, without the prior
permission of the Leicester University Press.

Designed by Douglas Martin
Typeset in IBM Journal by Joshua Associates, Oxford
Printed and bound in Great Britain by The Pitman Press, Bath

British Library Cataloguing in Publication Data

Party and management in Parliament, 1660–1784
1 Great Britain. *Parliament* – History
2 Great Britain – Politics and government – 1660–1714
3 Great Britain – Politics and government – 18th century
I. Jones, Clyve
328.41'09   JN536

ISBN 0-7185-1199-9

First published in the United States of America in 1984 by
St. Martin's Press, Inc., 175 Fifth Avenue, New York,
NY 10010

Library of Congress Cataloging in Publication Data

Main entry under title:

Party and management in Parliament, 1660–1784.

Includes bibliographical references and index.
Contents: The "Presbyterian" opposition and the emergence
of party in the House of Lords in the reign of Charles II /
Richard Davis – The "Country" interest and the party
system, 1689–c. 1720 / David Hayton – Ashby v. White: the
case of the men of Aylesbury, 1701–4 / Eveline Cruickshanks
– [etc.]
1. Great Britain. Parliament – History – 17th century –
Addresses, essays, lectures. 2. Great Britain. Parliament –
History – 18th century – Addresses, essays, lectures.
3. Political parties – Great Britain – History – 17th century
– Addresses, essays, lectures. 4. Political parties – Great
Britain – History – 18th century – Addresses, essays, lectures.
I. Jones, Clyve, 1944–.
JN521.P37 1984   328.41'09   83-40519

ISBN 0-312-59755-X

Contents

For G.S.H.   *but for whom*

Preface

The idea for this volume of essays arose from the work on *A Register of Parliamentary Lists, 1660–1761* (University of Leicester History Department Occasional Publications no. 1, 1979). It was clear that a good deal of new material had recently come to light concerning the history of Parliament in this period, which in many respects added to the known facts and altered the interpretations of previous work. This was particularly true in relation to areas of party development and parliamentary management. Four of the contributors to the *Register* were actively engaged on research into various aspects of parliamentary history, and were keenly interested in carrying on that partnership. Two others agreed to join. It is hoped that these essays will help to stimulate further work in the field.

The editor and contributors would like to thank the following individuals and institutions for allowing them to use and quote from manuscripts in their possession: the Duke of Devonshire and the Trustees of the Chatsworth Settlement; the Marquess of Bute; the Marquess of Downshire; the Marquess of Lothian; the Earl of Dartmouth; the Earl of Harrowby; Lord Binning; Lord Bolton; Lady Anne Bentinck; the Beinecke Rare Books and Manuscripts Library, Yale University, New Haven, Conn.; Berkshire Record Office; Bodleian Library; Boston Public Library, Boston, Mass.; British Library; Cambridge University Library; Cornwall Record Office; East Suffolk Record Office; Hertfordshire Record Office; House of Lords Record Office; Henry E. Huntington Library, San Marino, California; Kenneth A. Spencer Research Library, University of Kansas, Lawrence, Kansas; Kent Archives Office; Leicestershire Record Office; National Library of Scotland; Northamptonshire Record Office; North Yorkshire Record Office; Nottingham University Library; Public Record Office; Scottish Record Office; Staffordshire Record Office; and the William Andrews Clark Memorial Library, University of California, Los Angeles.

The contributors would also like to thank the following for their help: Dr J. V. Beckett, Dr Linda Colley, Professor Jess Stoddard Flemion, Professor Geoffrey Holmes, Professor Henry Horwitz, Professor Mary Frear Keeler, Dr F. P. Lock, Dr P. E. Murrell, Dr O. G. Pickard, Dr P. W. J. Riley and Dr Daniel Szechi. Eveline Cruickshanks, David Hayton and Bill Speck would like to thank the History of Parliament Trust for allowing them to use unpublished draft biographies and constituency articles and transcripts of manuscripts in its possession. Eveline Cruickshanks, Richard Davis, David Hayton and Clyve Jones would like to thank the Huntington

Library for awarding them visiting fellowships which enabled them to consult manuscripts and provided stimulating surroundings in which to work. Eveline Cruickshanks, David Hayton and Clyve Jones would also like to thank the Twenty-Seven Foundation for generous financial assistance towards their researches in America. Richard Davis and Clyve Jones wish to thank their universities and departments (Department of History, Washington University, St Louis, and the Institute of Historical Research, University of London) for their encouragement and support.

Finally, thanks are due to Mrs Sandra Herbert for typing a large part of this volume, and to Mr Alasdair Hawkyard for indexing it.

Clyve Jones October 1982

Notes on the contributors

Eveline Cruickshanks, B.A., Ph.D. (London), is editor of the 1690–1715 volumes of *The History of Parliament*. She is also editor of *Parliamentary History: A Yearbook*, which first appeared in 1982. Her publications include *Political Untouchables: The Tories and the '45* (1979) and (as editor) *Ideology and Conspiracy: Aspects of Jacobitism, 1689–1759* (1982).

Richard Davis, B.A. (Amherst), Ph.D. (Columbia), M. Litt. (Cambridge), is Professor of History at Washington University, St Louis. His publications include *Dissent in Politics, 1780–1830* (1971), *Political Change and Continuity, 1760–1885: A Buckinghamshire Study* (1972), *Disraeli* (1976), and *The English Rothschilds* (1983).

David Hayton, B.A. (Manchester), D. Phil. (Oxford), is Research Assistant on the 1690–1715 volumes of *The History of Parliament*. He has published (as co-editor) *Penal Era and Golden Age: Essays in Irish History, 1690–1800* (1979) and several articles, mainly on Anglo-Irish relations in the late seventeenth and early eighteenth centuries.

Clyve Jones, B.A., M. Litt. (Lancaster), M.A. (Sheffield), is Assistant Librarian at the Institute of Historical Research, University of London. He is co-editor with Geoffrey Holmes of *The London Diaries of William Nicolson, Bishop of Carlisle, 1702–18* (1984), and has published several articles, mainly on the House of Lords, 1689–1720.

Paul Kelly, M.A., D. Phil. (Oxford) worked in the University of London Library and as Assistant Keeper of Manuscripts at the National Library of Scotland, Edinburgh, until 1981. He has published several articles on late-eighteenth-century English politics.

W. A. Speck, M.A., D. Phil. (Oxford), is G. F. Grant Professor of History at the University of Hull. He has published extensively on early eighteenth-century politics and literature, including *Tory and Whig: The Struggle in the Constituencies, 1701–15* (1970), *Stability and Strife: England 1714–60* (1977), and *The Butcher: The Duke of Cumberland and the Suppression of the '45* (1981).

Abbreviations

Note Places of publication are given only for works published outside the
United Kingdom. Commonly recognized abbreviations such as
J. for *Journal, Rev.* for *Review*, have been used; other abbreviations
are listed below.

Add. MS	Additional Manuscript
BIHR	*Bulletin of the Institute of Historical Research*
BL	British Library
Bodl.	Bodleian Library
CJ	*Journals of the House of Commons*
Cobbett, *Parl. Hist.*	*Cobbett's Parliamentary History of England . . . 1066 to . . . 1803*, ed. William Cobbett (36 vols, 1806–20)
CSP Dom.	*Calendar of State Papers Domestic*
DNB	*Dictionary of National Biography* (63 vols, 1885–1901)
EHR	*English Historical Review*
HJ	*Historical Journal*
HLRO	House of Lords Record Office
HMC	Historical Manuscripts Commission
LJ	*Journals of the House of Lords*
NLS	National Library of Scotland
PRO	Public Record Office, London
RO	Record Office
UL	University Library

Introduction

If it has become something of a cliché to talk of a recent revival of interest in parliamentary history, it is none the less true that the last few years have seen an increase in the amount of research and writing on the history of the British parliaments from the medieval period to the twentieth century.[1] Effort has, however, been concentrated on certain periods — most notably on the reigns of the early Stuarts and the English Revolution 1640–60 — to the relative neglect of other areas. At the same time there has been a noticeable shift of emphasis away from the more traditional aspects of the subject, away from a study of parties, management and personalities, towards a study of the mechanics of the institution of Parliament, towards the nuts and bolts of procedure and the study of legislation, its initiation, progress and function. These new developments are to be welcomed, for without an understanding of how the two Houses of Parliament were organized and functioned on a day-to-day basis one cannot fully understand the major developments which were undoubtedly taking place.

The essays in this book, while not claiming to be the vanguard of the counter-revolution, do nevertheless return to a more traditional study of the growth of parties and the development of the techniques of management. The reasons for this are twofold. The chronological span of the book — from the Restoration in 1660 to the 1780s — is a period which has received scant attention since the publication in the 1960s and early 1970s of the important works of such historians as J. H. Plumb, Geoffrey Holmes, W. A. Speck and Henry Horwitz, and the first two sections of *The History of Parliament* (edited by Romney Sedgwick, and Sir Lewis Namier and John Brooke).[2] The fields tilled by these historians produced a rich harvest, the fruits of which are still being digested more than a decade later. The time has come to look afresh at some of the problems raised and to fill some of the gaps left by these earlier works.

One such gap was caused by the heavy concentration by previous publications on the House of Commons, largely to the detriment of the upper House.[3] This relative neglect of one partner in the parliamentary triumvirate is being rectified by a growing interest in the history of the Lords. Two of the essays in this volume concentrate solely on the Lords, one deals with the relationship between the two Houses which was often fraught with difficulty, while one of the remaining three touches upon aspects of the upper House.

The wide chronological span of these essays is matched by their range through the political spectrum, from the top to the bottom, so to speak, of the political nation. While Lord Oxford, the head of Queen Anne's last ministry, struggled to manage the House of Lords, the electorate in the constituencies was developing a system for instructing its M.P.s. Both the 'high' and the 'low' of politics played their part in the management of Parliament.

The problem Parliament presented to the executive was one of control. No matter how much the Crown or Court disliked Parliament it was a necessary evil, for it was the source not only of legislation, but more importantly of the money necessary for the running of government. The answer the Crown found to the problem of control was the management of the two Houses by the Crown servants. This had developed slowly, but by the late seventeenth and early eighteenth centuries it had become crucial. The increased importance of management had been brought about by the growth of parties, the coalescing of the natural groupings within parliaments — the factions, the family connections, the 'ins and outs', the personal followings, the government supporters. The reign of Charles II saw the emergence of the Whig and Tory parties from the crisis of Exclusion, while the post-Revolutionary period saw the earlier traditions of Court and Country appearing once again under William III.

Today parties seem part of the natural order of things, the obvious way two or more groups can gather strength from numbers and improved organization in order to support or oppose the government, in order to push the policies or legislation they particularly favour. To many in the late seventeenth and early eighteenth centuries the idea of parties was anathema. Sir William Hustler M.P., for example, complained of 'the scurrulous distinctions of Whig and Tory'.[4] This view was undoubtedly shared by some of those men whom before 1714 the Crown trusted to run its affairs in Parliament. When the parties were particularly strong the job of manager was difficult if not impossible. The 'first age of party' reached its climax in the reign of Queen Anne, when the two dominant strains of Whig and Tory overwhelmed those of Court and Country, though the latter were to survive within their host bodies to become important factors in the middle years of the eighteenth century. The Crown's servants found it increasingly difficult to steer a middle course between the parties, and Robert Harley, Earl of Oxford, was the last politician for many decades to try. At the beginning of his ministry he put forward his philosophy of government: 'The great care should be', he told Queen Anne, 'that the Bent and Disposition of the People [towards faction] should be guided and directed for the Queen's service and the Public good, and not be at the disposal of particular persons. The two chief methods to do this are 1st By a steady management 2dly Avoiding to give Jealousies.'[5]

Though successful in providing for the queen's service for much of his ministry, Oxford was forced by the party conflicts over peace with France and the Protestant Succession to rely increasingly on Tory support. He was a man out of joint with his times — an essentially non-party man forced to operate through the party system, a system which destroyed his ideal of middle-of-the-road management of the queen's government. Ironically his very success in 1714 in fending off the bid for power by the extreme Tories under Bolingbroke was achieved with Whig aid and assisted the triumph of the Whigs under the new dynasty. Oxford inadvertently acted as midwife to a new era of party rule after 1714, and one-party rule at that.

The Whigs, favoured by an indulgent monarch, proscribed the Tory party, or at least those sections of it who would not conform to the Hanoverian régime. Recent work has shown that the Tory party, however, did not die in 1714.[6] Though greatly weakened, it lived on to cause the Whigs and the Crown trouble whenever it could, and the Tories were usually provided with their best chance when in alliance with a faction of the Whig party which had split from the government.

It is almost a universal law of politics that when one party is dominant and lacks a credible opposition, that party will eventually split. This happened to the Whigs in 1717 when the two contending factions within the party went their separate ways. The logic of the party system necessitated that the 'out' faction, led by Walpole and Townshend, ally themselves with the Tory opposition to force home the message upon the 'in' faction, led by Stanhope and Sunderland, that they were indispensable to government. But the alliance of Walpolean Whigs and Tories was short-lived, for it barely lasted the summer of 1717.[7] Two parties who three years earlier had raged at each other during the heated days of Anne's last ministry were unlikely to prove ideal marriage partners in the calmer 'pudding time' of King George I. The following essays illustrate various facets of the two interrelated propositions that whatever groupings or factions emerge in Parliament (whether they eventually develop into clearly defined parties or not), management will be needed, and that, where there is management, parties will usually develop as a vehicle for the effective organization of opposition. Party and management are in many senses the obverse and reverse of the parliamentary coin.

NOTES

1. This is perhaps most evident in the recent establishment of a new annual publication, *Parliamentary History*, designed to act as an outlet for new work in the field of British parliamentary history.
2. *The History of Parliament: The House of Commons, 1754–90*, ed. Sir L. Namier and J. Brooke (3 vols, 1964), J. H. Plumb, *The Growth of Political Stability in England, 1675–1715* (1967), G. Holmes, *British Politics in the Age of Anne* (1967), W. A. Speck, *Tory and Whig: The Struggle in the Constituencies, 1701–1715* (1970), *The History of Parliament: The House of Commons, 1715–54*, ed. R. Sedgwick (1971), H. Horwitz, *Parliament, Policy and Politics in the Reign of William III* (1977).
3. *The History of Parliament*, which in 1981–2 produced volumes on the Elizabethan and early sixteenth-century periods, ignores the Lords as an institution.

4. North Yorkshire RO, ZQH 9/18/102 (Chaytor MSS): to Sir W. Chaytor, 15 Aug. 1710.
5. BL, Stowe MS 248, f. 2: 'Mr Harley's Plan for conducting the Business of the Public as proposed to the Queen in a conference with Her Majesty, October 30th 1710'.
6. E. Cruickshanks, *Political Untouchables: The Tories and the '45* (1979), L. Colley, *In Defiance of Oligarchy* (1982).
7. See C. Jones, 'The impeachment of the Earl of Oxford and the Whig schism of 1717: four new Lords' lists', *BIHR*, *lv* (1982), 66–87.

1 The 'Presbyterian' opposition and the emergence of party in the House of Lords in the reign of Charles II

Richard Davis

There has recently been considerable discussion about the writing of parliamentary history in general, and about that of the seventeenth century in particular. Geoffrey Elton has chided historians of Parliament generally for their preoccupation with controversy and division and their failure to 'realize that the normal condition of sessions was agreement, even harmony, and not conflict.'[1] But he applies his strictures especially to historians of the seventeenth century. Of course he does not deny that there was conflict, but far more characteristic of this century – as of the one that preceded and the one that followed – was 'the reasonable co-operation, in Parliament, of king, Lords and Commons'. Effective government management was the primary explanation of this harmonious co-operation.[2] Even for the eighteenth century, Elton is reluctant to use the term 'party'. Government parties were amalgamations of ministerial connections, and 'the formal organization of opposition "parties" was intermittent and inconsistent'.[3] Elton's stress is on agreement and continuity.

While much discussed in relation to the first half of the century, there has been little or no consideration of the application of Elton's theories to the period after 1660. Elton himself would seem to be slightly uneasy about the period. Apparently because of the preference of Charles II and James II for 'absolutist and Catholic France as a model', the relative harmony which he sees prevailing both before and afterwards applies only 'in great measure' to the period between 1660 and 1688.[4]

Such caution would appear to be more than justified. There can be no doubt that conflict and division begin to emerge, and to make a strong impression on men's minds, early in the period. This is reflected at least as early as 1667 in the language of Marvell's 'Last Instructions to a Painter'. The relevant instruction goes:

> Describe the *Court* and *Country*, both set right,
> On opposite points, the black against the white.

No agreement and harmony here.

This is the first use of the terms 'Court' and 'Country' in what he calls a party sense (by which he means two organized conflicting groups) that Perez Zagorin has been able to find, and I have not found an earlier one.[5] Thereafter, however, there is no doubt that they quickly become part of the common coin. By 1677 we find Lord Chancellor Finch in his speech at the opening of Parliament calling for an end to 'those ill-meant distinctions between the Court and the Country. . . . Let all who go about to persuade others that there are two several interests have a care of that precipice to which such principles may lead them,' he warned.[6] The conflict between Whig and Tory would not lie far beyond.

These divisions were as evident in the House of Lords as in the House of Commons, and for several reasons the upper House provides a particularly useful place for closer examination. One reason is that, while scholars have continued to throw important new light on isolated aspects of the history of the Lords in the period, there had been no attempt to draw all this work together since Turberville's two articles in the *English Historical Review* some fifty years ago.[7] This essay can only be a beginning. It will but touch on the critical question of management. Nor will it be concerned primarily with the growth of factional politics, which Clayton Roberts has emphasized.[8] Rather it will address itself mainly to that phenomenon which made management increasingly difficult, and upon which factions attempted to play – the rise of opposition and party.

The emergence of opposition and party in the House of Lords is especially striking, for pressures for the harmony and agreement that Elton stresses were perhaps never greater than at the Restoration. Relative to their previous position in society, probably no group suffered more from the Civil War and Interregnum than the lords, in their individual as well as their corporate capacity. Many peers were in serious financial difficulties, as a direct or indirect result of the late troubles. Not a few had lent or otherwise expended money in the royal cause. Others suffered from fines and confiscations between 1642 and 1660, as one régime followed another. The interest payable on money borrowed to meet the various sorts of expenditure added to the financial difficulties of the peerage. Not only was the burden of debt greater, it had been harder to bear – for more reasons than one. In ordinary times, the privileges of Parliament (or of the peerage – the Lords after the Restoration significantly tended to use the terms interchangeably) would have afforded some protection from arrest for debt as well as for other offences. But there was no privilege of Parliament for peers after 1649, because there was no House of Lords, its abolition having rapidly succeeded that of the monarchy. Neither was there any more trial by one's peers, since the peerage had now become completely subject to the ordinary courts. All that was left to lay lords were what must have seemed rather empty titles – the bishops were not even left those.[9]

The peerage had been a privileged and pampered class in society before

1640. Not all peers, however, had properly appreciated how fortunate they were. What happened thereafter was a rude lesson, and it was one they never forgot. It became a major object of their lordships that under no circumstances should the events of the 1640s be allowed to repeat themselves. Nor did this object acknowledge much, if any, limitation by previous loyalties — after 1649 there had not really been a right side for a lord. The Earl of Manchester, a former commander of the parliamentary armies and Speaker of the House of Lords, was not indulging in mere flattery when he welcomed Charles II back with these words:

> as the nation in general, so the peers with a more personal and particular sense, have felt the stroke that cut the Gordian knot which fastened Your Majesty to your kingdom, and your kingdom to your Majesty.
>
> For, since those strange and various fluctuations and discomposures in government, since those horrid and unparalleled violations of all order and justice, strangers have ruled over us, even with a rod of iron. But now, with satisfaction of heart, we own and see Your Majesty, our native king, a son of the wife, a son of the ancient kings, whose hand holds forth the golden sceptre.[10]

It was not of course that Oliver Cromwell had ever been in the literal sense a stranger to Manchester — he had known him only too well. The point was that only a king, and a son of ancient kings, could hold the golden sceptre of legitimate rule. And however much Manchester and the other parliamentary lords had once doubted the beneficence of that instrument, they, with their fellow peers, doubted it no more. The attachment of the Lords to the monarchy and their identification of their interests with the king's became one of the most important political facts of the post-Restoration period.

On general grounds, then, the Lords were anxious to support the restored monarchical government. The individual interests of the peerage tended to make the bonds even stronger. The king was the fountain of honour, the source of patronage and promotion, the dispenser of all good things — a factor of particular importance given the straitened circumstances of many peers in the post-Restoration period. There would have been very good reasons for lords to wish to remain in the king's good graces.

The bishops, who had probably suffered most from the Civil War and who were particularly dependent on the Crown for promotion, were another potential source of strength. Up to 1678, when the second Test Act excluded Roman Catholics from Parliament, the number of potentially active lay lords (i.e. excluding such categories as lunatics and minors) did not vary a great deal. There were 132 in 1661 and 131 in 1678, falling to 121 in 1680.[11] The attendance was likely to be closer to 50 or

60. Under such circumstances the 26 votes of the two archbishops and the 24 bishops were extremely important. They were a compact and relatively easily organized group; and, as proxies counted in votes in the House, it was unnecessary for all to be there in person. In fact, their attendance record varied and they were not as assiduous as is sometimes thought.[12] But they were easily mustered in a crisis. And from the beginning, careful attention was given to marshalling both their persons and their proxies, long before such attention was given to their lay brethren.[13]

With such promising potential for management, it is perhaps surprising that the Crown and its ministers were not more successful than they were. True, the Lords usually accommodated the king's ministers in the end, but this would appear often to have been more the result of good luck than of good management. Part of the difficulty undoubtedly lay in the policies of the later Stuart kings and their ministers, though in their dealings with the Lords lack of policy was perhaps equally important. For if it is true that eighteenth-century oppositions were intermittent and inconsistent, these terms have even more force in describing the parliamentary positions of Restoration 'governments', especially in the Lords. It was frequently difficult to determine where the king stood on a particular issue; that position often changed, and those of his ministers were all too apt to be at variance from the start.

In so far, however, as the problems of ministers in the Lords stemmed from the pursuit of certain policies, those that gave rise to controversy there were not always identical to those that stirred the Commons. If absolutism and Catholicism were the bugbears of the lower House, and concern for the religion and liberties of Englishmen their response, then it must be said that at least until the mid-1670s the Lords showed little concern for civil liberties, while at the same time they would have allowed considerably more latitude in religion than the Commons were willing to contemplate. Of all the secular issues that agitated the 'Country' opposition in the Commons in these years — taxation, war, abuse of the royal prerogative and stricter checks upon the Crown — there was only one issue, and that hardly one of liberty, that evoked any significant and sustained response in the Lords: the Irish Cattle Bill of 1666-7. Otherwise, and there is every reason to believe that they would have complied even on that issue in the end, the court could count on the strong backing of the Lords, with only minor dissent.[14]

Religion, on the other hand, gave rise to issues in which the Lords took a lively interest, and these caused early and potent conflicts in the upper House. Though the lines of conflict certainly did not always follow those in the Commons, they were none the less significant. Indeed, it would appear that religion was the single most important cause of organized opposition, and later of party, in the House of Lords. It is a complicated question, and one that has received too little attention.

Yet religion was not a divisive issue in the Lords at the beginning of the period. Modern scholarship is agreed that, at any rate as regards the upper House, designations such as 'Presbyterian' and 'Royalist' have little significance in 1660.[15] The soundness of this interpretation is underlined by the fact that a leading part in modifying the bill of that year for confirming and restoring ministers, in a manner more conciliatory to Anglicans, was played by Lord Wharton, about whose personal adherence to the 'Presbyterian' cause there can be no doubt.[16] (As will be suggested in more detail presently, contemporaries used the term to describe anyone favourable to the cause of those who would soon become Protestant Dissenters.) There was a general spirit of tolerance and conciliation in the Lords during the Convention, with no one apparently anxious to push to extremes, and this spirit would continue into the Cavalier Parliament. The Lords considered measures to ease the lot of Roman Catholics in June and July of 1661. Later in the same session they attempted to prevent a bill against Quakers being extended to other sects. On the other side there was no significant opposition to the passage of the Corporation Act in December.[17]

Up to this point there is little information about the exertion of government influence in the Lords. It is generally believed, however, that there is clear evidence of the importance of such influence, as wielded by Lord Chancellor Clarendon in persuading the Lords to attempt (unsuccessfully, as it turned out) to moderate the strong Anglican zeal of the Cavalier House of Commons in the spring of 1662, which saw the passage of the Uniformity Act. But what is usually held to be the most striking example is the fate of a bill earlier in the session to confirm the 1660 act confirming and restoring ministers. A widely accepted version is G. R. Abernathy's; this has it that a considerably modified bill sent up from the Commons was met on 29 January by a motion in the Lords 'to confirm without change the presbyterian and court inspired Act of 1660, which had specifically provided for the retention of ministers not episcopally ordained'. There was a tied vote, which according to the rules of the House defeated the motion. Clarendon, however, exerted strong Court influence, bringing around seven bishops, the Duke of York and the Catholic lords, and on 3 February the House in effect reversed itself and voted to confirm the 1660 Act unchanged.[18]

In fact, this is not quite what happened. The vote of 29 January, which was on an instruction to a Committee of the Whole House, was on whether the committee 'shall be restrained to the confirming the said act without the provisos, *only with a liberty to speak to the point of ordination?*'[19] What was defeated, in other words, was a motion which would have opened up precisely the critical question that Abernathy claims it would have settled. The vote of 3 February, therefore, was more in the nature of a confirmation of the previous action, and certainly not a reversal. There is no question that both now and later in the session Clarendon exerted his influence and invoked royal authority. With what appears to have been a

close division of opinion, the effect may well have been decisive, especially
in dividing the votes of the bishops, who had been readmitted to the
House in the previous December. But, even if this was the case, there
would seem to have been a large number of lords who were not being
persuaded against their inclinations.

   Such an impression is further strengthened by events the following
year, which might have been far more critical for the lord chancellor.
At the end of December 1662 the king issued a declaration in which he
stated his intention at the forthcoming session of Parliament of seeking
legislation endorsing his use of the dispensing power in such a way as to
achieve freedom for Protestant Dissenters to worship publicly, and for
at least the private exercise of their religion by Roman Catholics. The
legislation actually proposed in January 1663 by Lord Robartes, the lord
privy seal, addressed itself only to Protestants. The Lords, however, were
clearly concerned about whether it was possible to draw clear distinctions,
and Robartes was occupied as late as 19 March attempting to devise wording excluding 'Romish recusants'.[20] As so often, Clarendon's role is
obscure. It is clear that he did not, as he later hinted, put an effective
end to the bill's progress with his speech of 12 March (his first appearance
of the session). The violence of the Commons against both Catholics
and Dissenters did that. Clarendon was, however, widely blamed, and this
gave rise to the first organized opposition during this reign in the House
of Lords.[21]

   The occasion was provided by what has usually been seen as a hare-
brained attempt by the Earl of Bristol to impeach the lord chancellor.
G. F. T. Jones, however, has seen a much wider significance in the event,
arguing that it marked an effort not only to remove Clarendon but to
reverse the policies with which he was identified.[22] Though some scholars
have been inclined to be sceptical, a careful scrutiny of the evidence and of
surrounding events tends to confirm this interpretation. Among the papers
of Lord Wharton is a list of 44 peers, holding 15 proxies, whom he clearly
expected to support Bristol's attempt.[23]

   Of these 59, the largest single category is made up of 25 who are readily
identifiable as coming from what the Duke of York would later refer to as
'the Presbyterian and Commonwealth gang'.[24] By this he meant old
parliamentarians and Cromwellians, whom he presumed to be favourable
to Protestant Dissenters. These three elements, with primary emphasis
on the last, were what most contemporaries meant to imply when they
used the shorthand term 'Presbyterian', and used with care it is a helpful
one. The 25 are: the Duke of Albemarle, the Earls of Manchester (lord
chamberlain), Oxford, Bedford, Scarsdale, Suffolk, Clare, Warwick,
Carlisle, Salisbury and Pembroke, Viscounts Saye and Sele, Fauconberg
and Hereford, and Lords Robartes (lord privy seal), Eure, Wharton, Paget,
Hunsdon, Craven, Howard of Escrick, Delamere, Ashley, Crew and
Holles.[25]

There are almost as many Roman Catholics — 20: the Marquess of Winchester, Earl Rivers, the Earls of Shrewsbury and Bristol, Viscounts Montagu and Stafford, and Lords Morley, Abergavenny, Audley, Petre, Arundell of Wardour, Teynham, Howard of Charlton, Stourton, Powis, Cardigan, Langdale, Carrington, Widdrington and Bellasis.[26] The Earl of Newport was married to a Roman Catholic. The other 12 are a mixed group. The Duke of Buckingham, besides being a self-seeking opponent of Clarendon, was also a 'Presbyterian' by sympathy and connections. Others, such as the future Danby's brother-in-law Viscount Campden, may, like his famous relative, have been following the Duke's lead at this time. And there is at least one mistake: as well as placing him among Bristol's allies, Wharton has also placed the Earl of Bath in the list of Clarendon's supporters, where at this point he almost certainly belongs.

Bristol's attempt was a dismal failure. His charges against Clarendon were many, but it was by no means clear that they amounted to treason. Some were undoubtedly wild, such as his suggestion that the chancellor was attempting to alienate the affections of the king's subjects by creating the impression that Charles was a papist. It may well be, however, that the king did not want too close an investigation of these matters.[27] At any rate, he came to Clarendon's aid with a speed and vigour not always characteristic of him, and the impeachment effort soon fizzled out.

The most striking evidence for the existence of the formidable opposition suggested by Wharton's lists, and for its motivation, however, comes some ten days after these events. On 24 July a bill was sent up from the Commons allowing a late subscription for those ministers who by accident or illness had been prevented from making the required signification of adherence under the Uniformity Act. This was read a first time in the morning and again in the afternoon, upon which it was committed to a select committee made up of 18 lay lords and eight bishops. The committee was to meet the next morning before the House sat. It did so and made its report the same day.

The report transformed an apparently innocent bill into something quite different. For the committee had added a clause, 'that the Declaration and Subscription under the said Act . . . shall be understood only as to the practice and obedience to the said Act, and not otherwise.' The result would have been to restore conformity to a mere outward obedience, with no implication of inner conviction. Such an interpretation could probably have been accepted by a large number of those who had been ejected in 1662; and it is easy to understand why, when the clause was accepted by the House, there was a protest against it as 'destructive to the Church of England as now established'. Heading the protesters — which gives a clear indication of the Court's position — was the Duke of York.[28]

The Church suffered no permanent damage. When the Commons challenged the clause at a conference two days later, the Lords agreed to give it up.[29] The question is why it had got through the Lords in the first place. The evidence is not conclusive, but, taken in conjunction with Wharton's lists, it is at least highly suggestive. The fact that the one recorded vote at the committee meeting was eight to four, and that only four members of the committee, all temporal lords, signed the protest, suggests that the defenders of the Church had been neither vigilant nor active.[30] And the fact that not a single bishop appears on the protest suggests that they had been particularly lax: only those present at a vote could sign a protest.[31] As far as one can judge from the attendance lists for 25 July, on the other hand, Bristolians had turned out heavily in comparison with Clarendonians. Twenty-eight lay lords listed by Wharton as Bristol supporters, including eight Roman Catholics, were present, as against only 17 listed as Clarendon supporters.

In his speech at the end of the session the king remarked that he had been led to expect bills against conventicles and the growth of popery: 'But it may be that you have been in some fear of reconciling those contradictions in religion in some conspiracy against the public peace, to which, I doubt, men of the most contrary motives in conscience are inclinable enough.'[32] It had already happened — and it would happen again.

There is no indication of a formidable opposition in the Lords for another three years — not until the last session in which Clarendon was chancellor, 1666–7. There are probably several reasons for this. First, after the 1663 session the lord chancellor's dominance was clearly over. He became but one voice among several. As I. M. Green has pointed out, his dominant role in religious affairs was certainly at an end.[33] Though in 1664, on the question of the first Conventicle Act, the Lords resumed their role of moderating the Commons' zeal and softening their measures, the leading figure now was the Earl of Anglesey, who might best be described as a 'Court Presbyterian'. In the November 1664 to March 1665 session religion was not an issue. It became one again at the session held at Oxford in the autumn, which saw the passage of the Five-Mile Act, but attendance at this session was small, and the bishops were in a much higher proportion to the temporal lords than was usual. On 30 October there were only 29 temporal lords present, compared with 11 bishops; and according to Bishop Henchman's journal, a powerful combination of the bishops and the Duke of York rode over all opposition.[34] Clarendon was not even present.

None the less, he may not entirely have escaped the blame. It is perhaps significant that the following session of 1666–7, which saw renewed violence against Catholics, also saw the emergence of a hectoring and sometimes formidable opposition to Clarendon and to measures which at least purported to be those of the king's ministers.

Though the next session, autumn 1667, provides much more information on the identity of Clarendon's opponents at that time, it is possible

to read too much into the events of this later session. This is especially
true of the fact that a number of prominent Presbyterians in the Lords
seem either to have remained neutral, as in the cases of Wharton and
Manchester, or like Anglesey, Denbigh and Holles, actually defended
Clarendon in the bitter onslaught upon him after his fall. But the fact
that he was already out of office and that the Commons' handling of
the impeachment raised not only questions of justice but also of the
Lords' privileges in matters of judicature, had profoundly altered the
situation in the later period. Clarendon was not without Presbyterian
opponents even then, and other old opponents reappear.

The only extensive list for the period is that of the 28 lords who
protested against the decision on 20 November not to imprison the earl,
as the Commons had requested.[35] Of the 25 lay lords who protested,
eleven had appeared as Bristolians on Wharton's 1663 list. These included
the Duke of Albemarle, the Earls of Pembroke, Carlisle and Dover, and
Viscount Saye and Sele, all old Presbyterians. For three there is subsequent evidence about their religious attitudes. Carlisle had almost
certainly been the mover of the unsuccessful motion to recommit the
Five-Mile Bill in 1665,[36] and of the three still alive in 1670, Carlisle,
Dover and Saye and Sele, all signed at least one of the two protests
against the second Conventicle Act.[37] Three more of the former Bristolians were Roman Catholics — Bristol himself, Lord Howard of Charlton
and Lord Teynham. Of the three remaining old Bristolians, the Duke of
Buckingham had long been in opposition to Clarendon, as well as Presbyterian in sympathy. Lord Berkeley of Stratton could have had a variety
of motives, and I know of no good grounds to speculate on those of
Charles Goring, Earl of Norwich.

Among the newcomers to opposition represented on the protest,
several are worthy of comment. Lord Lucas had been among Clarendon's
supporters in 1663, but he had gone over to opposition early in 1664 and
had taken a prominent part from that time forward as a spokesman for
'Country' causes. Though an Anglican and a former Cavalier, he had
opposed the Five-Mile Bill. Lucas had endorsed the arguments of the Earl
of Southampton, who warned against further provocation of Dissenters
and pleaded instead for toleration.[38] He had thus come to be at least a
supporter of Presbyterian causes. The Earl of Kent, the future Exclusionist, was married to Lucas's only child. Finally, Lord Powis was a Roman
Catholic, who had recently succeeded his father, a Bristolian of 1663.

The protesters of the autumn of 1667, therefore, include a number who
might reasonably be presumed to have been opposed to the religious
policies associated with Clarendon's name. It is likely that most of the
rest of the names on the protest, including three bishops (there would
have been four[39]) and a number of well-known courtiers, represent another
factor: the strong and consistent royal influence exerted against the
former lord chancellor in this session.[40] Lord Arlington represents

that too, as well as the long history of division among the king's chief advisers.

Clearly, the steady and consistent use of royal influence against him had not been a factor in the previous session, the last in which Clarendon had been in office. The chancellor had, however, been in serious difficulties in the 1666–7 session. The passage of the Irish Cattle Bill over his strenuous opposition is one example, but there had been special circumstances. The prohibition of the importation of Irish cattle was naturally very popular with English landowners. The chancellor of the Exchequer, Lord Ashley, gave a strong lead in this, as well as in other, Country measures during the session. Arlington wavered. And finally, when the backing of the Lords against the Commons could have been secured, the king himself gave way.[41] The management of the Lords on this issue left much to be desired.

More revealing of what might be called the ordinary opposition to Clarendon is evidence in connection with the impeachment, in the same session, of Viscount Mordaunt for alleged abuses of his office of constable of Windsor. The evidence is unfortunately sketchy, as it all too often is. It clearly reveals, however, the existence in the Lords of a substantial opposition to the chancellor on an issue on which the Court was probably as firmly united as it ever was in this period, and when therefore he ought to have been in a position of maximum strength. Mordaunt was, it is true, an old and close associate of Clarendon's, but in this instance it was evident that some of the actions he was charged with had been carried out at the king's express command. Charles did not waver in his support, and there is no indication that any of his close advisers did.

The Commons for their part, apparently not greatly impressed with their own case, soon became involved in one of those procedural struggles with the Lords which actually served to mask what was primarily a political conflict. In this case the pretext was the Commons' attempt to dictate detailed arrangements for the trial. More fundamentally, this represented a successful ploy by the opposition in the lower House to obstruct the king's business.[42] What is of interest for the purposes of this essay is the evidence of the considerable backing the ploy received in the Lords. On 5 February 1667 the Commons requested a free conference to discuss the impeachment procedures. The Lords refused to grant one, but the entry of the vote in the 'Draft Journal' shows that the margin of victory among those present was not wide. The original vote was 34 to 29, and only the proxies made it a more respectable 49 to 38.[43] A list of the minority would be invaluable. Unfortunately, no extensive lists have been discovered between Wharton's on the Bristol impeachment attempt in 1663 and the 1667 list of protesters against the failure to commit Clarendon.[44] But seven lords did register a protest against the failure to grant a conference. Three were old Presbyterians — Lord Robartes, the Earl of Denbigh, and Dover, a protester of the autumn. A fourth was

1. The 'Presbyterian' opposition and the emergence of party

the Earl of Bolingbroke, the only peer to protest against the Corporation Bill in 1661.[45] A fifth was the Roman Catholic Lord Audley.[46]

Denbigh would later be one of two peers to speak on 15 October 1667 against the Lords joining the Commons' address of thanks to the king for dismissing his lord chancellor, on the ground among others that 'since the king had not acquainted them with the reasons of his so doing that this thanks was a kind of condemning of a man unheard and unaccused.'[47] A comment in Lord Robartes's journal that the Commons' 2 December message berating the Lords for their refusal to commit was 'a vote unprecedented unless anno 1648 when the House of Commons voted the House of Lords dangerous and useless', suggests that he too would have been on Clarendon's side of the question in the autumn.[48] None the less, and especially in Robartes's case, given his normally high view of the Lords' privileges in matters of judicature, it is difficult to ascribe their actions in February to anything but opposition to the then lord chancellor. Later reluctance to act vindictively against a fallen opponent is no proof to the contrary.

To sum up, then, there seems to be considerable evidence of formidable opposition to Clarendon in the Lords, especially in the sessions of 1663 and 1666-7. The most prominent and consistent element in this opposition appears to have comprised opponents of religious restrictions, as many had demonstrated in the past or would in the future — Denbigh and Bolingbroke as well as Dover, for example, being among those registering their protest against the second Conventicle Act in 1670.[49] There would have been good reason for such people to be attracted to an opposition most of whose major spokesmen were men such as Bristol, Buckingham, and Lucas, who, however diverse their backgrounds, had come to espouse tolerationist principles.

There is no doubt that similar objections to religious restrictions and a similar alliance were the basis of the most formidable and effective opposition of the period in the Lords — the 'Country lords', as they called themselves, of 1675.[50] The continuity of personnel which, as will be seen, existed between this and the earlier oppositions underlines the importance of such factors in the Lords, from 1660 at least until the later date: that is to say, for by far the greater part of the parliamentary history of the Restoration period. The fact that the situation — the personnel to a lesser extent — altered radically with the Exclusion crisis must not be allowed to obscure the earlier importance of what might be called the 'tolerationist' factor in opposition.

The existence of a large number of lords inclined towards the easing of religious restrictions would also explain the apparent lack of any group sufficiently organized and coherent to be called an opposition to Clarendon's immediate successors. There was political conflict aplenty in the period when the so-called Cabal was emerging and exercising its dominance — to the extent that it ever did either.[51] The conflict, however, tended to be between Lords and Commons, with ministers in the Lords taking the side of their own House. That this created serious problems for the king's government is undoubted. Indeed it seems to have prompted the king, beginning in 1670, to take a direct and personal role in the management of the Lords. But the problem was not primarily one of opposition. The closest-run issue of which there is any record is the Roos Divorce Bill in March 1670, when, excluding proxies, votes were 42 to 41 for a second reading and 48 to 44 to commit. Yet not only did the issue divide the king and the Duke of York, a glance at the debates and the extensively sub-scribed protest will demonstrate that it split every major group in the House.[52]

On the other hand, in its religious policy – perhaps the only major policy on which it was united and consistent – the Cabal received easy and apparently willing co-operation from the Lords. The House blocked two conventicle bills sent up by the Commons in 1668 and 1669 and made every effort to draw the teeth of the third, successful, one in 1670.[53] In 1671 a bill against the growth of popery and an additional conventicle bill both died in the Lords. Both bills were committed to the same committee, chaired by the Presbyterian Anglesey. The last action taken on the Popery Bill was on 13 April, when it was resolved 'that a subcommittee shall be named to draw up . . . a test or oath according to the debate of the Committee this day, which being taken may obtain a mitigation of the penalties of the law'.[54] The committee never even got round to discussing the additional conventicle bill.

It is true that the Lords in 1673 could not be lured into a battle with the Commons in support of the royal prerogative as exercised in the Declaration of Indulgence in 1672. They were, however, quite prepared to embody most of the Declaration's intended effects in legislation, and they gave way only reluctantly to the fury of the Commons, which found vent in the Test Act. The Lords were clearly sympathetic to a greater tolerance in religious matters.[55]

It is uncertain whether there remained any real possibility of co-operation between the friends of Protestant Dissent and Roman Catholics in the Lords after 1673 to extend the religious privileges of both groups. In the violent reaction which followed the revelation of the Duke of York's Catholicism, noble friends of Dissent were among the leaders of the hue and cry against papists. So, however, was the Roman Catholic Bristol,[56] and the political flexibility of the traditional Catholic leadership should probably not be underestimated. Yet whether or not Presbyterian and papist could again have co-operated in formulating a positive policy of their own, they showed themselves quite capable of co-operating to block someone else's. Not only did they prevent Danby from giving legislative formulation to his Anglican policy in 1675, they came nearer than any opposition in the Restoration period to inflicting a major defeat on a minister in the House of Lords.

The occasion was provided by Danby's Test Bill, introduced in the spring 1675 session, which would have imposed on all office-holders and members of both Houses of Parliament an oath not to attempt to alter the existing establishments in Church and state. The policy had been suggested in the king's speech and there was no doubt that his influence was fully behind the bill, especially as he had now been personally attending the Lords for several years. The bishops were firm and united in their support, and undoubtedly important. If, for example, one can assume that the 17 bishops listed as attending on 26 April were actually present for the vote on committing the bill and therefore part of the majority of 53 to 37, simple arithmetic indicates that without them the committal would have been lost by one vote.[57] Yet, even with such impressive backing, the progress of the bill was slow and painful; and it ultimately died in the great controversy between the two Houses over *Shirley* v. *Fagg* — a controversy which Shaftesbury and the opposition fanned for all they were worth.

Viscount Conway wrote to the Earl of Essex during the course of the debates that 'nothing is gained but by inches, and every line contested till 10 o'clock at night, the weaker party every day entering their protests'. In describing the divisions, he went on to say, '*Duke* and *Papists* divided and *Papists* and *Presbyterians* united.'[58] He was suggesting, in other words, that York was siding with Danby, while the opposition was made up of papists and Presbyterians. The analysis which follows helps to demonstrate why the progress of the bill was so painful, as well as the essential correctness of Conway's observation, at any rate on the nature of the opposition.

K. H. D. Haley, who unfortunately relies on Turberville's inaccurate figures and non-existent protests,[59] is none the less in one sense right in the point he makes about them. The largest number to sign an individual protest was 23. Eleven peers signed all four connected with the issue, three signed three, nine signed two, and three signed one. If protests were votes, this would undoubtedly not add up to the performance of a 'coherent, disciplined "party" ', which is the point Haley wishes to make.[60] But protests are not votes, and they measure not those who went out to debate and vote, but those who got up early enough the next day to sign the protest.

Attendance is probably a more significant measure. In his calculations for 1680, E. S. De Beer has chosen to take the king's attendance, which as he points out was almost entirely voluntary, as a measure of that of an interested politician.[61] In the spring of 1675 Charles attended 43 of a possible 49 sittings. Interestingly, only four bishops equalled or surpassed this record. Thirty-eight temporal lords did so. Of these no fewer than 19 appear on the opposition lists. Only 14, including the four bishops, appear on the lists of Danby's supporters.[62] Assiduous attendance was probably the main factor that made the opposition of the spring of 1675 such a formidable one. This would have been especially important in the Committee of the Whole House, where the normal rules were suspended and a lord could speak to the issue any number of times. The result would have been to maximize what would already appear to have been an edge in debating power.

Who made up this opposition? The point of continuity with earlier oppositions has already been suggested. If, for example, one compares Wharton's list of Bristolians with the spring 1675 opposition, one finds, after eliminating 22 who are dead and 16 who do not appear on the lists of Danby's supporters or opponents, 14 Bristolians also on the opposition lists in the spring of 1675: the Duke of Buckingham, the Earls of Bedford and Bristol, Viscount Hereford, Lords Audley, Wharton, Paget, Petre, Howard of Charlton (Earl of Berkshire in 1675), Delamere, Ashley (Shaftesbury), Crew, Herbert of Cherbury and Holles. Four were Roman Catholics — Bristol, Audley, Petre, and Berkshire. The rest, with two exceptions, came from that category of Wharton's list whose pre-Restoration pasts suggest the likelihood of sympathy with Dissent. The exceptions, Buckingham and Herbert of Chirbury, both proved their sympathy in the Restoration period, the latter as a friend of the Quakers.[63]

If one moves to the autumn session of 1675, the connection between the 1663 Bristolians and the opposition is strengthened even more. Though the Test issue was not formally revived, it remained the basic explanation of division in the autumn as in the spring. And on 20 November the opposition came close to scoring a major victory, when a vote to address the king to dissolve Parliament failed by only two votes, 50 to 48, with only a superiority in proxies saving the day for the Court. On the division list one finds the names of a further five Bristolians among the opposition.[64] Lord Bellasis had switched sides. The Earl of Scarsdale, Viscount Fauconberg, and Lords Morley and Arundell of Wardour had not previously appeared on the lists of either side. Thus of the 25 peers active both in 1663 and 1675, 19 are ultimately to be found on opposition lists in the latter year as well as the former.

The autumn additions conform to already noticed patterns. Scarsdale was a former parliamentarian, Fauconberg a Cromwellian and one who had spoken against the Five-Mile Bill. Morley and Arundell of Wardour were Roman Catholics. So was Bellasis, who had deserted Danby for the opposition. The continuity between 1663 and 1675 further establishes the significance of Wharton's 1663 list and the interpretation put on it. It is difficult to doubt the existence of a substantial number of peers strongly and consistently concerned with the question of religious restrictions. The analysis so far suggests that the basic components of this group were former parliamentarians and Cromwellians on the one hand and Roman Catholics on the other.

An analysis of the 1675 opposition as a whole, though it adds some new elements, further emphasizes the importance of this group. In the spring 36 peers in all have been identified as having opposition associations, of whom we have already noticed the 14 Bristolians. Of the remaining 22, at least 12 would fit into more or less the same moulds. The Marquess of Winchester, though not himself one, was the son of a Roman Catholic Bristolian. The Earl of Salisbury's and Lord Eure's fathers had also been Bristolians. The Earl of Rutland had been a parliamentarian. So had the Earl of Denbigh, and, as has already been noticed, he, as well as the Earl of Bolingbroke, had evidenced opposition to Clarendon. Like both of them, Lord Sandys had registered his protest against the Conventicle Bill on 26 March 1670. Lord North had also been a parliamentarian, and Lord Grey of Rolleston was his son. Lord Townshend had held office during the Interregnum. The Earl of Stamford and Viscount Saye and Sele came from families active both as parliamentarians and Cromwellians.

Of the remaining 10, an element not previously noticed in opposition is represented by the old Clarendonians. As well as the earl's son and heir, the Earls of Bridgwater, Burlington and Carnarvon can probably be classed among this group.[65] It is perhaps significant that both the Earls of Devonshire and Dorset were listed as uncertain in Wharton's 1663 lists, and were undoubtedly of moderate opinions. The Earl of Ailesbury, Viscount Halifax, and Lords Fitzwalter and Mohun are less easy to classify according to their pasts.

The opposition of the spring remained intact to an impressive degree in the autumn — 28 of the 36 names reappear.[66] The largest single accession of strength came from the Catholic peers. Besides Bellasis, the Earls of Norwich and Powis and Lord Carrington had switched to the opposition; and in addition to the Bristolians, Morley and Arundell of Wardour, the Earl of Cardigan and Lords Teynham and Stourton were newcomers to the opposition lists. The remarkable unity of the Catholic peers in this session, broken only by Bristol who had perversely switched in the other direction, was doubtless connected with the fact that York had also swung over to opposition. Clearly, however, the duke could not command the blind and undiscriminating allegiance of the Catholic lords.

At least two other autumn accessions to the opposition conform to a traditional pattern — the Earl of Manchester, the son of the parliamentary leader, and Lord Brooke. Clarendon's opponent of the 1660s, the Earl of Kent, had been moving in similar circles since that time. The Earl of Peterborough's appearance on the opposition list arose from his closeness to York. It is more difficult to speculate on the motives of the Earls of Chesterfield, Mulgrave and Sunderland, and Viscount Yarmouth. Chesterfield had previously entrusted his proxy to two lords now also among the opposition, Fauconberg and Halifax.[67] Mulgrave, Sunderland and Yarmouth, for their parts, were normally among what might be called the habitual courtiers. Perhaps they were demonstrating that they ought not to be taken for granted. If so, the manoeuvre worked for Yarmouth. He was made lord lieutenant of Norfolk on 6 March following. None of the four seems to have adhered to opposition for long, all being noted as of varying degrees of 'vileness' in Shaftesbury's 1677 calculations of the political complexion of the Lords.

True, Shaftesbury also lists Viscount Newport as 'vile'. In fact, however, Newport, the Earls of Westmorland and Essex and Lord Lovelace, all listed as 'worthy', suggest a new shift towards opposition.[68] Like an earlier convert, Kent's father-in-law Lord Lucas, all came from Cavalier pasts. But it would appear that for them, like him, present issues outweighed past ones.

Up to and including the sessions of 1675, the existing evidence, fragmentary though it is, points strongly to the conclusion that the single most important element in opposition in the House of Lords was an alliance to block the tightening of religious restrictions. Taken together, this would seem to be the meaning of the events of 1663, 1667 and 1675. And numerous instances, both before and between these years, of the Lords' willingness to extend religious privileges or to curb harsh restrictions proposed by the Commons, argue as well for the centrality of the issue in the minds of many peers. Nor is it possible to identify any alternative focus for opposition in the Lords.

Clearly, in order to be effective — even to exist — these oppositions were dependent on an extremely fragile and unstable coalition of friends of Protestant Dissent on the one hand, and Roman Catholics on the other. Together they were formidable, by themselves relatively powerless. The coalition had fallen apart between 1673 and 1675. It dissolved after the latter year and became irretrievable after the Popish Plot scare of 1678. Yet, while the possibility of the coalition had lasted, it had been a critical factor in the politics of the House of Lords.

Meanwhile, as the appearance of new names in opposition in 1675 suggests, the nature of the issues had begun to change. The existence of a Roman Catholic heir to the throne had the effect of making Protestants of all varieties more sensitive to the question of royal power. At the same time, there was evidently a growing feeling that this should not be made an excuse for freezing the institutions of the country into an Anglican — as Danby was attempting to do — or any other sort of rigid mould. Both factors probably worked to bring about a continuity between the opposition of 1675 and the Whig party that emerged after 1678; for the solution to both problems could be seen as a more limited monarchy and greater freedom for Parliament and the subject. In any event, contrary to some authorities, there was a significant continuity.

The accepted wisdom on this subject seems still to be Turberville's.[69] The argument against continuity is based on the following contention. According to Turberville, 32 lords signed the 'six great protests relating to the Test Bill of 1675'. But, he says, the names of 'only nine of them are included among those who voted for the Exclusion Bill in 1680, while eight of them voted against the Exclusion Bill, which,' he resoundingly concludes, 'is sufficient indication of the extent to which Shaftesbury's pertinacious support of the spurious claim of the duke of Monmouth eventually broke up the powerful phalanx of the whig party in the house of lords.'[70]

Unfortunately, there are several problems with Turberville's conclusions. Aside from the fact that Shaftesbury did not press Monmouth's claims in 1680, one must agree with J. R. Jones that it is much too early to talk about a Whig party in 1675. Jones prefers not even to use the term 'party' at this time, though he says one can justifiably talk of 'a real, if not always consistent, Opposition since it opposed the principles of government as well as the person of Danby'.[71] It is probably a useful distinction. In any case, it would seem evident that one could not possibly describe the coalition of interests of 1675 as the 'Whig party', if for no other reason than the Catholic element in it. But this is just the beginning of the difficulty with Turberville's case. In the first place, diligent searching of the *Lords' Journals* reveals not six but only four protests, great or small, relating to the Test Bill of 1675. In the second place, on none of these four do three of the eight names Turberville lists as voting against Exclusion in 1680 appear! Lord Audley's name does, but he did not vote against Exclusion in 1680 — as a Roman Catholic he had been excluded from the Lords by the Test Act of 1678!

It is perhaps better to start again. If one takes the names appearing on the four protests and adds those identified in *A Letter from a Person of Quality* as members of the opposition, one emerges, as has been seen above, with a list of 36 peers.[72] After removing those who are dead by 1680 and two Roman Catholics — a total of 16 of whom Turberville's figures take no account — one is left with 20 who might have cast a vote on the Exclusion issue. Of these, eight voted for Exclusion: the Earls of Stamford, Salisbury, Shaftesbury and Bedford, and Lords Wharton, Delamere, Grey of Rolleston and Eure. Four voted against it: the Earls of Clarendon, Halifax, Bridgwater and Ailesbury. Two more may have voted against Exclusion: the Earls of Carnarvon and Burlington. Six were absent: the Duke of Buckingham, the Marquess of Winchester, the Earls of Bolingbroke and Devonshire, and Viscounts Saye and Sele and Townshend.[73]

The names of the opponents of Exclusion deserve a closer look. Halifax (though a special case), Ailesbury and Clarendon can certainly by no stretch of the imagination be classed among the Whig opposition. Bridgwater's is a much less clear-cut case. Despite his vote against Exclusion on 15 November he was one of those who voted the Catholic Viscount Stafford guilty of high treason on 7 December 1680.[74] This made him the promoter of a Whig issue, though by no means all who voted for Stafford's guilt could be considered Whigs.[75] Perhaps more significant, he also appears on Wharton's list of those who protested in connection with the failure to commit Lord Chief Justice Scroggs on 7 January 1681.[76] (Scroggs was being attacked mainly for blocking the Duke of York's indictment as a papist recusant.) Though Bridgwater's name does not appear in the *Lords' Journals*, Wharton was a careful observer,[77] and Bridgwater's inclusion on his list must be taken as strong evidence of sympathy in what was much more clearly a party demonstration than the Stafford vote.

As to the two who possibly voted against Exclusion, the Earls of Burlington and Carnarvon, their names appear on only one of two surviving lists (each on a different one) as voting against the issue.[78] Against this must be set their protest on the Scroggs vote and, in Carnarvon's case, appearance in the minority in an earlier division on 23 November for a joint committee with the Commons to consider the state of the kingdom.[79] Thus, while there is certainly no evidence of their voting for Exclusion, there is evidence of subsequent support for Whig measures, which must cast doubt on the likelihood of their having opposed Exclusion. Carnarvon's support for Whig causes was not undiscriminating. Unlike Burlington, who voted for Stafford's guilt, Carnarvon was in the minority which held him not guilty.

Of the six absentees from the Exclusion vote, no one is likely to dispute the classification of Buckingham and Winchester as Whigs. Townshend and Saye and Sele, though both were members of the opposition in the spring 1679 session, had ceased to be active in this one. There is no evidence to connect Bolingbroke and Devonshire with either side.

An analysis of the 20 'Country lords' of the spring of 1675 still in the House in the autumn of 1680 suggests, therefore, a different conclusion from that reached by Turberville. In fact, besides the eight who voted for Exclusion, Buckingham and Winchester must be classed as Whigs. There is evidence for giving a similar classification to Burlington and Carnarvon. And there is also evidence that a thirteenth, Bridgwater, though one of the four who voted against Exclusion, gave the Whigs some support thereafter.

It is not easy to say precisely what went wrong with Turberville's calculations. As anyone who has ever attempted such analyses can attest, it is not difficult to become confused. What is clear is that he included some who do not appear in opposition until the autumn, and since the issues remained basically the same between spring and autumn, it seems evident that a full picture requires an extension of the analysis to the later period — which does not much alter the impression gained from looking at the earlier one.

If one includes the autumn 1675 accessions to the opposition, one finds the names of five more lords who voted for Exclusion: the Earls of Kent, Manchester, Sunderland and Essex, and Lord Lovelace. A sixth, the Earl of Westmorland, appears as for on one list and against on another.[80] But as he appears on both subsequent opposition lists, as well as giving a guilty vote at Stafford's trial, it appears safe to include him as a Whig supporter in 1680.

The autumn 1675 opposition list also includes seven peers who voted against Exclusion. These, however, include four — Chesterfield, Peterborough, Mulgrave and Yarmouth — whose adherence to the Country lords of the mid-1670s was, as has been seen, a fleeting one. Nor would there be any reason to suspect the reconversion of any of them, except Mulgrave. He voted with the opposition in May 1679 on the key question of the presence of bishops in capital cases, the underlying issue of which was whether this loyal band of Court supporters might have a voice in determining whether Danby's plea for a royal pardon was valid against impeachment.[81] The question, therefore, was no longer one that could be viewed as opposition to the fallen minister alone, but had to be seen as opposition to the Court. J. R. Jones is right to consider it a critical test.[82] Nevertheless, Mulgrave, though a gentleman of the Bedchamber, voted against the Court on the issue. What is more, he would go on to vote with the minority on the joint committee on the state of the kingdom on 23 November 1680. If, as De Beer argues, he should be classified as a capricious Tory, he was clearly a highly capricious one.[83]

The remaining three of the autumn 1675 opposition who voted against Exclusion are of a different sort. The Earl of Scarsdale and Viscounts Fauconberg and Newport all appear in the minority against the presence of bishops in capital cases in May 1679. This makes even more significant Newport's name on the two opposition lists subsequent to the Exclusion vote, those of 23 November 1680 and 7 January 1681. Clearly Newport, like Bridgwater, despite a vote against Exclusion, did not entirely desert Whig causes thereafter. But Scarsdale and Fauconberg, who also voted with the Court majority on 23 November, seem to have done so.

The above calculations include all the autumn 1675 additions to the opposition who were still in the House in the autumn of 1680 (i.e. excluding ten who were Roman Catholic, dead, or both), with two exceptions. These are York and his loyal follower Lord Darcy, whose proxy York held at the earlier date. For obvious reasons neither could be considered a potential Whig. Nor, as has already been suggested, would it be sensible to so consider Chesterfield, Peterborough, Yarmouth or probably even Mulgrave. Neither, on the other side, can Sunderland be included in that category, despite his vote for Exclusion.

This leaves us, then, with four more from among the autumn 1675 opposition who can safely be identified as Exclusionists and Whigs in 1680-1. In addition, though he may not actually have voted for Exclusion, it is probably safe to call Westmorland a Whig at this time, especially as he would also be one of the protesters against the failure to proceed with the Fitzharris impeachment at the subsequent Oxford Parliament.[84] Of the three remaining members of the autumn 1675 opposition (those who opposed Exclusion in 1680), Newport supported the Whigs on the other three issues of which there is a record, as he also voted Stafford guilty. Scarsdale and Fauconberg likewise voted for Stafford's guilt; but this was the sole issue on which these supporters of the spring continued their adherence to Whig causes, and they are the two clear cases of a change of sides.

In short, there was a good deal more continuity between the opposition of 1675 and later Whiggery than is usually allowed for. To turn the question around and consider only those who actually voted for Exclusion, we find that of the 30, 13 were on the opposition lists in 1675 (this is including Sunderland). The Earl of Clare, a prominent Country lord in the previous session, almost certainly would have figured there had he not been out of the kingdom in 1675. Eight more could not have figured because they had either been under age or had not yet succeeded to the title. The Presbyterian antecedents of a number are, however, evident from the titles they bore — Brooke, Crew, Grey of Wark, Herbert of Chirbury, Howard of Escrick, Leicester and Paget. Cornwallis was the sole exception. Of the eight remaining who were entitled to sit in 1675, the Earl of Suffolk was himself one of the 1660 Presbyterians. Earl Rivers had apparently renounced his earlier Catholicism. Both had been Bristolians in 1663.

I have not been able to discover anything significant in the background of Lord Rockingham, who had succeeded in 1653 to a peerage created by Charles I in 1645. Like Cornwallis, he first appears on an opposition list among the 21 lords who protested against alterations in the Bill for Disbanding the Army on 20 December 1678.[85] The five remaining had all been on the lists of Danby's supporters in 1675. The Earl of Anglesey, lord privy seal in both years, can best be described, as has already been suggested, as a Court Presbyterian. The Duke of Monmouth was an adventurer. It is difficult to account for the Exclusionist vote of the king's old friend, the recently elevated Earl of Macclesfield. The last two are the Earls of Northampton and Huntingdon.

These two names particularly should serve as a reminder that, if, as it undoubtedly did, the Exclusion issue provided an effective rallying point for a cohesive opposition party, the Whigs too, like earlier oppositions, were a coalition of diverse interests. As Huntingdon wrote to a clerical ally in Leicester about his fellow-Exclusionist, Lord Stamford, 'I believe you know that there are but few things relating to government either in church or state wherein we agree.'[86] Both Huntingdon and Northampton had been consistent high Anglican opponents of Dissent throughout their previous careers. Only the Exclusion issue brought them together with men of quite opposite backgrounds.

What this investigation of opposition in the House of Lords in the reign of Charles II suggests is the central importance of Presbyterians and the Presbyterian tradition. To a far greater degree apparently than in the Commons, the old champions of Protestant Dissent and those who came to share their views formed the solid nucleus around which oppositions gathered, from the Bristolians of 1663 to the Whigs of 1680–1.[87] These

oppositions were diverse and their ideas inconsistent, both within themselves and in contrast with one another. What is consistent and inescapable
is the key role of Presbyterians and Presbyterian objectives.

NOTES

1. *British Studies Monitor, ii,* no. 1 (Summer 1971), 4–14.
2. G. R. Elton, *Studies in Tudor and Stuart Politics and Government* (2 vols, 1974), II, 162.
3. *Ibid.*
4. *Ibid.*
5. Perez Zagorin, 'The Court and the Country: a note on political terminology in the earlier seventeenth century', *EHR, lxxvii* (1962), 310.
6. *LJ, xiii,* 39.
7. A. S. Turberville, 'The House of Lords under Charles II', *EHR, xliv* (1929), 400–17 and *xlv* (1930), 58–77.
8. Clayton Roberts, *The Growth of Responsible Government in Stuart England* (1966), 70–1.
9. The Ellesmere and Hastings MSS at the Huntington Library, San Marino, California, provide an interesting variety of examples of the problems, stemming from the Civil War and Interregnum period, experienced by two noble families.
10. *LJ, xi,* 48.
11. These calculations are based on calls of the House in *ibid., xi,* 259; *xiii,* 150–1, 628–9.
12. On the bishops' attendance, see Walter G. Simon, *The Restoration Episcopate* (New York, 1965), 69–71.
13. See Robert S. Bosher, *The Making of the Restoration Settlement* (1951), 237; Simon, *Episcopate,* 73–5. Proxies could not be used in committees, either select or Committees of the Whole House.
14. On the Commons, see W. T. Witcombe, *Charles II and the Cavalier House of Commons, 1663-1674* (1966).
15. J. R. Jones, 'Political groups and tactics in the Convention of 1660', *HJ, vi* (1963), 159–77; G. F. T. Jones, 'The composition and leadership of the Presbyterian party in the Convention', *EHR, lxxix* (1964), 307–54.
16. See *LJ, xi,* 165–8.
17. John Miller, *Popery and Politics in England, 1660-1688* (1973), 98–9; Cobbett, *Parl. Hist.,* IV, 233; Douglas R. Lacey, *Dissent and Parliamentary Politics in England, 1661-1689* (1969), 37.
18. G. R. Abernathy, 'Clarendon and the Declaration of Indulgence', *J. of Ecclesiastical History, xi* (1960), 58.
19. *LJ, xi,* 373. Italics mine.
20. HLRO, Minutes of Committees, 19 March 1662/3.
21. A recent and excellent discussion of the vexed question of Clarendon's position on religious questions will be found in I. M. Green, *The Re-Establishment of the Church of England, 1660-1663* (1978), 203–36.
22. G. F. T. Jones, 'The Bristol Affair, 1663', *J. of Religious History, v* (1968-9), 16–30.
23. See Appendix 2, col. 1.
24. J. S. Clarke, *The Life of James II* (2 vols, 1816), I, 426.
25. Besides standard reference works such as *The Complete Peerage,* ed. G. E. Cokayne (12 vols, 1910–59), and the *DNB,* identifications are made from a list drawn up with similar categories obviously in mind, Bodl., MS Carte 81, f. 63: Wharton's 'List of the Lords of England, 1660' (see Appendix 1). Included are 'Lords who sate' (i.e. in the later years of the Long Parliament); 'Who

withdrew a little' (i.e. those who vacillated); 'Lords who sate in both houses' (i.e. also in Cromwell's Parliaments).

26. Wharton also includes a list of 'papists' (see Appendix 1). Other useful lists are to be found in K. H. D. Haley, 'Shaftesbury's lists of lay peers and members of the Commons, 1677–8', *BIHR*, *xliii* (1970), 86–95 and J. P. Kenyon, *The Popish Plot* (1974), 310–11.
27. Green, *Re-Establishment*, 227–9.
28. For the proceedings on the bill, see *LJ*, *xi*, 570–3.
29. *Ibid.*, 575–7.
30. HLRO, Minutes of Committees, 25 July 1663. The Minutes do not give names, only numbers.
31. BL, Harleian MS 2243, f. 62: the Earl of Radnor's (then Lord Robartes) note-book observes that the Bishop of St Asaph had to blot out his name on the protest against the failure to commit Clarendon on 27 November 1667 'because he was not there present at the passing of the vote.'
32. *LJ*, *xi*, 579.
33. Green, *Re-Establishment*, 229–32.
34. Bodl., Rawlinson MS A 130, 30 Oct. 1665. The journal's author is uniden-tified in the document, but see my 'Committee and other procedures in the House of Lords, 1660–1685', *Huntington Library Q.*, *xlv*, no. 1 (Winter 1982), 29.
35. *LJ*, *xii*, 142.
36. Caroline Robbins speculates that it was either Coventry, Carrington or Crofts ('The Oxford session of the Long Parliament of Charles II, 9–31 October 1665', *BIHR*, *xxi* (1946–8), esp. 221). But Lord Coventry was not present, and Carlisle is a much more likely choice than the Bishop of Coventry or the other two Cs suggested by Robbins.
37. *LJ*, *xii*, 326, 340.
38. Robbins, 'The Oxford session', 221.
39. See above, n. 31.
40. See Clayton Roberts, 'The impeachment of the Earl of Clarendon', *Cambridge HJ*, *xiii* (1957), 1–18.
41. Carolyn A. Edie, 'The Irish Cattle Bills: a study in Restoration politics', *Trans-actions of the American Philosophical Society*, *lx*, part 2 (1970).
42. Witcombe, *Cavalier House of Commons*, 48–50.
43. HLRO, Draft Journal, 5 Feb. 1666/7 a.m. This division is not mentioned in J. C. Sainty and D. Dewar, *Divisions in the House of Lords: An Analytical List, 1685–1857* (1976), 4n., which notices divisions between 1660 and 1685, but see my 'Recorded divisions in the House of Lords, 1661–80', *Parliamentary History*, *i* (1982), 167–71.
44. For manuscript lists, see *A Register of Parliamentary Lists, 1660–1761*, ed. David Hayton and Clyve Jones (University of Leicester History Department Occasional Publication no. 1, 1979).
45. *LJ*, *xi*, 353.
46. The sixth and seventh were the Earls of Northampton and Lindsey (*ibid.*, *xii*, 103).
47. Bodl. Rawlinson MS A130: (Bishop Henchman's journal) 15 Oct. 1667 (but folios out of place and opposite 21 Oct.).
48. BL, Harleian MS 2243, f. 64.
49. *LJ*, *xii*, 326, 340.
50. 'A Letter from a Person of Quality, to his Friend in the Country', in *The History and Proceedings of the House of Lords from the Restoration in 1660 to the Present Time*, ed. Ebenezer Timberland (7 vols, 1742), I, 135, 137.

51. See Maurice Lee, *The Cabal* (1965).
52. The proxies were 15 to 6 and 16 to 6 respectively. F. R. Harris, *The Life of Edward Montagu, K.G., First Earl of Sandwich* (2 vols, 1912), II, 318–24. A slightly different list of protesters is published here than in *LJ*, *xii*, 311.
53. J. R. Jones, *Country and Court: England, 1658-1714* (1978), 167.
54. HLRO, Minutes of Committees, 13 April 1671.
55. K. H. D. Haley, *The First Earl of Shaftesbury* (1968), 321–6; Witcombe, *Cavalier House of Commons*, 135–8.
56. Haley, *Shaftesbury*, 355.
57. *Ibid.*, 375; *LJ*, *xii*, 668.
58. *Selections from the Correspondence of Arthur Capel, Earl of Essex, 1675-1677*, ed. C. E. Pike (Camden Soc., 3rd ser. XXIV, 1913), 8.
59. See below, p. 17.
60. Haley, *Shaftesbury*, 376.
61. E. S. De Beer, 'The House of Lords in the Parliament of 1680', *BIHR*, *xx* (1943–5), 26 and n. 2.
62. The lists of Danby's opponents and supporters are published in A. Browning, *Thomas Osborne, Earl of Danby and Duke of Leeds, 1632-1712* (3 vols, 1951), III, 122–5. See also Appendix 2, col. 2.
63. *DNB*, XXVI, 180.
64. See Appendix 2, col. 3.
65. *Ibid.* This would also probably be the explanation of the Duke of Newcastle, who had previously entrusted his proxy to Clarendon, transferring it to Bridgwater in the autumn 1667 session; and of York holding Carnarvon's throughout the mid- and later 1660s (HLRO, Proxy Books, V).
66. See Appendix 2, col. 3.
67. To Fauconberg on 24 Feb. 1667/8, and Halifax on 26 Jan. 1673/4 (HLRO, Proxy Books).
68. Haley, 'Shaftesbury's lists', 86–95.
69. See, for example, Haley, *Shaftesbury*, 376.
70. Turberville, 'The House of Lords', 58.
71. J. R. Jones, *The First Whigs* (1961), 20–1.
72. See Browning, *Danby*, III, 124–5.
73. There are two lists of the division on Exclusion: BL, Add. MS 36988, f. 189 and Northamptonshire RO, Finch-Hatton MS 2893A. The two lists agree on 45 names as voting against Exclusion. In addition to these two manuscripts, a third lists only those who voted for Exclusion, Bodl., MS Carte 81, fos 4, 654 (Wharton Papers). This is the list printed by De Beer, 'The House of Lords', 37, and it contains the 30 names on which all three lists agree. A composite list is printed in Appendix 2, col. 5. Viscount Fauconberg, however, reported to the Earl of Tweeddale that 31 voted for Exclusion (NLS, MS 14407, f. 72).
74. See Appendix 2, col. 7.
75. Jones, *The First Whigs*, 144.
76. See Appendix 2, col. 8.
77. See, for example, n. 73.
78. See Appendix 2, col. 5.
79. *Ibid.*, col. 6.
80. *Ibid.*, col. 5.
81. Browning, *Danby*, III, 137–40; *LJ*, *xiii*, 570.
82. Jones, *The First Whigs*, 72 and n.
83. See Appendix 2, col. 6; De Beer, 'The House of Lords', 28.
84. *LJ*, *xiii*, 755. Westmorland's known Whig sympathies may explain Fauconberg's report to Tweeddale that 31 voted for Exclusion (see n. 73).

85. Bodl., MS Carte 81, fos 3, 455 (Wharton Papers); *LJ*, *xiii*, 426. See Appendix 2, col. 4.
86. Huntington Library, HA: Huntingdon to J. Gery, 4 March 1680/1.
87. The contrast with the Commons is suggested, for example, by J. R. Jones's analysis in *The First Whigs*, 10–19.

Appendix 1 Lord Wharton's 'List of the Lords of England, 1660' (Bodl. MS Carte 81, f. 83)

What follows is substantially a reproduction of Wharton's list, omitting several illegible words written to the side and apparently not critical to its meaning. A few comments may make the list easier to understand.

Asterisks indicate that a name has been struck out. In Viscount Hereford's case, however, his original inclusion among the 'Lords who sate' is probably significant. These were the hard core of the old parliamentary lords of 1648, a hard core to which some of the Presbyterians wished to limit the restored House of Lords in 1660 (for a recent discussion, see Patricia Crawford, *Denzil Holles, 1598–1680* [1979], 189). Hereford's original inclusion among them, though inappropriate in the sense that he did not accede to the title until 1654, very likely indicates Wharton's assessment of his trustworthiness on religious questions. The other cases of excision occur under 'Lords whose fathers sate' and 'Lords sonnes whose fathers have been in armes', and including as these lists do peers on both sides during the Civil War, their significance for present purposes is at best slight.

Titles in square brackets indicate the title under which the peer actually sat. 'The printed booke', listing 'Lords made since the wars', is not with the manuscript list.

'Lords who sate'	*'Who withdrew a little'*	Hereford
Northumberland	Bedford	Chirbury*
Rutland	Clare	Exeter
Lincoln	Leicester	Strafford
Manchester	Craven	Bridgwater
Suffolk		Winchilsea
Saye	*'Lords who sate in both houses'*	Oxford
Denbigh		Middlesex
Hereford*	Salisbury	Banbury
Nottingham	Pembroke	Purbeck
Delawarr	Stamford	Anglesey
Wharton	Dacres	Sandys
Montagu	Eure	Windsor Q[uery]
Robartes	Howard [of Escrick]	
Rochford [Hunsdon]		*'Lords sonnes whose fathers have been in armes'*
North	*'Lords whose fathers sate'*	
Maynard	Warwick	Carnarvon
Grey of Wark	Poulett	Chesterfield
Elgin [Bruce]	Brooke	Huntingdon*
	Bolingbroke	Dorset

Fauconberg

Scarsdale

Holland

Capel

Conway

Mohun

Spencer [Sunderland]

Finch

'Lords with ye King'

Newport

Southampton

Hertford

Lindsey

Newcastle

Dorchester

Carlisle

Westmorland

Dover

Monmouth

Berkshire

Carrington

Peterborough

Derby

Northampton

Portland

Thanet

Devonshire

Cleveland

Marlborough

Buckingham

Trowbridge [Seymour]

Cromwell

Wentworth

Andover [Howard of Charlton]

Paget

Coventry

Poulett

Lovelace

Darcy

Willoughby

Goring

Chirbury

'Infants'

Mulgrave

Kent

Norreys

Richmond

'Papists'

Petre

Arundell of Wardour

Shrewsbury

Brudenell

Viscount Montagu

Abergavenny

Audley

Rivers

Winchester

Worcester

Bristol

Morley & Monteagle

St Albans

Stafford

Vaux

Stourton

Gerard

Teynham

Arundel

'Lords made since the wars'

'The printed booke'

'Vacated for want of issue'

Dunsmore

Wotton

Hervey

Bath

Danvers

Cambridge

Somerset

Sussex

Essex

Appendix 2   Some House of Lords lists, 1663–81

The following are the lists on which this essay is largely based. With the exception of the spring 1675 list, they have never, as far as I know, been published. Column numbers correspond to the numbering of the lists as given below.

Some of the following lists are composite ones based on a number of different originals. Where the original lists do not agree as to the voting or intentions of a peer, two symbols indicating the difference will be given in the columns.

1. *13 July 1663*, Lord Wharton's forecast of the division on the Earl of Bristol's motion to impeach Clarendon, Bodl., MS Carte 81, fos. 2, 224.

2. *April–June 1675*, composite list of supporters and opponents of the Non-Resisting Test, in A. Browning, *Thomas Osborne, Earl of Danby and Duke of Leeds, 1632–1712* (3 vols, 1951), III, 122–5.

3. *20 Nov. 1675*, 'A List of Lords who voted in the vote for an Address to the King for dissolving of this Parliament', Huntington Library, EL 8418.

4. *20 Dec. 1678*, 'Lords that protested against alterations in the Bill for disbanding [the] Army', Bodl., MS Carte 81, fos. 3, 455 (Wharton papers).

5. *15 Nov. 1680*, a composite list of those for and against the Exclusion Bill (and those absent from the division) based on Bodl., MS Carte 81, fos. 4, 654; BL, Add. MS 36988, f.159; and Northamptonshire RO, Finch-Hatton 2893A and 2893C (list of absentees only). I am indebted to the History of Parliament Trust for my information on the last three lists. Where the original lists disagree over the voting of a peer the sources of the differences are indicated in column 5.

6. *23 Nov. 1680*, division on a motion 'That a Committee be appointed by this house in order to join with a Committee of the House of Commons to debate of the safety of the Kingdom', Bodl., MS Carte 81, fos. 4, 669 (Wharton Papers).

7. *7 Dec. 1680*, division on Viscount Stafford's guilt or innocence: a composite list based on Bodl., MS Rawlinson A 183, f.62 (Pepys Papers); MS Carte 80, f.823 (Wharton Papers); and Cheshire RO, DCH/K/3/4 (Cholmondeley of Cholmondeley Papers). The last list has only recently been brought to my attention through the kindness of Miss Irene Cassidy. It exactly confirms the other lists of those voting not guilty. (Beside 'Lord Aron' is written his English title of Butler of Weston.) The list of those voting guilty is torn off at the end, just as the votes of the dukes are about to begin; this probably accounts for their absence and for that of the three high officers of state — Anglesey, Finch and Radnor.

8. *7 Jan. 1680/1*, 'Names of the Lords who protested upon the previous question about committing Lord Chief Justice Scroggs', Bodl., MS Carte 81, f. 656 (Wharton Papers).

A	absent (Finch–Hatton 2893C only)	b	baron
C	content (CP = proxy)	d	duke
G	guilty	e	earl
NC	not content (NCP = proxy)	m	marquess
NG	not guilty	v	viscount
O	no designation		
P	protest		
U	uncertain		

	1	2	3[1]	4	5	6	7
Abergavenny, b, 1662–6	C						
Ailesbury, e, 1664–85		NC	NC		C		NG
Albemarle, d, 1660–70	C						
Albemarle, d, 1670–88						NC	G
Anglesey, e, 1661–86[2]		C	NC		NC	NC	G
Arlington, b & e, 1665–85[3]					C	NC	NG
Arundell of Trerice, b, 1664–88		C	NC		C	NC	NG
Arundell of Wardour, b, 1643–94	C		C				
Astley, b, 1662–88					C		G
Audley, b, 1663–84[4]	C	NC					
Bath, e, 1661–1701	C&NC	C	NC		C	NC	NG
Bedford, e, 1641–94	C	NC		P	NC	C	G
Bellasis, b, 1645–89	CP	C	C				
Berkeley, b & e, 1658–98	C				C		NG
Berkeley of Stratton, b, 1658–78	C	C	NCP				
Berkshire, e, 1669–79[5]	C	NC&C[6]	C				
Berkshire, e, 1679–1706					C	NC	G
Bolingbroke, e, 1646–88		NC	C		A		
Bridgwater, e, 1649–86	NC	NC&C	C		C	NC	G
Bristol, e, 1653–77	C	NC	NC				
Bristol, e, 1677–98					C(BL[7])	NC	G
Brooke, b, 1658–77[8]			CP				
Brooke, b, 1677–1710					NC	C	G
Buckingham, d, 1628–87	C	NC	C	P		C	G[9]
Burlington, e, 1664–94[10]	NCP	NC			C(FH[11])		G
Butler of Moor Park, b, 1666–July 1680[12]			NC				
Butler of Weston, b, 1673–86					C		NG
Byron, b, 1652–79	U	C	NC				
Byron, b, 1679–95							NG

	1	2	3	4	5	6	7	8
Campden, v, 1643–82	C	C	NCP		A		O	
Cardigan, e, 1661–3	CP							
Cardigan, e, 1663–1703			C					
Carlisle, e, 1661–85	C				C(FH)	C	G	P[13]
Carnarvon, e, 1643–1709	NC	NC			C(BL)	C	NG	P
Carrington, b, 1643–65	CP							
Carrington, b, 1665–1701		C	C					
Chandos, b, 1655–76	NC	C						
Chandos, b, 1676–1714				P	NC(BL) C(FH)		G	
Chesterfield, e, 1656–1714	NC		C		C	NC	NG	
Clare, e, 1637–66	C							
Clare, e, 1666–89				P	NC	C	G	P
Clarendon, e, 1661–74[14]	NC							
Clarendon, e, 1674–1709		NC&C	C		C	NC	NG	
Cleveland, e. 1626–67	NC							
Colepeper, b, 1660–89	NC				A			
Conway, v & e, 1655–83		C			C		G	
Cornwallis, b, 1662–73	NC							
Cornwallis, b, 1673–98				P	NC	NC	G	P
Coventry, b, 1661–15 Dec. 1680					C(BL) &A	C?[15]	O	
Craven, b & e, 1627–97	C		NC[16]		C		NG	
Crew, b, 1661–79	C	NCP						
Crew, b, 1679–97					NC	C	G	P
Crofts, b, 1658–77	C							
Cromwell, b, 1653–68	CP							
Cromwell, b, 1668–82					C		G	
Cumberland, d, 1644–82[17]	U	C			C(BL)	C	G	
Danby, e, 1674–94[18]		C	NC		A			
Darcy, b, 1654–82[19]			CP		C&A	C?	G	
Deincourt, b, 1680–1					C	NC	NG	
Delamere, b, 1661–84	C	NC	C	P	NC&A	C[20]	O	

	1	2	3	4	5	6	7
Delawarr, b, 1628–87	U				A		
Denbigh, e, 1643–75		NC	CP				
Denbigh, e, 1675–85					C	NC	NG
Derby, e, 1651–72	NC						O
Derby, e, 1672–1702					A		
Devonshire, e, 1628–84	U	NC	NCP		A		O
Dorchester, m, 1645–80	C	C	NCP				O
Dorset, e, 1652–77	U	NC&C	C				
Dorset & Middlesex, e, 1677–1706[21]		C	NC		C(BL)&A		O
Dover, e, 1666–77[22]	C						
Essex, e, 1661–83		C	C	P	NC	C	G
Eure, b, 1652–72	C						
Eure, b, 1672–1707		NC			NC	C	G
Fauconberg, v, 1653–1700	C		C		C	NC	G
Ferrers, b, 1677–1711					C	NC	NG
Feversham, e, 1677–1709[23]		C			C	NC	NG
Finch, b, 1674–81[24]		C	NC		C(FH)		G
Fitzwalter, b, 1670–9		NC					
Freschville, b, 1665–82		C	NC		A		
Grey of Wark, b, 1624–74	NC&U						
Grey of Wark, b, 1675–1701				P	NC	C	G
Halifax, v & e, 1668–82		NC	C	P	C		NG
Hatton, b, 1643–70	C						
Hatton, b, 1670–83		C			C	NC	NG
Herbert of Chirbury, b, 1655–78	CP	NCP	CP				
Herbert of Chirbury, b, 1678–91					NC	C	G
Hereford, v, 1654–76	CP	NC					
Holland, e, 1649–75	CP						
Holles, b, 1661–80	CP	NC	CP	P			NG
Howard of Escrick, b, 1628–Apr. 1675	C						

	1	2	3	4	5	6	7	8
Howard of Escrick, b, 1675–8			NC					
Howard of Escrick, b, 1678–94				P	NC		G	P
Huntingdon, e, 1656–1701			NCP		NC	C	G	P
Kent, e, 1651–1702			C	P	NC	C	G	P
Langdale, b, 1661–1703	CP						O	
Lauderdale, d, 1672–82[25]		C	NC		C	NC	G	
Leicester, e, 1677–98				P	NC		G	
Leigh, b, 1672–1710				P	C		G	
Lexinton, b, 1645–68	NC							
Lincoln, e, 1619–67	NC							
Lincoln, e, 1667–92							O	
Lindsey, e, 1642–66[26]	U							
Lindsey, e, 1666–1701[27]		C	NC		A			
Lovelace, b, 1634–70	NC							
Lovelace, b, 1670–93			C	P	NC	C	G	
Lucas, b, 1645–71	NC							
Lucas, b, 1671–88			NC		C	NC	NG	
Macclesfield, e, 1679–94[28]	NC	C	NC		NC		G	P
Manchester, e, 1642–71[29]	C							
Manchester, e, 1671–83			C		NC	C	G	P
Marlborough, e, 1665–79			NCP					
Maynard, b, 1640–99	NC	C	NC		C	NC	G	
Mohun, b, 1665–77		NC	C					
Monmouth, d, 1663–85		C			NC	C	G	P
Montagu, v, 1629–82	C							
Montagu, b, 1644–84			NCP		A			
Mordaunt, v, 1659–75	NC							
Mordaunt, v, 1675–89					A			P
Morley, b, 1655–97[30]	C		C		C		NG	
Mowbray, b, 1678–84					C		NG	
Mulgrave, e, 1658–94		C	C		C	C	G	
Newcastle, m & d, 1643–76	NCP		NCP					

	1	2	3	4	5	6	7
Newcastle, d, 1676–91					C		NG
Newport, e, 1628–66	C						
Newport, e, 1675–9					A		
Newport, b & v, 1651–94			C		C	C	G
Norreys, b, 1657–82		C	NCP		C	NC	NG
North, b, 1666–77		NCP	CP				
North & Grey, b, 1677–91[31]		NC	C	P[32]	NC	C	G
Northampton, e, 1643–81	NC	C	NC		NC	NC	G
Norwich, e, 1663–71	C						
Norwich, e, 1672–7[33]		C	C				
Nottingham, e, 1642–81	U	C	NCP		A		
Ormond, d, 1661–88[34]			NCP		A		
Oxford, e, 1632–1703	C				C		G
Paget, b, 1628–78	C	NC					
Paget, b, 1678–1713					NC	C	G
Pembroke, e, 1650–69	CP						
Pembroke, e, 1674–83					A		
Peterborough, e, 1643–97	U	C	C		C	NC	NG
Petre, b, 1638–84	C	NC&C	C				
Portland, e, 1663–5	NC						
Poulett, b, 1649–65	U						
Poulett, b, 1665–79			NC				
Poulett, b, 1679–1706				P			
Powis, b, 1656–67	CP						
Powis, e, 1674–87		C	C				
Radnor, e, 1679–85[35]	C				C(FH)	NC	G
Rivers, e, 1654–94	C				NC		G
Rochester, e, 1658–80		C					
Rockingham, b, 1653–89				P	NC	C	G
Rutland, e, 1641–79		NCP					
Rutland, e, 1679–1703					C		NG
St Albans, e, 1660–84	NC				C		NG

	1	2	3	4	5	6	7	8
Salisbury, e, 1612–68	CP							
Salisbury, e, 1668–83		NC	C		NC	C	G	P
Sandwich, e, 1672–88					A			
Sandys, b, 1660–8	U							
Sandys, b, 1669–80		NCP	C		A			
Saye & Sele, v, 1662–74	C							
Saye & Sele, v, 1674–98		NC	CP		A		O	
Scarsdale, e, 1655–27 Jan. 1681	C		C		C	NC	G	
Seymour, b, 1641–64	NC							
Shaftesbury, e, 1672–83[36]	C	NC	C	P	NC		G	P
Shrewsbury, e, 1654–68	C							
Southampton, e, 1624–67[37]	NC							
Stafford, v, 1640–80	C	C						
Stamford, e, 1673–1720		NC	C	P	NC	C	G	P
Stourton, b, 1633–72	CP							
Stourton, b, 1672–85			C					
Strafford, e, 1641–95	NC	C			A			
Suffolk, e, 1640–89	C				NC	C	G	P
Sunderland, e, 1643–1702	U	C	C		NC	C	G	
Sussex, e, 1674–1715					C		G	
Teynham, b, 1628–73	C							
Teynham, b, 1673–89			C					
Thanet, e, 1631–64	U							
Thanet, e, April 1680–4					C	NC	NG	
Townshend, b & v, 1661–87	NCP	NC	C		A			
Vaughan, b, 1643–86	NC		NC		A		O	
Ward, b, 1644–70	NC							
Ward, b, 1670–1701			NCP		C	NC	NG	
Warwick, e, 1653–73	C							
Wentworth, b, 1640–65	U							
Westmorland, e, 1666–91			C		C(FH) &NC(BL)	C	G	P

	1	2	3	4	5	6	7
Wharton, b, 1625–96	C	NC	C	P	NC	C	G
Widdrington, b, 1651–75	CP	C					
Widdrington, b, 1675–95							O
Willoughby, b, 1680–92					A		
Winchester, m, 1629–5 March 1674/5	C						
Winchester, m, 1675–89		NC	C	P	A	C	
Winchilsea, e, 1639–89		C	NCP		C		G
Windsor, b, 1660–82			NC		C	NC	NG
Worcester, m, 1667–82		C			C	NC	NG
Wotton, b, 1650–83	CP				C	NC	NG
Yarmouth, v & e, 1673–83		C	C		C&A		O
York, d, 1644–85	U		C				

THE BISHOPS

As bishops are fully listed in only one of the above lists, I have not included them in the table. The comments on them in the several lists are as follows:
1. York, Oxford, Llandaff, Norwich and Bangor: all NCP.
2. 'The 24 Bishops': C.
3. 'Bishops who were all that were in the house at the vote' (but Bangor, Exeter, and Norwich whose names follow were all proxies, so they must be *in addition*): NC.
6. Bath: C. Rochester, Llandaff, Ely, Exeter, London, St Asaph, Oxford, Worcester, Durham and Peterborough: NC.

NOTES

1. Also noted are 'Lords absent and sick who have attended this session and most usually voted with the [opposition] Lords': besides Denbigh and Holles, who appear in the table, these are Bedford and Burlington. Bedford held Lord Crew's proxy (HLRO, Proxy Book, v). Lords Eure and Fitzwalter are mentioned elsewhere as sympathetic (Browning, *Danby*, III, 126 n.2).
2. Lord privy seal, April 1673–82.
3. Lord chamberlain, 1674–85.
4. Earl of Castlehaven.
5. Lord Howard of Charlton, 1640–69.
6. In this and the other cases of double listing in this column, the evidence favours 'not content' as the correct designation.
7. Indicates appearing thus only in BL, Add. MS 36988, f. 189.
8. Lord Greville.
9. So listed only in Bodl. MS Rawlinson A 183, f.62 (Pepys Papers).
10. Lord Clifford, 1643–64.
11. So listed only in Northamptonshire RO, Finch-Hatton 2893A.
12. Lord Ossory.

13. Carlisle is not on the list but appears as a protester in *LJ, xiii*, 738.
14. Lord chancellor, 1660–7.
15. The usual designation on this list is a solid stroke to the right of the name for 'content', to the left for 'not content'. In this case, there are simply three dots to the right of the name.
16. A list in HLRO, Hist. Coll.215/7, misdated 22 Nov., lists Dover instead of Craven.
17. Prince Rupert.
18. Lord treasurer, 1673–9.
19. Lord Conyers.
20. Listed Delawarr, but almost certainly a mistake.
21. Earl of Middlesex, 1675.
22. Lord Hunsdon, 1640–66.
23. Lord Duras, 1673.
24. Lord keeper, 1673–5; lord chancellor, 1675–82.
25. Earl of Guilford.
26. Lord great chamberlain.
27. Lord great chamberlain.
28. Lord Gerard of Brandon, 1645.
29. Lord chamberlain, 1660.
30. Lord Monteagle.
31. Lord Grey of Rolleston, 1673.
32. The list is unclear and this may be Charles, Lord Grey, or De Grey (1676–9).
33. Earl marshal.
34. Earl of Brecknock and lord steward, 1660.
35. Lord Robartes, 1625; lord privy seal, 1661–73; lord president, 1679–84.
36. Lord Ashley, 1661; lord chancellor, 1672–3; lord president, 1679.
37. Lord treasurer, 1660.

2 The 'Country' interest and the party system, 1689-c.1720

David Hayton

Studying news of the 1698 general election, Secretary of State James
Vernon was alarmed to discover 'a strange spirit of distinguishing between
the Court and the Country Party'; in 1702 a pamphleteer wrote that
'Court and Country are as opposite as ever heretofore'; and six years
later another commentator observed that in the House of Commons itself
'the notion of extinguishing the names of Whig and Tory, and assuming
the distinctions of Court and Country party' was being 'taken up'.[1]
On such occasions the two-party system characteristic of politics in
this period seemed to be giving way to a more traditional pattern, for
while the Whig and Tory parties had originated in the Exclusion crisis of
1679–81, the terminology of 'Court and Country' was of a much older
vintage, antedating the Civil War. According to one historian, 'in 1689
the received view of the constitution saw politics as a struggle between
Court and Country'.[2] At times during William III's reign, especially
in the early 1690s, the real conflict in Parliament seemed to be between
Court and Country rather than Whig and Tory, and even under Queen
Anne issues arose which temporarily united 'Country' Members on both
sides. The apparent slow fragmentation of the Whig and Tory parties in
the first half of the eighteenth century; the persistence of the old
'Country' attitudes on the Commons' back benches, independence from
and chronic suspicion of central government and an obsession with the
need for 'good husbandry' in administration; and the employment by
opposition writers in the 1720s and 1730s of 'Country' rhetoric — have
all encouraged the view that 'Court and Country' re-emerged as a
dominant theme under the Hanoverians. It has even been suggested that
the 'rage of party' was only a brief aberration from this norm, and that
Court and Country rather than Whig and Tory was still after 1688 the
fundamental division in English political life.[3] Although this point of
view is an extreme one, many if not most students of the period would
concur that 'party is not the only concept that historians should employ
in their explanation of the workings of the political system in the age of
William III and Anne'.[4]

To admit the importance of Country attitudes, and the existence of

a Country interest in politics capable of transcending Whig and Tory party
loyalties, is one thing; to suggest, as some historians have done, that the
division between Court and Country is as important as that between Whig
and Tory, or that it constitutes some kind of basic political structure
underlying the temporary superstructure of the party system, is another.
Such an argument would go against the conclusions of the most authoritative of recent detailed studies of the parliamentary politics of the late
seventeenth and early eighteenth centuries. The efforts of Dennis Rubini
to prove that under William 'most of the important issues were fought on
a Court–Country basis', that 'contemporaries usually spoke in these terms',
and that therefore the 'character' of politics was 'predominantly Court-
Country', have not survived the criticisms of other scholars. Notable
among these is Henry Horwitz, who, while making every allowance for
the confusions and cross-currents of politics in the 1690s and for the fact
that Whig–Tory and Court–Country alignments might quite easily co-exist
in the same House of Commons, none the less concluded his systematic
survey of the parliamentary history of the reign with a statistical examination of division lists to demonstrate the remarkably high degree of consistency in party voting in the Commons, and with the observation that in
1702, 'as in 1689, the major issues of the day divided men along Whig-
Tory lines'.[5] Geoffrey Holmes's monumental study, *British Politics in
the Age of Anne*, while it gave full weight to 'the Country tradition',
still stressed that from 1702 to 1714 England was 'a divided society with
two nation-wide parties', the Whigs and the Tories, 'whose rivalry increasingly permeated the life, the work and even the leisure of the politically-
conscious classes' – a conclusion which has been borne out not only by
numerous analyses of parliamentary lists but also by the investigations of
W. A. Speck and others into the behaviour of the electorate.[6] And work
on the politics, as opposed to the political journalism, of the reigns of the
first two Georges by, amongst others, Eveline Cruickshanks and Linda
Colley, has shown that the clash of Whig and Tory remained their most
marked feature. Debate there may be over the extent to which Tories
were, or were not, Jacobites; the party's existence as a coherent political
grouping until at least the 1750s is agreed.[7]

But while historians of parliamentary politics in the period 1688–
c.1760 have been emphasizing the conflicts of Whigs and Tories and consistently underplaying the theme of Court against Country, historians of
political ideas have to some extent been reversing this process. Considerable attention has been paid to the 'Country party' writers of the 1690s
and 1720s, men like John Trenchard, Walter Moyle, Robert Molesworth
and John Toland, who, it is argued, formed a vital link between the
radicalism of the mid-seventeenth century and that of the later eighteenth,
by resurrecting some republican ideas, transforming them into a 'Country'
canon acceptable to Tories as well as Whigs, and transmitting this to the
'patriot' opposition which spoke and wrote against the Walpolean

oligarchy and which included Tories like Bolingbroke as well as unrecon-
structed Country Whigs – or, as Trenchard and his collaborator Thomas
Gordon preferred it, 'independent Whigs'. This interpretation represents a
confluence of two streams of investigation. On the one hand historians such
as Caroline Robbins and Bernard Bailyn, tracing the pedigree of colonial
American radicalism, have connected the opposition writers of the 1720s
and 1730s with their radical Whig predecessors of William's reign.[8] On the
other hand J. G. A. Pocock, pursuing the ideas and intellectual influence
of James Harrington and other 'classical republicans', has discovered in
Moyle, Trenchard, Molesworth and other members of the Grecian Tavern
circle the rediscoverers and popularizers of Harrington's ideas. These 'neo-
Harringtonians' (to use Professor Pocock's terminology) forged the
Country ideology which Trenchard and Molesworth themselves were to
carry forward into George I's reign.[9] Pocock has recognized a difference,
and an important one, between the two elements in the Country opposition to Walpole – the 'urban radical Whigs' as he has described them, and
the 'Tory country gentlemen' – but has argued persuasively that the
ideology they shared was essentially Whig, 'Old Whig', and derived from
Harrington; so persuasively, in fact, that his picture of the 'neo-Harringtonians' and their influence has become generally accepted.[10]

This emphasis on the continuity of Country ideology between the
1690s and 1720s and on its importance to English political development
needs to be squared with the observations of the parliamentary historians,
who place the conflict between Whig and Tory unquestionably at the
centre of the stage, and regard effusions of Country sentiment as diver-
sions from the main plot. One means of reconciling the two derives from
the work of an earlier parliamentary historian, Robert Walcott, whose
interpretation of the 'structure' of early eighteenth-century politics is now
otherwise disregarded. Walcott's main aim had been to apply to the reign
of Anne the conclusions drawn by Sir Lewis Namier from his studies of
Parliament in the 1760s, denying any real meaning to the party labels of
Whig and Tory and insisting that the dynamic forces on the political
scene were family-based 'connections'. This theory, carefully constructed
from elaborate genealogies, proved as flimsy as a house of cards. Amidst
the debris of its demolition, however, one element of Walcott's analysis
remained intact: his imaginative attempt to accommodate both Whig–Tory
and Court–Country alignments in one model of political 'structure' – the
framework within which his entirely bogus connections were supposed to
have operated. To do this he made use of an image which subsequent historians have been loth to discard, the compass. Court and Country was
envisaged as an alternative polarity to that of Whig and Tory – north-
south, say, as against east–west. In surveying the political attitudes of
Members of Parliament (as distinct from their obligations to particular
connections) one could 'box the compass', travelling for instance from
Whig through Court Whig to Court, then to Court Tory, Tory, Country

Tory, Country Whig and so on back to Whig again.[11] This image underlies Professor Horwitz's characterization of politics in William's reign, when 'the Commons as a whole wavered or oscillated between orientation along a Whig–Tory or a Court–Country axis'; and even Walcott's most trenchant critic, Geoffrey Holmes, who dismantled the fake 'connections' with ruthless skill, nevertheless still speaks of both Whig and Tory parties as having possessed a Court and a Country wing.[12]

Here then we have an explanation — Court and Country and Whig and Tory as conflicting polarities — to account for the emergence of a potent cross-party ideology in the 1690s and its reappearance in the 1720s. The dominant themes of political argument can be seen as having altered as first one polarity, and then the other, was in the ascendant. Under William the balance was frequently in motion, and in the years 1697–c.1701 at least, it was the Court–Country polarity that prevailed, because of the nature of the various issues arising; under Anne the Whig–Tory polarity reasserted itself, while after 1714 'the Tory party lost its Court wing', the 'Country Whigs . . . went into opposition' and 'together they allied with the Tories in attempts to form a Country party to oppose the Court.'[13] This 'chronology of political structure', so to speak, fits in quite well with the accepted version of political history for 1688–1714. For the period after 1714, however, it is much more contentious. As we have already noted, recent studies of parliamentary politics under the first two Georges, even though disagreeing on some important points, are united in emphasizing the continuity of Whig–Tory divisions. Yet historians of political ideology have argued quite the reverse — that the Tory party collapsed in 1714 and that in consequence 'the structure of politics changed from a division along Whig–Tory lines to one along the lines of Court and Country'.[14]

In part such statements show the influence of studying political ideology in a vacuum, of concentrating on what men wrote to the exclusion of what they did; in part the influence of another Namierite historian, J. B. Owen, whose examination of politics in the 1740s produced a view of the House of Commons in which the only meaningful party distinction was between Court and Country, and who then extended this interpretation as a 'pattern' for the entire eighteenth century;[15] in part the influence of the compass image. In asserting the primacy of Court and Country politics after 1714, H. T. Dickinson, for example, leans heavily on the assumption that there were already powerful Court and Country interests in Parliament under William and Anne, claiming in particular that the Country element in the House of Commons was 'of substantial proportions . . . perhaps as much as half the House'; that there were 'strong backbench elements in both parties which could not bring themselves to give unequivocal support to any ministry'; and that the 'Country interest' 'prevented the development of a simple two-party structure'.[16]

The presence of a substantial 'Court interest' in the Parliaments of William and Anne is undeniable. Perennial Court party men are relatively easy to identify, because they held office (if successful) and because they are more likely to show up on the various parliamentary lists of the period, whether 'management lists' drawn up by ministers or their aides, or 'black lists' of Members against whom the compilers felt it necessary to warn the unsuspecting electorate. The Court stooge was the principal bogyman on such occasions: thus we have lists of placemen, and of those who had supported the Court in such unpopular causes as the defence of the standing army (1699) and the resistance to the 'place clause' in the Regency Bill (1705–6).[17] It is with confidence therefore that Geoffrey Holmes can enumerate Court adherents in the reign of Queen Anne. Even so, he is still more inclined to define them as 'Court Tories' and 'Court Whigs', and he refers to the 'government Members' in both Houses as a 'tiny group', consisting of 'civil servants' such as Treasury Secretary William Lowndes, Secretary at War William Blathwayt, Admiralty Secretary Josiah Burchett and Under-Secretary John Ellis; professional soldiers and sailors; and 'inveterate placemen' like the egregious James Brydges, paymaster to Marlborough's armies, and Thomas Coke, who though originally a Tory squire came to be a permanent feature of Court life, surviving as vice-chamberlain from 1706 until 1727.[18] Some of these men, and other similar types, had been returned to William's Parliaments: officials like Blathwayt's nephew John Povey, 'a little inconsiderable supernumerary clerk of the Council'; and placemen like Richard Jones, Earl of Ranelagh, one of Brydges's predecessors as paymaster, who held a government post of some kind, whether in England or in Ireland, continuously from 1668 to 1702.[19] In the upper House Holmes finds only three strictly 'Court' peers — Lords Delawarr, Hunsdon and Strafford — but to these we should probably add at least some of that bedraggled troop of 'poor lords' whose votes any ministry was able to buy, and others whom the crack of a government whip and the threat of dismissal or promise of advancement could quickly bring into line.[20] The Place Bill of 1692–3 was finally defeated in the Lords, after early Country successes, by a combination of the votes of army officers, gentlemen of the Bedchamber, aspirant courtiers and four penurious pensioners, not to mention the bishops.[21]

When we move away a little in either direction from the Court pole in Walcott's compass, we can find more considerable numbers of Tories and Whigs, in the Commons and the Lords, who found the pull of the Court as strong, if not stronger, than the pull of party. In the years 1690–3, for example, when the king was leaning towards the Tories, there were Whigs willing and eager to hold on to office: men like William Jephson, secretary to the Treasury from 1689 until his death in 1691; Sir William Forester, once a conspirator against Charles II, who had come over with William and been given the clerkship of the Green Cloth; Sir Robert Howard, playwright and placeman, whom William confirmed in his life patent as auditor of the Exchequer and who in 1691 was warning the king of the anti-monarchical designs of the Country opposition in 'extravagant'

terms; the Suffolk Presbyterian Sir Robert Rich and his fellow defector
from the accounts commission in 1691 and fellow lord of the Admiralty
from 1691 onwards, Robert Austen.[22] Then there are the so-called 'Leeds
Tories', followers of the former Danby, now Duke of Leeds, who stayed
in office after the Tory ministry had been replaced in 1693–4 by a Whig-
dominated administration; the 'Harleyites' of 1704–8, most prominent
among them Henry St John, Simon Harcourt and Thomas Mansel, who
had floated into office with Robert Harley on the Tory tide at the beginning of Anne's reign, but broke with the great men of the Tory party in
1704 and continued to support the Court until in February 1708 their
leader was finally forced out of office by the Whig Junto; the 'Lord
Treasurer's Whigs', men of the stamp of Robert Walpole, John Smith and
Spencer Compton, who had been prepared to co-operate in Harley's last
attempted coalition of 'moderates' in the winter of 1707–8, and who afterwards stood by Lord Treasurer Godolphin against the attacks of the Junto
and the bitter criticism of old comrades; and lastly the moderate Whigs,
principally independent-minded grandees like the Dukes of Shrewsbury,
Somerset and Newcastle, who helped Harley to his successful coup in
1710 against what was now a Marlborough/Godolphin-Whig Junto
ministry, and subsequently held office with the Tories.[23]

   While the 'Court interest' thus appears in sharp focus, the same cannot
be said of its opposite. The 'Country interest' is less easy to fix on, since
essentially it represented a way of thinking, a set of principles, attitudes
and prejudices. In this respect Sir Lewis Namier's assertion that the term
'country gentleman' denoted a way of life, and that the country gentleman
outside the House was also a Country Member inside — 'the distinguishing
mark of the country gentleman was disinterested independence' — can be
misleading.[24] Independence was indeed a quality which the well-to-do
country squire could afford, a luxury one might say, but it does not follow
that every country gentleman was a Country Member, or *a fortiori* that
every supporter of Country measures was a landowner with large private
means. Before examining the strength of the Country interest, and
especially its importance in relation to the two-party system, we would do
well to rid our minds of the stereotype of the Country M.P.: a landed
gentleman, pure and simple, untainted by any dependence on government
or by any connection with the commercial world of London, preferring
the peaceful innocence of rural life to the turmoil and corruption of the
capital and the obsequiousness of the Court, and thus more often to be
found at home than in Parliament.

   Such idealized 'independent country gentlemen' existed in our period,
but not in the kind of numbers that Namier envisaged. A few Country
Members did indeed live like *grands seigneurs*: Sir John Brownlow at
Belton House in Lincolnshire; or Sir William Ellys in the same county at
Nocton, 'like a prince' in his 'palace'.[25] Others scraped along on a humbler
scale, 'middling gentry' or 'small fry', or were themselves 'moneyed' rather

than 'landed' men, and not just 'provincial merchants' at that, but in some cases representatives of the great London 'moneyed interest'.[26] The 33 Whigs who opposed the Septennial Bill in 1716 included ten closely connected with the City of London, and of those, two were directors of the Bank of England, two directors of the East India Company and one a director of the South Sea Company.[27] Many leading Country Whigs in fact had City associations of some kind or another: Sir Peter Colleton, the West Indian; the Barnardistons, active in the Turkey trade and the East India Company; the Onslows in the Levant Company; Thomas Lewes, son of a Levant merchant and himself an East India stockholder; Sir John Cropley, also descended from a London merchant and an inveterate dabbler in stocks; and Robert Eyre, Sir Peter King, James Stanhope and Edward Wortley Montagu, all substantial proprietors of Bank stock in 1710. There were 'moneyed' men among Country Members on the Tory side too. The October Club in 1711 contained Samuel Shepheard junior, East India Company director; George Pitt, a director of the South Sea Company; Alderman Robert Child, East India Company director and warden of the Goldsmiths' Company; Sir Richard Child, son of the great merchant Sir Josiah and himself a heavy investor in the Bank; Abraham Blackmore, son of a London common councilman and brother of a City merchant; and Sir Nicholas Morice, another merchant's son, whose own considerable investments were guided by his cousin Humphry, a director of the Bank.

And if the Country party was not composed exclusively of substantial landed men, neither did it have a monopoly of those who were habitual absentees from Parliament. It was indeed a Country Tory who pleaded 'very good hunting weather' as an excuse for not coming up to the House, but among those M.P.s with the worst record of attendance were men on the Court rather than the Country side in politics, like Richard Chaundler, John Cloberry, Hugh Fortescue, William Howard, John Michell and Richard, Lord Newport. One Court Whig, the Duke of Bolton, reacted to news of the disappointment of his hopes for the Irish viceroyalty by announcing his resolution 'of retiring for good and all into the country'; another, Aubrey Porter, was so neglectful of his parliamentary duties that his irritated constituents at Bury St Edmunds proposed not to re-elect him.[28] Nor was it only Country Members who rejoiced, or affected to rejoice, in the pleasures of the country, and Court men who were transfixed by the glitter of the town. It was a Country Whig, Maurice Ashley, a Dorset man invited to stand for Wiltshire in 1701, of whom it was said that he 'do not express any liking for this country nor takes . . . much delight in his own'.[29]

Very rarely indeed could a Member of Parliament, country gentleman or not, affect *complete* independence from central government. This was as true at the end of the seventeenth century as it had been at the beginning. A Country politician still required the resources of Court patronage to maintain his position in his own shire. As Derek Hirst has observed of the period before 1629, a purely Country stance was politically 'non-viable'.[30] The local magnate needed to hold the great offices of lord lieutenant or *custos rotulorum*, the country gentleman to retain his seat on the commission of the peace, and both needed to be able to advance and protect their dependants. 'What I call substantials,' wrote the high Tory Duke of Beaufort in 1711, 'is that I may not be oppressed in my county of Hampshire'.[31] Even that archetypal Country Whig the third Earl of Shaftesbury allowed himself to be nominated in 1701 as vice-admiral of his county, Dorset; he was succeeded a year later by a Country Tory, Thomas Strangways. There would be requests too for places under the central government for children, relations, friends. Between 1710 and 1714 Robert Harley was inundated with begging letters of this kind from the Tory back benches. Often the desired favour would be something of an essentially local character: Sir William Barker wanting a post in Suffolk for his uncle; Sir William Carew asking for the appointment of a kinsman as postmaster at Camelford; Sir Richard Vyvyan needing to have 'a particular friend' named for a vacant customs collectorship at Helston.[32] Others would be on a somewhat grander scale: Sir Robert Davers, Suffolk knight of the shire, looking for a customs or Exchequer office for his son and also for his son-in-law, the M.P. Clement Corrance; or Sir James Etheridge proposing the comptrollership of wine licences for his son Charles.[33] The correspondence of the Country Tory Sir Arthur Kaye shows the extent to which he was preoccupied at this time with trying to secure titbits from the Tory government for his friends in Yorkshire.[34] And if it was not appointments to office as such, there might well be some other connection, some other link of dependence between the Country M.P. and the Court: Sir John Barker in Suffolk expecting to sell his timber to the Crown; Sir Henry Johnson, the Blackwall shipbuilder, enjoying the profits of naval contracts; Sir Nicholas Morice hoping in 1713 for the renewal of the lease of a manor he held under the Duchy of Cornwall.[35]

Yet if no 'country gentleman' could be wholly independent of government — and only a minority, probably, of the Country Members were 'country gentlemen' pure and simple — there was still a sense in which the term was used by contemporaries as Namier used it, namely to distinguish those M.P.s who were not placemen or pensioners of the Crown, especially the back-bench supporters of the party in power. In 1697 Robert Yard reported that in the Commons 'the country gentlemen were still possessed by their notions against a standing army'; in 1712 Sir Humphrey 'Polesworth' appealed 'to all country gentlemen (if there was any such thing left among them)'; in 1713 the Tory rebels on the French Commerce Treaty Bill were described in one account as 'the country gentlemen'.[36] It is this self-distancing from the *ministry*, rather than from government as such, which is characteristic of the Country Member; the cast of mind which saw in all courts the potentiality for corruption and therefore required protection against a standing army, and supported place bills, bills to make elections freer and more frequent, bills to keep military men and government financiers out of the Commons, all to safeguard the liberties and the purity of Parliament. The first place bill after the Revolution, introduced in 1692, was not intended to bar every placeman from the House but to exclude Members who accepted office after their election — in other words to stop the Court from 'corrupting' them once they had been freely chosen.[37]

The notion of 'patriotism', of representing the true interests of the country, was also involved. The word 'patriot' was in common currency in this period, the cant term for any politician in opposition, and used, simply or ironically, at the head of many a published 'white' or 'black list' — 'worthy patriots', 'true patriots' and so on. 'Patriotism' was the obvious justification for any kind of opposition, high-minded or factious; there was indeed no other. But it also represented what was publicly accepted as the rationale for entering Parliament. Major-General Charles Trelawney, pressing in 1702 his claims to a seat, stressed 'what I have done for the true interest of our English monarchy in former Parliaments' and how 'in the last reign I always opposed with pleasure the designs against the true English interest'. In proposing his fellow Tory William Bromley for the Speakership in 1710, Sir Thomas Hanmer made it his chief recommendation that here was a man 'who had given signal proofs of his abilities and willingness to serve his country'.[38] Patriotism and suspicion of the Court were bound up together: an M.P. served his country by exposing ministerial 'mismanagements' and by defending its liberties. These were the attitudes which contemporaries recognized as marking out the Country Member. They were characteristic of the 'independent country gentleman', but were not his exclusive property.

Most modern historians would agree that at least by the reign of Anne 'Country' sentiments had come to be more common on the Tory than on the Whig side. Geoffrey Holmes writes of the 'Country Tories' forming 'always . . . much the largest single group on either side in the Commons' and a substantial squadron too in the House of Lords. According to H. T. Dickinson, the Country Tories were 'the major element in the party', the 'Country element' in the Commons including 'a high proportion of the Tory back-benchers'.[39] What had happened during the 1690s was that the Whig party had been transformed from a natural party of opposition — the Whigs had after all been the Country party of the late 1670s and 1680s — into a natural party of government, while the Tories and a few former Whigs led by Paul Foley and Robert Harley had combined to form a 'New Country Party', which led the opposition to the Whig ministry in the 1698–1700 Parliament and thereafter turned itself into a new Tory party, in many respects a natural party of opposition. Such a complete reversal of roles could not of course be accomplished without confusion, and the changeover left stragglers on either side. There were

Court Tories, and, even after the small Harley–Foley group had departed, there were still Country Whigs. Leaving aside the matter of how far the pre-1688 Tory party had indeed been a *Court* party (and some reservations have recently been expressed on that score[40]), the most important question as far as the present essay is concerned is the size of the Country remnant in the Whig party.

The process by which the Whigs moved from opposition to government can be traced through the evidence of parliamentary lists. Of those M.P.s classed as Whigs by Lord Carmarthen in an analysis of the new Parliament in 1690, about 125 were marked as opposition, or 'Country', by Robert Harley in a list of April 1691, with some 85 as 'Court'. By the spring of 1693, when the nonjuror Samuel Grascome compiled his list of the Court party, he could include 121 of these Whigs, leaving at the most some 68 among the Country opposition. At this stage there were still a number of important Whigs who were opposing the ministry less out of a commitment to Country principles than because of their impatience with William's failure to employ them. Such future Court Whigs as Goodwin Wharton and Thomas Pelham, for example, spoke in favour of the Triennial Bill in February 1693.[41] The king's decisive turn towards the Whigs in 1693–4 and the establishment of an administration under the leadership of the 'new Whigs' of the Junto completed the turn-round, and using the various division lists from 1696 we find that of our original 1690 Whigs some 100 now voted consistently Court and only 27 consistently with the opposition. The year 1696, however, with the assassination plot against William, saw probably the high-water mark of Whig party unity in William's reign. In the succeeding two years some opposition developed within the party to the policies and personalities of the Junto ministers, and lists of the old and new Parliaments after the 1698 election show a slight alteration in the trend of previous figures. Of 128 Whigs from the 1690 list whose names still appear (oddly enough the same number as in 1696), 93 are classed as 'Court' and 35 as 'Country'.[42] These sets of figures are suggestive, but they cannot tell us what we want to know. We can see which Whigs opposed the government, but not necessarily which were on principle Country Whigs. For this we need to look for evidence on specifically Country issues.

One of the difficulties in finding Country Whigs in this period lies in the nature of the available evidence. Aside from the generalized lists classifying Members as 'for' or 'against' the administration, the only surviving Commons *division lists* on issues of Country principle are those on the Disbanding Bill of 1699, the 'place clause' of the Regency Bill in 1706 and the Septennial Bill in 1716; and none but the last actually gives the Country side in the vote, the two former being 'black lists' of Court supporters.[43] It is still possible, however, to make some use of the two Court lists, by identifying those Whigs who were *not* included, but even after known absentees have been eliminated the numbers remaining in both cases are much too high. Fortunately, the Disbanding Bill list can be supplemented by two analyses of the House in the 1698–9 session, one distinguishing Members as 'Court' or 'Country', the other almost certainly a forecast for the opposition in the disbandment division itself: taken together these clarify considerably the picture of the Whig element in the Country party. Even then, this and the Septennial Bill list are too far apart in time to enable any meaningful correlation to be made between them: of the 80 or so Whigs missing from the Court list in 1699, no more than 15 were still in the House in 1716. For the Lords there are three full division lists on Court against Country questions, all from William's reign: two on the Place Bill of 1692–3, and the third on the retention of the Dutch guards in 1699.[44] These are close enough together chronologically to make a comparison worthwhile, and their evidence discloses only one Country Whig peer: the volatile and untrustworthy Earl of Peterborough. As for that other staple source, reports of debates, these are much more useful before 1702 than after. There is no equivalent for Anne's reign of the lengthy Commons diaries of Anchitell Grey (to 1694), Narcissus Luttrell (1691–3) and Sir Richard Cocks (1699–1702).[45] Thereafter we are left with scraps of diaries, accounts of proceedings inserted into private correspondence, and the odd published debate. One such fragment does contain notes of speeches on the Regency Bill place clause, though like all parliamentary reporting it reveals the attitudes of only the more important or vociferous Members: in this case some six or seven of the Country Whigs.[46]

In spite of the sparseness of the sources, Geoffrey Holmes has made a valiant attempt to enumerate the Country Whigs in Anne's reign. On the basis of 'correspondence and electoral interest' as well as the negative evidence of the Regency Bill division list, he has identified as such some three peers and 30 M.P.s.[47] This is an impressive analysis, but is none the less open to several reservations. In some cases Professor Holmes employs as criteria to define a Country Whig those qualities of the stereotype Country politician which, we have seen, might be found among Court-orientated Members too. For example, of the two 'occasional' attenders he names, one, Henry Henley, was certainly not a Country Whig: a Court man in the 1690s, voting for the standing army, and after 1714 literally a courtier, as a gentleman of the Privy Chamber. Of the other, Sir William Bowes, little or nothing is known. Another dubious qualification used for a Country Whig — one derived from the notion of boxing the political compass — is habitual cross-voting. Whigs who straddled the party-political fence, who voted with Tories in Parliament or co-operated with them in the constituencies, may indeed have been motivated by Country principles, but equally by bloody-mindedness or pique. It is possible that Professor Holmes is correct in putting down John Morgan of Tredegar as a Country Whig on the strength of his wavering support for the Duke of Marlborough against Tory allegations of corruption in 1712, and his

evidently cordial relations with the high Tory Duke of Beaufort in Monmouthshire. On the other hand Sir John Guise, in the neighbouring county
of Gloucestershire, whose 'wayward' voting record earns him inclusion
alongside Morgan, was not enough of a Country Whig to support the place
clause in 1706, and himself explained his erratic career after 1702 in a
quite different way — that having left his former Tory friends and joined
the Whigs he in turn abandoned them when the Whig ministry refused him
office.[48]

A further reservation about this list of Country Whigs derives from
Professor Holmes's foreshortened perspective. Had he looked back as far
as the disbandment controversy of 1697–9, for example, or forward to
1716 and the Septennial Bill, it would in some respects have strengthened
his case — as to Sir Richard Onslow, who had spoken against a standing
army, and Sir William Ellys, Robert Eyre, William Harris, John Rudge and
Richard Vaughan, who had also been Country Whigs in the 1690s and had
probably voted for disbandment; and as to Sir John Cope, and Rudge
again, who both voted against the Septennial Bill. But it would have cast
doubt on the inclusion of such men as Sir John Hawles, John Hervey,
Richard Neville, Sir Isaac Rebow, Sir William Robinson and John Thornaugh, Court Whigs under William and some of them placemen, who had
all voted *for* the maintenance of a standing army.

This question of chronological perspective raises a more fundamental
problem in the definition of a 'Country' Member: how far should one
expect consistency of belief or conduct over any length of time in men
whose circumstances, connections and attitudes might well undergo drastic
change? We have been reminded, in the context of the controversy over
the post-1714 Tory party's commitment to Jacobitism, of the folly of
studying eighteenth-century politicians like 'butterflies in an album'.[49]
There are numerous examples of Whigs who turned Tory or Tories who
turned Whig; of ex-Jacobites who became reconciled to Hanover, and
even of pro-Hanoverians like Sir Henry Bunbury and Lord Barrymore,
who eventually turned to Jacobitism.[50] Similarly we can find Courtiers
transmogrifying into Country party men, and vice versa. John Beckett
has demonstrated how, in the case of the Cumberland Whig James Lowther, Ordnance office placeman from 1696 until the beginning of Anne's
reign, 'a windfall inheritance transformed him into an independent
country Member opposed to some of the values he had earlier represented'.[51]

The economic breezes could of course blow chill as well as warm. A
financial crash and the spectre of the bailiffs — 'my house will be rifled,
myself and family exposed' — reduced the Lancashire Tory Sir Roger
Bradshaigh to an abject pensioner of the Harley administration of
1710–14, and afterwards persuaded him to go over to the Whigs.[52] In
the case of Sir George Downing, an independent-minded country gentleman involved in the preparation of the Place Bill of 1710–11, it was not

poverty that laid him open to offers, for he was always a wealthy man, but what seemed the irrevocable loss of his Commons seat. His interest at Dunwich, which represented a considerable investment, had collapsed in 1715, but the grant of a 99-year lease of the borough from the Crown shortly before the 1722 election helped put the nomination of both Members in his pocket, and he repaid the debt with years of loyal service to Walpole.[53] In 1698 at nearby Orford electoral disappointment produced a change in the opposite direction in the mind of Sir John Duke, a Whig who was suddenly enlightened as to the iniquities of the Junto ministry by the prospect of being elbowed out of a parliamentary seat by Lord Somers's brother-in-law.[54] A similar conversion might be wrought by an alteration in a man's career prospects, or in his own appraisal of them. The continued intractability displayed by the former Whig solicitor-general Sir John Hawles in his later years, after his speeches 'against officers' in the Regency Bill debates, his defence of the high Tory pamphleteer James Drake in 1706 and cross-voting during the 1708-9 session, doubtless stemmed from the Junto's failure to obtain him a place on the judicial bench and from a well founded belief thereafter that time had passed him by.[55] He was one of those of whom it might be said, as it was of the Whigs who brought forward a place bill in 1709-10, that they 'see to whose share soever places are like to fall, they are not like to fall to them'.[56]

What makes the translation from Court to Country, or from Country to Court, significantly different from other changes in party allegiance, is the nature of Country principles themselves. Since a Country stance in politics involved much emphasis on personal moral rectitude and staunchness of principle, it rendered its holder acutely vulnerable to any cynical examination of his conduct. Hence the enormous care with which Sir Thomas Hanmer, Tory Speaker of the 1713-14 Parliament, protected his own near-legendary reputation for 'honesty', refusing offer after offer from Robert Harley of a place in his ministry, even while assisting the Court in an unofficial capacity in 1712-13.[57] For a self-conciously 'Country' M.P. to change sides and take office called into question the genuineness of his previous commitment in a special way. Someone who could thus be bought could not ever have been possessed of the 'honesty' he had claimed for himself: this was the obvious conclusion for contemporaries to draw, and draw it they did. There was the opinion of Lord Poulett, for example, that place bills in particular 'arose from the dregs of the discontented of both parties'; and the more general explanation offered by Francis Hare of the activities of Country politicians as conventional, self-serving hypocrisy: 'when men are out,' he wrote, 'they have nothing to do but to act the patriot, to spy faults in those that are in, to make themselves popular by invectives against the ministry, or by self-denying motions, in order to be taken off by the prince, or to ingratiate themselves with the people.'[58]

It does not require a deeply pessimistic view of human nature to recognize a degree of justice in this assessment. Naturally, it would be as wrong to assume that no politician ever believed what he said as to profess the opposite, and unfair to seek ulterior motives everywhere, but the very fact that an M.P. might vote for a place bill in one session and calmly take office the next, might declare against all ministries and then promptly join one, must mean that we take his Country allegiance less seriously. No one would argue that the votes of Nicholas Lechmere and John Fane against the Septennial Bill in 1716 were influenced by anything more profound than resentment at dismissal from office, Lechmere having lost the solicitor-generalship, and Fane his army command. Other examples may be less clear-cut, but the circumstantial evidence is telling. Sir Robert Clayton's opposition in 1699, for example, may have stemmed from his association with radical Whigs, his past connection with John Wildman and present patronage of John Toland, or from his removal from the customs commission in 1697;[59] and even the impressive Country Whig record of Sir Richard Onslow, 'Stiff Dick', who from the mid-1690s until about 1708 backed many popular measures — not just place bills but inquiries into government grants, landed qualification bills and so on — pales somewhat when viewed as a long interlude between periods in office, from 1690 to 1693 as a lord of the Admiralty, and after 1714 as succes- sively chancellor and teller of the Exchequer (the latter a particularly lucrative place). Then there are the young men in a hurry, anxious to impress ministers and win a reputation in the House by the espousal of 'patriotic' causes, but essentially careerists; as Professor Holmes has put it, 'men who had donned a "Country" mantle largely for the sake of political convenience'.[60] A prime example was Robert Eyre, the Wiltshire lawyer who had been the original proposer of the 1705–6 place clause but who ratted at the last minute after a meeting behind closed doors with Junto lords, and 'in the most audacious as well as infamous manner that ever was seen in the House gave up his cause, his friends and himself'.[61] Less flagrant was Peter King, Eyre's comrade in the Regency Bill agitation, who saw through to the end the battle for 'the clause' and stayed a 'whimsical' for several more years, but who none the less had 'certainly no antipathy to preferment'.[62] Knighted in 1708, he became under the Hanoverians lord chancellor and a peer of the realm. A third leader of the Country Whigs in 1705–6, James Stanhope, enjoyed an even more spectacular later career: great offices of state and the leadership of a ministry. Although already a brigadier-general in 1706, he was pushing for further promotion and had been soliciting plum diplomatic appointments. After 'acting the patriot' he was named envoy extraordinary to Charles III in Spain and in 1707 was advanced to major-general.[63]

Many similarly unedifying stories can be told: Edward Wortley Montagu, self-styled Country Whig spokesman, presenter of five place bills in four years in Anne's reign, became a Treasury commissioner in 1714; Richard

Edgcumbe, in 1710 teller for a Country motion to introduce into the
Commons voting by ballot, also became a Treasury lord; Grey Neville,
prominent among the Country Whigs in 1707–8, was yet another to take
office under George I, as was Richard Vaughan, who after years of unpre-
dictability settled down to a judgeship in his native Wales. Even Sir
Richard Onslow's stout-hearted son Thomas, whose enthusiasm for 'self-
denying' legislation was still undiminished in 1715, eventually crossed
over, succeeding his father as teller of the Exchequer.[64] But perhaps the
most remarkable instance was the author of the *Principles of a Real Whig*
himself, Robert Molesworth. The necessity of providing for a numerous
family out of limited resources drew Molesworth towards the source of patronage. Godolphin made him 'assurances' after he had supported the 1704–5
Place Bill. These came to nothing and he again opposed the Court over the
Regency Bill, but the appointment of his son Jack to a place in the Stamp
Office in 1706 won him over to the administration. He was even willing to
make approaches to Robert Harley when his patron Godolphin fell from
power, and at the accession of George I became a placeman himself and
for a time a spokesman for the 'Court interest', amongst other things supporting (with considerable embarrassment) a standing army. His biography,
it has been said, 'amply demonstrates the force of self-interest . . . in politics'.[65]

   We can see, therefore, that in the case of the Regency Bill agitation in
particular, which has been described as 'the only considerable defection
of Whigs that we know of during Queen Anne's reign',[66] nearly all the
principal figures among the Country Whigs had feet of clay. Far from
being disinterested patriots, they appear as peevish or ambitious oppor-
tunists. It is also possible to explain this episode in a different, though
equally cynical way, as a piece of political calculation, arising from the
struggles of the Junto to secure a stronger foothold inside the Marlborough–Godolphin ministry. Given the peculiar circumstances of 1705–6,
the Junto assisting the 'duumvirs' without receiving what they regarded
as proper reward, we might expect to find pressure being brought to bear
by devious means. The virtues of 'place' legislation for this purpose had
indeed been sketched in by Halifax in November 1705. Observing that to
keep up a 'mixed ministry' of Whigs and 'moderate' Tories was akin to
trying to blend 'oil and vinegar', he noted that 'a bill of offices' would
probably prove an excellent method of separating out the two by tempting
Tories to desert the government.[67] There is evidence to support the
speculation that, at least in part, the place clause in the Regency Bill was
one such scheme: the connections between the Junto and several of the
Country Whig leaders, especially Sir Richard Onslow, Stanhope and
Hawles; the involvement of the same group in other ploys, more obviously
Junto-inspired, to vex the ministry by joining Tories in opposition or taking an independent line on matters with which the Court was intimately
concerned, over the Regency Bill itself and the 'Hanover motion' that preceded it, and over Scottish affairs in December 1705; and lastly the fact

that the place clause which the Country Whigs put forward was actually rather a moderate measure, less than Tory extremists wanted and even in its strongest form a modification of the more sweeping exclusion pre-scribed in the Act of Settlement.[68]

None of this of course does more than point in the direction of the clause being a Junto tactic, and what has been said applies only to the leaders of the Country Whigs. If the measure originated as a calculated manoeuvre, it quickly gathered some force of its own and attracted back-bench Whigs who were genuinely independent. Even so, the momentum did not finally prove unstoppable, and with Robert Eyre deserting, Stan-hope leaving London to embark for the Peninsula, and Onslow also unable to last out to the end, the Country Whig crusade petered out in a com-promise acceptable to the Court.[69] Certainly at other times in Anne's reign the Junto used 'whimsical Whigs' in a similar fashion – as guerrilla troops to harass the Marlborough–Godolphin administration, for instance in the winter of 1707–8, when they were themselves co-operating with high Tories in attempts to smash Harley's 'moderating scheme'.[70] And at other times too they showed a fondness for the place bill in particular as a device to sow discord among supporters of a Tory government. In 1702 Sir John Holland, a Whig later to hold office as comptroller of the House-hold, had proposed just such a measure; in 1704–5 the Junto had given some support to a bill, fathered by Peter King and Onslow, which looks like a trial run for the Regency Bill clause; and in 1710–11 a place bill was 'brought in by the Whigs designedly that the Tories may discover themselves, they being violently for it last year'.[71]

If, then, we discount the posturing of the pseudo-patriots, what remains of the Country wing of the Whig party? The only estimates of numbers that we can make are in the three recorded divisions noted earlier.[72] While there were considerably more Country Whigs early on in William's reign, the figure in the standing army division of 1699 is unimpressive, probably about 36 in all out of 221 on the Country side. For the Regency Bill we have the contemporary estimate of one 'whimsical', Sir John Cropley, a man moreover given to bragging, who put the entire strength of the 'squadron' at about 30, and this before the late desertions, out of some 196 in opposition to the Court in the crucial divisions.[73] A similar result is yielded by the Septennial Bill division list: 33 Whigs out of 186 listed against the bill. Two obvious conclusions are to be drawn from this politi-cal arithmetic: the surprising consistency of the figures, and the relatively low level of Whig participation in these Country oppositions. Furthermore, when we separate wheat from chaff, the real Country Whig from the bogus, not only does this level of participation become even lower, but the Country Whigs who are left often display characteristics which mark them out as declining parliamentary species.

Three broad types may be distinguished among the more genuine Country Whigs in the Commons. First there were the older men, many veterans of the Exclusion crisis and some, like the wealthy London alderman Thomas Turgis or Francis St John, returned for Peterborough in 1698 after a gap of 17 years, who had begun their parliamentary careers before the Restoration. A few of these lived on into Anne's reign, the Lincolnshire baronets Sir William Ellys and Sir Edward Hussey being two examples, but the majority seem to have died or retired from politics before 1702. From the death of the octogenarian Sir John Maynard, Strafford's prosecutor, in October 1690, what was left of Shaftesbury's Whig party began steadily to disappear. During the course of the 1690 Parliament some 18 identifiable Country Whigs died, including John Birch (1691), Henry Powle (1690), William Sacheverell (1691) and John Swinfen (1694); two more were called to the Lords, Henry Capel and Sir Vere Fane; and a further seven did not seek re-election in 1695. Robert Harley's father, Sir Edward, was numbered among subsequent casualties, retiring in 1698 although in truth he had been a spent force ever since coming back into Parliament in 1693; and 1702 saw the last of Sir Robert Cotton, the Cheshire knight of the shire, and his fellow Exclusionist Sir Samuel Barnardiston, so much a 'Country party' man that he joined with a high Tory to defeat Court Whig candidates in the Suffolk election of 1698 and was blacklisted in 1701 for having opposed the war with France.

Alongside these old hands we find the young sparks, parliamentary tyros innocent of parliamentary worldliness, impatient with the political establishment and anxious to cut a figure, who began as 'patriots' but eventually changed their spots. Their early vigour in the Country cause was a recognizable syndrome: one observer noted in 1705 that James Stanhope and Peter King 'like novices of Whigs have been very zealous and forward in procuring a bill . . . for disabling men in office'.[74] Of the 36 or so Whigs likely to have rebelled against the standing army in 1699, no less than 12 had been elected for the first time the summer before. It is a similar story in 1706, and the proportion of young men (at least in the parliamentary sense) in the Whig opposition to the Septennial Bill in 1716 is still higher: 11 out of the 33 had been newcomers to the House in 1715, and five more, making altogether just under half the total, had not sat prior to 1713.

The third type is distinguished not by age but by character and association, for it consists of those who from about 1696 onwards set themselves up as 'old' or 'true' Whigs, guardians of what they regarded as their party's heritage against the apostates of the Junto. Foremost among these were of course the Grecian Tavern circle — Moyle, Trenchard, Molesworth and the rest of Professor Pocock's 'neo-Harringtonians'. Important as these various individuals were to the Country party, especially in carrying on the paper war against the standing army, they did not themselves make much impact in Parliament. Moyle's career in the House lasted just three years, from 1695 to 1698; Trenchard was not elected until 1722. Only Molesworth sat for any appreciable length of time, and he was out of Parliament at the time of the disbandment controversy.

Nevertheless there was an 'old Whig' grouping in the Commons, active in the late 1690s and again in 1705–6, a small connection grouped around the third Earl of Shaftesbury.[75] The grandson of the founder of the Whig party, Shaftesbury considered himself the keeper of the faith. As M.P. for Poole in 1694–9, he 'persevered in the same way of acting, always heartily concurring in every motion for the better . . . securing our liberties . . . though the motions frequently came from people who were of a differently denominated party'.[76] Although, because of chronic ill-health, not personally active in national politics after leaving the Commons, he put his intellectual and literary abilities to the service of his principles, offered his patronage to Molesworth, Toland and others, and also tried to turn his electoral interest to the advantage of 'real' Whiggery. His influence can probably be seen in the absence of his friend Thomas Trenchard and of three of Trenchard's fellow Dorset M.P.s (Dorset being Shaftesbury's county) from the Court list on the standing army; and even more clearly in 1705–6, when he appears as the *éminence grise* behind the Country Whig revolt. Not only were Molesworth (in its early stages) and the earl's close confidant and nominee at Shaftesbury, Sir John Cropley, avid supporters of the place clause, but Shaftesbury himself was also on intimate terms with Peter King and James Stanhope, and there were again Dorset M.P.s missing from the Whigs on the Court side of the division, this time six in all, including Cropley and Shaftesbury's own brother Maurice.[77] For some time after the Regency Bill crisis Cropley's letters to his patron, in which, it must be admitted, vanity and flattery were much in evidence, suggest that both the ministry and the Junto regarded the earl as a man worth cultivating. In the winter of 1706–7 the Junto made professions of friendship; a year later Godolphin was telling Cropley, via Molesworth, that 'he was of his mind to have true Whigs [elected] that would be your [Shaftesbury's] Whigs and not the Junto's'.[78] How seriously Godolphin viewed this approach is a question which cannot be answered, for the fall of Harley in February 1708 so transformed the political scene as to render such minor considerations wholly insignificant. And besides, Shaftesbury's own influence was now declining sharply. The 1708 election saw his electioneering efforts reduced in scope and less successful than they had been for some while, and after the Tory landslide in 1710 he was left with no more than two possible followers in the Commons.[79] By this time his own health did not permit him to remain in England, and he died in Naples in 1713.

By the second half of Queen Anne's reign, therefore, the Country element in the Whig party consisted of a handful of men of principle, lacking now any political magnate, even one as remote as Shaftesbury had been, around whom to collect; together with eccentric individualists, rash young men, restless place-seekers and embittered grudge-bearers. In practical terms the 'Country interest' seemed to have become almost synonymous with the Tory party, so much so that in 1711 Swift could

reassure Country Tories doubtful of the integrity of the new ministry
that since Harley and his colleagues had come to power 'the Court and
Country are of a side'.[80] Five years later a combination of Tories and dissident Whigs against the Whig administration in a Commons debate 'about
the grants' could be described as 'the old Whigs' siding with 'the Country
party'.[81]

This identification of Country and Tory had begun even earlier. We
have seen from the forecast and division list that in practice in 1699 the
bulk of the Commons opposition to the standing army came from the
Tory side, and from the Lords division lists how scarce were Country Whig
peers even in the 1690s. The Whig Joseph Paice, in his account of the
1701 Parliament, divided the lower House 'principally into two parties,
the Court and the Country', but to him 'the Court party' were the Whigs
and 'the Country party' consisted of 'Sir Edward Seymour, *etc.*'; a Scots
visitor, William Cleland, viewing the Commons in November 1706, also
considered 'the proper division' to be between Court and Country but
seemed to think this identical with 'Revolution and Jacobite'.[82]

The number of former Country Whigs who under William and Anne
transformed themselves into Tories, and some high-flyers at that, confirms the general acceptance of the alignment: not only the Harleys and
Foleys of the 'New Country Party', but former Exclusionists like Edward
Harvey of Combe, who surfaced again in the Parliament of 1705 as a Tory
and was subsequently a Jacobite; Sir Eliab Harvey, who acted consistently
with the Tories after the Revolution; and Morgan Randyll, who became
a member of the October Club. The fierce Whig Sir John Thompson had
become by Anne's reign the hot Tory Lord Haversham; and Sir Michael
Warton — still a Country Whig, it would appear, in the early 1690s — was
also, by 1701 at least, a 'staunch Tory'.[83] And even where a Country Whig
might himself remain loyal to his party, his descendants would still follow
the path to 'High Church'. George England, who in 1710 succeeded his
Country Whig uncle and namesake as M.P. for Great Yarmouth, sat as
a Tory; so did Sir William Carew, returned for Saltash the following year,
another to break with his family's Whig traditions. Perhaps the most
striking example are the Leveson Gowers, once Whigs, who became in
due course the pillars of the Church party in Staffordshire. But above all
it is the very behaviour of Tory M.P.s themselves which underlies the
strength of the Country interest within their ranks: the fact that Whigs
expected, and secured, substantial Tory support for place bills and the like
— even when the Tories were themselves the party of government — and
indeed relied on this as a habitual tactic; and the barrage of Country
measures brought forward by Tory back-benchers in the 1710 Parliament
against a Tory-led Court party which, as one Tory Member wrote, 'we
opposed . . . in our own interest'.[84]

The Whig contribution to Country politics is not, however, to be considered strictly in terms of parliamentary votes. While the infantry of the

Country party, so to speak, may have been mostly Tory, those who provided the weapons, the theoreticians and pamphleteers, were preponderantly Whig. In the 1690s the 'neo-Harringtonians' led the way, exposing the menace of the standing army and in more general terms denouncing what they saw as a Court-inspired programme to 'corrupt' the constitution. In George I's reign it was again one of their number, John Trenchard, abetted by Thomas Gordon, who in *Cato's Letters* spearheaded resistance to the Whig oligarchy.[85] While accepting that there were separate Whig and Tory strains in Country ideology, Professor Pocock and his followers have sought to minimize the Tory elements and assert the primacy of the Whig. Certainly these 'neo-Harringtonians' were, and remained, staunch Whigs: Molesworth and Trenchard, for example, insisted on styling themselves so, Molesworth actually delighting in the title of 'Commonwealthman'; Walter Moyle, though hob-nobbing with exceedingly high Tories, was in November 1699 anxious that 'the Church party see they are not like to be our governors in the ministry'; all three were sharply anti-clerical.[86] What is more, the most important of the tracts against the standing army — Moyle and Trenchard's *Argument showing that a Standing Army is inconsistent with a Free Government*, Trenchard's *A Short History of Standing Armies in England*, Andrew Fletcher's *A Discourse concerning Militias* and Toland's *The Militia Reformed* — all presented their case in Harringtonian terms: that the standing army overbalanced the constitution and rendered it corrupt and 'violent', and that the proper mode of defence of the country was a militia.[87] Trenchard and Toland extended the analysis to denounce the proliferation of placemen, and Molesworth to call for a return to a reliance on landed men in Parliament, in both instances as part of an endeavour to preserve the balance.[88] These pamphlets found a ready market among Country Tories as well as Country Whigs, and so too did earlier republican works, now published or republished: Harrington's *Oceana*, Algernon Sydney's *Discourses*, the *Memoirs* of Denzil Holles, and those of the regicide Edmund Ludlow (suitably edited, probably by Toland).[89] Anthony Hammond, a Grecian Tavern crony of Moyle, was one Tory admirer of Sydney's writings; and even a less complex character, Norfolk knight of the shire Sir William Cook, could recommend the *Discourses* to his son-in-law as 'worth your reading', though he added, 'it's possible you may wonder I should buy Algernon Sydney's [book], being on a subject not very agreeable to a Church of England man, but really I must confess, though I am not very well pleased with the matter, yet the manner is inviting'.[90]

While acknowledging the 'old Whig' leadership of the Country agitation in the press, at least before the appearance of Bolingbroke's *Craftsman* in the 1720s, we should not underestimate the distinctively Tory contribution to the development of Country ideology. Fear of the corrupting influence of the Court did not have to originate with a belief in Harringtonian constitutional theory: as early as 1693 a Tory M.P., John Hungerford, could declare that 'corruption is digging the grave of our English liberties'.[91] Distrust of the 'courtier' was endemic,[92] and a general awareness of the debilitating effects of bribery on the independence of the House of Commons had long since been awakened by Danby's methods of management in the 1670s. On another aspect, the question of influence over elections, there was a Cavalier tradition of upholding the liberties of the subject against the incursions of central government, and a recent painful experience too for Tories to be guided by. 'A free parliament' had been one of the slogans of the Restoration — as it was to be the great demand of the Tory party after 1714 — and although local Tories had enthusiastically co-operated with the Crown in its campaign to remodel the parliamentary boroughs after 1681, they had been thrown into great alarm by James II's efforts in 1687–8 to reverse this process and, by an alliance with the Dissenters, to pack a Parliament which would set aside the penal laws. The effects of James's policies, against the Church of England and against Churchmen in the corporations, in preparing the Tory party for its character-change in the 1690s, have been hinted at elsewhere.[93] Nor did a belief in the right of the landed interest, and the landed interest alone, to represent the country in Parliament, have to depend on Harringtonian doctrines. It was a Tory reflex to look to the shires while the Whigs looked to London and to the larger boroughs for their popular support, and the closer associations of the Whigs with the wealthier City merchants and financiers, many of whom were Dissenters — associations that the foundation of the Bank of England in 1694 and the New East India Company in 1698 turned into a firm alliance — were a matter of simple observation. But the presence of a specifically Tory element in Country ideology is perhaps best illustrated by a brief examination of what were the two most important issues in the Country campaign of c. 1697–1701, the standing army and the project to resume the Irish forfeitures. It was these that Swift dwelt on when in an *Examiner* in May 1711 he set out the Tory claim for a monopoly of 'Country' virtue:[94] 'I shall take leave to produce some principles, which in the several periods of the late reign, served to denote a man of one or t'other party. To be against a standing army in time of peace, was all High Church, Tory and tantivy . . . to resume the most exorbitant grants that were ever given to a set of profligate favourites, and apply them to the public, was the very quintessence of Toryism.'

On the standing army, which was undoubtedly the most important issue at stake for the Country party in the Commons and the 'neo-Harringtonians' in the press between 1697 and 1699, and which remained a litmus test of Country sentiment into the Walpolean era, there was a common tradition of opposition shared by Tories as well as Whigs. In 1685 Tory leaders like Sir Thomas and Sir Walter Clarges and Sir Edward Seymour had defied King James over this very question.[95] Professor Pocock has made the telling point that the most obvious Tory objection to a standing army, the memory of Cromwell, 'received curiously little emphasis' in the pamphlet debate before 1714. There are references in Moyle and Trenchard's *Argument*, a hint in the introduction to Ludlow's *Memoirs*, and a comment by Swift (characteristically ahead of his time) in another *Examiner*, insinuating a link between the Whigs and absolutist government via this route.[96] Nor in the debates of the late 1690s can we find Tories in Parliament making much play with the argument. The one possible example is a comment by Robert Harley to the effect that 'an army will choose Members of Parliament'.[97] This failure to make any explicit reference to the New Model Army and the major-generals may not, however, be particularly significant, at least in regard to speeches in Parliament. In the first place, Country Tories would obviously wish to emphasize matters of agreement rather than matters of difference with their Country Whig allies; and secondly, and more important, it seems to have been acknowledged in the Commons as axiomatic (and without having to be explained) that a standing army threatened the liberty of the subject. Court Whigs professed it equally, sometimes even when in the act of opposing disbandment or defending increased military expenditure.

In William's reign the maintenance of a powerful army was usually justified as a temporary emergency measure, required by the presence of even greater dangers in the shape of enemies abroad or plotters at home. Thus Sir John Somers, the future Junto lord, could declare in 1692, 'I am against a standing army as much as any in this House, but yet as long as an army is necessary for your service I am for using them well', and his follower Edward Clarke, Whig M.P. for Taunton, could echo this admission when attacking the Disbanding Bill of 1698–9, 'a standing army will enslave us, but this [is] not the question'.[98] Opponents sometimes cited instances of the dire effects of standing armies abroad; Robert Harley once mentioned Caesar, but rhetoric of this kind was unusual.[99] A debate in December 1698 may serve as a more typical sample: a standing army was said to be illegal; unpopular; too much of a drain on the kingdom's resources; contrary to William's declaration of 1689; too great a risk in the hands of a less sympathetic sovereign; and of course 'always destructive to liberty', though the way in which it was 'destructive' was taken for granted.[100] After the Hanoverian succession, when government speakers broke this consensus, abandoned the argument from expediency and fell back on the wording of the Declaration of Rights to claim that a standing army 'with the consent of Parliament' could not constitute any threat because it remained under parliamentary control, opposition Tories were driven to take their explanations further, and, as William Shippen did in 1717, touch upon Civil War experiences and the 'outrages' that a 'parliament army' had once committed.[101]

There were other distinctively Tory objections to a standing army, which did not derive from the party's Cavalier heritage or Restoration traditions but from events in the more recent past, the Glorious Revolution itself and the war that followed. It was a Tory rather than a Country response, for example, to answer the defence of a standing army on security grounds by pooh-poohing talk of Jacobite conspiracy and even making light of the danger from France. It also became characteristic of the Tory view of foreign policy to display a strong preference for the Navy over the Army as the principal means of national defence, and an aversion to the use of foreign troops, both of which were elements in the case against a standing army. There was nothing specifically Tory about either of these prejudices before 1688. The idea that 'the walls of our kingdom are the navy', as one M.P. had expressed it in 1621, was common to all sides in the political conflicts of the seventeenth century, and Whigs as well as rebel Tories had argued on this basis against a standing army in 1685.[102]

Xenophobia had also been no respecter of parties. There were Whig as well as Tory critics of 'foreign officers' in the Commons in 1691 and 1692, and it was a Country Whig, Robert Molesworth, who singled out 'standing armies of mercenaries' as the worst type, and in his *Account of Denmark . . . in . . . 1692* noted how the absolutist régime there depended on 'a standing army composed for the most part of foreigners, who have no value for the natives'.[103]

However, in the Nine Years War these two issues — reliance on the Navy and opposition to foreign troops, in particular foreign officers — became fused into a Tory view of grand strategy which was anti-Dutch and by clear implication anti-William. This 'blue-water' approach, deeply sceptical of the value of any military involvement on the continent of Europe, produced suspicions that England had been 'drawn in . . . by the Dutch' to take part in a war that was for Holland's advantage and probably England's disadvantage. 'England bears almost the charge of the war.' said Paul Foley in 1692, 'and others reap the benefit.'[104] The previous year a Tory Member had asked 'that we may know what sums of money have been sent to the Duke of Savoy, the Dutch, and the beggarly princes of Germany', and there were 'some unseasonable reflections made on the Dutch'; while in 1693 Nicholas Barbon commented, 'I should be loth to see trade regulated at Amsterdam, and war at The Hague'.[105] There were some more neutral, Country feelings at work here too, the desire for 'good husbandry' and the simple resentment of the taxpayer at the size of army salaries, but the thrust of the attack was against the king himself, his Dutch connections and, in this respect, his double loyalty. It was an argument which of course was to apply equally to the Hanoverians, whom Tories disliked just as much. Moreover, by 1714 the 'blue-water' policy had become a Tory 'party line', manifested under Queen Anne in consistent opposition to fighting in Europe, and finding its most notorious expression in Swift's *Conduct of the Allies.*

The relationship between this debate over strategy and the conflicts over the standing army are obvious. Although strictly speaking the standing army issue arose only when peace was concluded in 1697, Tory and Country opinion had been developing during the war. Opposition Members became used to undertaking a rigorous examination of army estimates, and resisting Crown demands to increase the numbers of troops. As early as 1691 Sir John Thompson was protesting that the request for a large force for a descent was 'only a colour' and that for himself 'I am against a standing army'.[106] Criticism of foreign officers in November 1692 included the remark from the Tory John Granville that 'till the French King had German troops and Italian ministers, he never could enslave his country'.[107] And throughout came the repeated refrain that it was sailors rather than soldiers on whom the country should rely. Sir Robert Sawyer in 1691: 'all agreed to have as good a fleet at sea as we can, not so land forces'; Sir Edward Seymour in 1692: 'the interest of England, and its security to be found only in the fleet'; Sir Thomas Clarges in 1693: 'I always told you, that our safety is the sea.'[108] The natural progression in discussions on the question of the standing army was to point out that while England still had an effective Navy she need not fear invasion, and expensive regular troops would therefore serve no useful purpose, or as Sir John Bolles reminded the Commons, 'that in the late war you were saved from an invasion without an army'.[109] So when Walter Moyle, who was a particularly keen advocate of naval reconstruction, and John Trenchard stated in 1698 that a standing army would be redundant 'if we keep the seas well guarded', they may, as has been suggested elsewhere, have been thinking in terms of Protectorate traditions and a type of 'Macchiavellian economics', but they were also reiterating what was by then a well established Tory point of view.[110]

The resumption of William's grants of forfeited estates in Ireland, which in 1699 succeeded disbandment as the prime objective of the Country party in Parliament, was largely a Tory-inspired scheme. It was a Country measure in that it constituted a blow against Court 'corruption', and also went towards reducing the tax burden on the country gentleman. Moves to confiscate Crown grants continued to be part of the Country platform as late as 1712. Charles Davenant's *Discourse of Grants and Resumptions*, the key pamphlet on the Irish forfeitures issue, put the case succinctly: 'it would be very hard if all this should be intercepted from the public, and . . . we should waste our blood and treasure only to enrich a few private persons.'[111] More specifically, he also tried to show that the £4,000,000 of English 'treasure' spent on reducing Ireland had been a prime cause of that vast debt which he regarded as the most pernicious legacy of the Junto ministry.[112] Other reasons advanced for the Resumption Bill, had, however, a pronounced party flavour. The most important consideration in any such measure was the chronological scope: Tories would only go back to the Revolution, Whigs to James II's reign at least. As a contemporary Whig satire put it,

> Of William's grants you now complain,
> Without regard to merit;
> For the lewd gifts of former reigns
> To whores and papists, you maintain,
> And bastards may inherit.

When in February 1696 the Commons discussed a motion to resume 'all the lands given away from the Crown in England and Ireland', it was reported that 'some would have gone back as [far as] 1660, others from [the] first year of King James II, others only since the Revolution'.[113] To take back William's grants alone was a direct insult, since the greatest sufferers were the king's own friends and favourites and his former mistress Lady Orkney. There was a sharply personal element in Davenant's attacks, Whig ministers and Lady Orkney herself recognizable in his historical analogies, and an emphasis, in pamphlets and in Parliament, on the fact that so many of William's grants had been to foreigners. One pro-resumption broadsheet proclaimed that *'our hereditary kings*, and the good old English parliaments, understood the interest of England much better than to let foreigners have any lands in England'.[114]

Moreover, the Resumption Act had major implications for Ireland, and Irish politics, which marked it out as Tory rather than Whig in character. Any tampering with the land settlement frightened Irish Protestants, many of whom had purchased or leased land from the grantees, and Irish politicians led a campaign against the act as an unwarranted assault on the Protestant interest there, the so-called 'national remonstrance'.[115] Now in so far as there was any difference between the parties on Irish policy, Whigs believed in supporting the Protestant interest to the utmost, while Tories were less sympathetic to the excesses of Irish Protestant opinion, less violently opposed to Irish Catholic claims, and less fearful about the future of the Williamite establishment.[116] The 'neo-Harringtonian' position — if one can be constructed from the fleeting references to Ireland in Harrington's own works and in the writings of his late-seventeenth-century interpreters and their pronouncements about colonies in general — would seem to have favoured the Irish protesters, since Moyle and his friends advocated large-scale colonization and the exercise of restraint in governing the colonists, with encouragement being given to the growth of local assemblies.[117] Defenders of the act made a great deal of the rights of the English Parliament to legislate for Ireland, and accused the organizers of the remonstrance of seeking to throw off this dependence on England.[118] A burlesque on 'the several addresses of some Irish folks' portrayed its subjects as avaricious bigots who adhered to the English Crown 'for their own sake' but in practice wished to enjoy complete freedom from English supervision, presumably to oppress the Catholics.[119] The fact was that the Williamite land settlement in Ireland had principally been managed by Irish Whig politicians, many of whom were now leading the agitation against resumption. Davenant's cool answer to their complaints was that anyone trafficking in forfeited estates should have been forewarned by the repeated interest shown by the English Parliament since the Revolution in putting the Irish forfeitures 'to the use of the public'. But others went so far as to denounce the Williamite settlement itself as unfair to the Irish Catholics.[120]

With the important exception of John Trenchard, it was Tories rather than Whigs in the Country party who made the running on the forfeitures question. Other Country Whig authors had little to say. Robert Molesworth, an Irishman, was himself adversely affected, and in 1703 chaired a committee of the Irish House of Commons which produced a 'representation' of the grievances of the kingdom including bitter criticism of the Resumption Act and the trustees appointed to put it into effect.[121] Walter Moyle treated the episode as merely another chance to indulge in the 'noble sport' of 'ministry hunting'.[122] In the Commons, Junto Whigs supported the Irish Protestant cause, and the Country side was led by Tories, Sir Edward Seymour, Simon Harcourt, Arthur Moore, Sir William Drake and Jack Howe. The committee named to bring in the Resumption Bill had included eight Tories and only one Country Whig (Sir Richard Onslow), and apart from James Sloane, an Irishman but one whose connections aligned him against the 'remonstrance' group, the only prominent Whig speaker in favour of resumption seems to have been Sir Richard Cocks; and his opinions, preserved in his diary, show just how far he had strayed from orthodox Whiggery on this issue. Having acknowledged that 'if this land had been divided amongst the conquering army, they would have planted colonies and bred up people in the religion and interest of England', he went on to show a remarkable degree of generosity to the deprived Irish Catholics:

> the poor Irish who stood by their natural prince, whose chiefest fault and misfortune was his being of their religion . . . and being extremely partial and favourable to them on all occasions. Methinks it is a great hardship to be reckoned a traitor for only adhering to one's natural prince . . . But I had almost forgot, the traitor is still he that is beaten. Well, then, since the Irish are traitors, it is more reasonable that they should be traitors to the people of England than to a few Court minions.[123]

The most notable Country Whig on the pro-resumption side was of course John Trenchard, a member of the commission of inquiry into the forfeitures in 1699 and the author of its report, on which the Resumption Bill was based; he was elected a trustee the following year and was the author of the principal defence of the conduct of the trustees, the *Letter to a Soldier*.[124] As an undoubted Whig, with an interest himself in Irish property, Trenchard represented the perfect answer to the charge that resumption was a Tory measure, and one Tory pamphleteer disposed of

a reference to 'Tory commissioners' simply by invoking his name.[125] In
the commission's report, and the *Letter to a Soldier,* he was careful to
avoid the excesses of Tory commentators, and sometimes justified resumption in Whig, or pseudo-Whig, terms. He included accusations that the
Williamite government's administration of the forfeited estates had itself
worked to the benefit of Irish Catholics; and emphasized the connection
between the resumption scheme and the claims of the still unpaid veterans
of the Revolution war, noting especially Parliament's objective that the
forfeitures be applied to the purpose originally intended, paying off the
soldiers whose exertions had secured them in the first place — a classic
Whiggish line. Yet he could not divorce himself from the approach and
the arguments of his confederates, and in his reactions to the Irish 'remonstrance' his tone became offensive, sneering at Irish ideas of 'independence' and even at the Irish Protestants themselves and their spokesmen,
'these Trinculos, and fantastic viceroys, these errant Sancho Panzas and
squire-like governors of this wild and enchanted island'.[126] On the trust of
1700 he was the leader of the Whig minority, which consisted of himself,
his cronies Thomas Rawlins and John Cary, and two Irish Whigs, one of
whom died before operations could get properly under way; on the other
side were seven, later eight, Tories.[127]

The trust was, to all intents and purposes, a Tory political job. The
trustees co-operated closely with leading Tory politicians like Sir Edward
Seymour, Simon Harcourt and Robert Harley, and it was recommendations from this quarter which usually carried the day when clerks, receivers
and so forth came to be appointed. There was a good deal of such patronage available, and some of it went to Tories of a very high strain. Richard
Nutley is one example: a young lawyer, later to become a judge in Ireland
under the Tory administration of 1710–14 and to be strongly suspected
of Jacobitism, he was brought over as secretary to the trust.[128] The conduct of the trustees became the subject of fierce criticism, Irish Whigs
denouncing their supposed bias in favour of Catholics and against the
'poor Protestant purchasers'.[129] In these matters Trenchard was no different from his Tory colleagues. After some misgivings about the company
he was obliged to keep, he seems to have participated fully in the work
of the trust.[130] His Irish associations were no barrier, for he was not an
Irishman like Molesworth, but a Somerset man who happened to be the
heir to a Limerick estate. And like Sir Richard Cocks, he was a Whig who,
in this instance, had been drawn into thinking and acting like a Tory.

As well as these Tory components in the opposition to the standing
army and the agitation on the forfeitures question, there was also a distinctively Tory contribution to the more general 'Country' interpretation
of the English political malaise of the 1690s — the growth of that hydra
called 'Court corruption', one of whose heads was a standing army, the
others being placemen and pensioners, high taxation and the national
debt. The 'real fear' of the 'Country interest' was that 'war, money and

patronage would undermine the constitution, subvert the liberties of the subject and corrupt the nation at large'. This was the legacy of the neo-Harringtonians to the 'patriot' opposition of the 1720s. And in the process of developing and transmitting this analysis two Tory writers played significant parts: Charles Davenant and his distant 'cousin', Jonathan Swift.[131] It was Davenant's *The True Picture of a Modern Whig* (1701) which created the classic caricature Tom Double, the embodiment of Junto vices, entirely self-seeking and unprincipled, in contrast to the 'old Whig' Whig-love. The idea was not new, but Davenant gave it concrete form, at the same time bringing together the various criticisms of the Junto administration into a coherent and persuasive picture. Both as a piece of propaganda and as a timely synthesis of different strands in Country ideology, *The True Picture of a Modern Whig* was of crucial significance. Davenant produced a sequel, *Tom Double returned out of the Country*, and brought the story up to date in 1710 with *Sir Thomas Double at Court* and *New Dialogues upon the Present Posture of Affairs*, which dovetailed neatly with Swift's work for the new Tory ministry.

Many of Davenant's ideas were taken up by Swift in his attacks on the Junto and the Marlborough–Godolphin ministry. The main theme of Swift's political journalism between 1710 and 1714 is pure Davenant, ascribing the ills of the country to the malign effects of 'new Whig' governments in 1694–1700 and 1708–10. In this scenario the Junto appeared as a corrupt political interest, only nominally Whig and in essence a mercenary faction, which to sustain itself in power and make itself rich had artificially enlarged two of the heads of the 'Court Corruption' monster — the Army and the institutions of public credit like the Bank and New East India Company — and to maintain them had brought the 'landed interest of England' to its knees. What was for Swift the 'moneyed interest', profiting by the War of the Spanish Succession, had been for Davenant the pernicious 'new funds' and the increasing national debt which he had written against since at least 1694; where Swift exposed an enormous vested interest, from Marlborough downwards, anxious to prolong the war against Louis XIV, Davenant in his *Essays* in 1701 had urged caution in foreign policy, limited involvement in any war with France and prevention of the return of the old gang of ministers whose grandiose strategy and deficit-financing had proved disastrous before. Most important, perhaps, was the way Davenant's attitude towards the Dutch and the other European allies prefigured the vehemence of Swift's prose: Holland to him was as much England's rival as was France, and in 1695 he had observed that the waging of a war in Europe was to Holland's advantage and England's disadvantage, even though the two countries were allies.[132] It is, above all, this attitude to foreign policy which renders Davenant and Swift (despite the various Country Whig influences on their writing) Tory as much as Country. Davenant's reluctance to support a war in 1701, which brought him into close touch with the French king's representatives in

London, separated him and his fellow 'Poussineer' Anthony Hammond from the Whigs at the Grecian.[133] The difference between this and the staunch anti-French posture adopted by such Country Whigs as Shaftesbury, Molesworth and Henry Maxwell, was fundamental.[134] So while Molesworth's 'old Whig' remained a Whig, the 'Whiglove' of Davenant's *True Picture* reappeared in 1710 in a new guise as a Tory, having succeeded to the family baronetcy of 'Comeover'.

If we are to retain the interpretation of 'Whig and Tory' and 'Court and Country' as different sets of points on the political compass, the least that should be done is to alter their arrangement. Rather than view them as competing polarities, the line from Court to Country cutting across that from Whig to Tory at right angles, we should set the two alignments much closer together. Certainly from the Junto's assumption of power in 1693–4, the bulk of the Country interest was accommodated within the Tory party, and by Anne's reign Country sentiment seems to have been largely absorbed into back-bench Toryism, though Country ideology retained in it enough that was traditionally Whig to enable rebel Whigs to make common cause with Tories on a Country basis if need be. But perhaps it would be wiser to throw away the compass altogether. Because Country Members were to be found so much more on the Tory than the Whig side, it does not follow that the Tory party was simply a Country party, for it always contained a substantial Court-orientated element too. The fact that the Tories were in power only for three brief spells between 1689 and their proscription in 1714 — 1690-3, 1702-4 (as a party, although a number of moderate Tories stayed in office until 1708) and 1710-14 — can create a false impression. When the opportunity arose Tories scrambled for place with quite as much keenness as Whigs. According to Bolingbroke in 1710 the Tories 'came to court in the same dispositions as all parties have done'; and the first back-bench pressure group to challenge the new ministry, the October Club, was as much concerned with replacing Whigs in office as it was with pursuing a Country programme: together with the enthusiastic new Members, it consisted of 'some of the old Tories, who are not yet provided'.[135]

Although the area of the Country interest on any pattern of politics can still be mapped out, it may be better to treat 'Court and Country' separately from 'Whig and Tory', as something quite different: 'another level of political consciousness' has been one suggestion.[136] Certainly in this period 'Court and Country' ceased to represent a standing political division. *A* Country party manifested itself from time to time; *the* Country party did not have a continuous existence. Whigs and Tories co-operated — in Parliament on Country measures, at elections sometimes, on a Country platform — but they did not lose their identity. They still remained Whigs and Tories first and foremost. In constructing a model of political structure, therefore, we should take as our basis the two-party system of Whig versus Tory, and regard the conflicts between Court and Country rather as

'superstructural'; or even, for this limited purpose, leave the Country
interest entirely on one side, as in itself too complex a phenomenon to
fit properly into any such conventional forms of historical pattern-making.

NOTES

1. *Letters Illustrative of the Reign of William III from 1696 to 1708* . . ., ed.
G. P. R. James (3 vols, 1841), II, 142–3; James Drake, *The History of the
Last Parliament* . . . (1702), preface (no pagination); HMC, *Portland MSS*,
IV, 490. I regret that Jonathan Duke-Evans's thesis on 'The political theory
and practice of the English commonwealthsmen 1675–1725' (D. Phil., University of Oxford, 1980), which bears directly upon my theme, came to my attention too late for its conclusions to be considered in this essay. However, they do
not, I believe, significantly affect its main arguments.
2. B. W. Hill, *The Growth of Parliamentary Parties 1689–1742* (1976), 26.
3. By W. A. Speck, in *The Whig Ascendancy: Colloquies on Hanoverian England*,
ed. John Cannon (1981), 72.
4. Frank O'Gorman, *The Rise of Party in England: The Rockingham Whigs
1760–82* (1975), 16.
5. Dennis Rubini, *Court and Country 1688–1702* (1968), 259–60; Henry Horwitz,
'Parties, connections and parliamentary politics 1689–1714: review and revision', *J. British Studies, vi* (1966); 'The structure of parliamentary politics', in
Britain after the Glorious Revolution 1689–1714, ed. Geoffrey Holmes (1969);
Parliament, Policy and Politics in the Reign of William III (1977), esp. 317–19.
See also I. F. Burton, P. W. J. Riley and Edward Rowlands, 'Political parties
in the reigns of William III and Anne: the evidence of division lists', *BIHR*,
Special Supp. *vi* (1968).
6. Geoffrey Holmes, *British Politics in the Age of Anne* (1967), 116–47, 418; 'The
Commons' division on "No Peace without Spain", 7 December 1711', *BIHR,
xxxiii* (1960); J. G. Sperling, 'The division of 25 May 1711, on an amendment
to the South Sea Bill: a note on the reality of parties in the reign of Anne',
HJ, iv (1961); W. A. Speck, 'The choice of a Speaker in 1705', *BIHR, xxxvii*
(1964); H. L. Snyder, 'The defeat of the Occasional Conformity Bill and the
Tack: a study in the techniques of parliamentary management in the reign of
Queen Anne', *BIHR, xli* (1968); 'Party configurations in the early eighteenth-
century House of Commons', *ibid., xlv* (1972); 'The contribution and limita-
tions of division lists to the study of parliamentary parties', in *The Parliament-
ary Lists of the Early Eighteenth Century: Their Compilation and Use*, ed.
Aubrey Newman (1973); W. A. Speck, *Tory and Whig: The Struggle in the
Constituencies 1701–1715* (1970).
7. *The House of Commons 1715–54*, ed. Romney Sedgwick (2 vols, 1970); Linda
J. Colley, 'The Loyal Brotherhood and the Cocoa Tree: the London organization of the Tory party 1727–1760', *HJ, xx* (1977); *In Defiance of Oligarchy:
The Tory Party 1714–60* (1982); Eveline Cruickshanks, *Political Untouchables:
The Tories and the '45* (1979).
8. Caroline Robbins, *The Eighteenth-Century Commonwealthman* (Cambridge,
Mass., 1959); *Two English Republican Tracts*, ed. Caroline Robbins (1969);
Bernard Bailyn, *The Ideological Origins of the American Revolution* (Cambridge, Mass., 1967).
9. J. G. A. Pocock, 'Macchiavelli, Harrington and English political ideologies in
the eighteenth century', reprinted in *Politics, Language and Time* (1972); *The
Macchiavellian Moment* (Princeton, 1975); *The Political Works of James Harrington*, ed. J. G. A. Pocock (1977).

10. J. G. A. Pocock, '*The Macchiavellian Moment* revisited: a study in history and ideology', *J. of Modern History, liii* (1981), 63. For an example of Pocock's influence, see H. T. Dickinson, *Liberty and Property: Political Ideology in Eighteenth-Century Britain* (1977), esp. chs. 3, 5.

11. R. R. Walcott, 'English party politics, 1688-1714', in *Essays in Modern History in Honor of Wilbur Cortez Abbott* (Cambridge, Mass., 1941), 83-5; *English Politics in the Early Eighteenth Century* (1956), 92-3, 157-8. See also Sir Lewis Namier, *Crossroads of Power* (1962), 32-3.

12. Horwitz, 'Structure of parliamentary politics', 108; Holmes, *Politics in the Age of Anne*, 220-30, 249-52, 253-7.

13. W. A. Speck, *Stability and Strife: England 1714-1760* (1977), 7.

14. Pocock, '*Macchiavellian Moment* revisited', 62-3; Dickinson, *Liberty and Property*, 123.

15. J. B. Owen, *The Rise of the Pelhams* (1959); *The Pattern of Politics in Eighteenth-Century England* (1962), esp. pp. 4, 14-15. Cf. J. C. D. Clark, 'The decline of party, 1740-60', *EHR, xciii* (1978), 499-501, 508. In the fashion of Namier, Owen divided the Commons membership broadly into professional politicians and 'independent country gentlemen'. Competition between the 'ins' and the 'outs' among the politicians for the allegiance of the country gentlemen was what produced 'Court' and 'Country' parties. Reliance on this Namierite analysis, by historians professing to rise above the mundane preoccupations and excessive cynicism of Namier's approach to understanding eighteenth-century politics, is somewhat ironic.

16. Dickinson, *Liberty and Property*, 91, 102. But see Linda Colley and Mark Goldie, 'The principles and practice of eighteenth-century party', *HJ, xii* (1979), 242-3.

17. *A Register of Parliamentary Lists 1660-1761*, ed. David Hayton and Clyve Jones (University of Leicester History Department Occasional Publications no. 1, 1979), 5-6, 37-50, 65-7, 71-2, 81-106.

18. Holmes, *Politics in the Age of Anne*, 355-7. Cf. Walcott, *English Politics*, 36-9, 68-9, 198-200.

19. Gertrude A. Jacobsen, *William Blathywayt: A Late Seventeenth-Century English Administrator* (New Haven, Conn., 1932), 313. For Ranelagh, see the *DNB*.

20. Holmes, *Politics in the Age of Anne*, 391-5. See also Edward Gregg and Clyve Jones, 'Hanover, pensions and the "poor lords", 1712-13', *Parliamentary History, i* (1982), 173-80.

21. Eveline Cruickshanks, David Hayton and Clyve Jones, 'Divisions in the House of Lords on the transfer of the Crown and other issues, 1689-94: ten new lists', *BIHR, liii* (1980), 69-73.

22. *CSP Dom. 1691-2*, 353; *1690-1*, 465, 481; J. A. Downie, 'The commission of accounts and the formation of the Country party', *EHR, xci* (1976), 40, 44-6, 50; Horwitz, *Parliament, Policy and Politics*, ch. 3; Mark Goldie, 'The roots of true Whiggism 1688-94', *History of Political Thought, i* (1980), 225. For Howard, see H. J. Oliver, *Sir Robert Howard* (Durham, N. Carolina, 1963); for Rich, Douglas R. Lacey, *Dissent and Parliamentary Politics in England, 1661-1689* (New Brunswick, New Jersey, 1969), 438-9.

23. Burton *et al.*, 'Political parties', 38-9; Horwitz, *Parliament, Policy and Politics*, 217; W. A. Speck, 'The House of Commons, 1702-14' (D. Phil. thesis, University of Oxford, 1965), ch. 3; Holmes, *Politics in the Age of Anne*, 260-9, 229-30; Walcott, *English Politics*, 66-8, 214-15; Godfrey Davies, 'The seamy side of Marlborough's war', *Huntington Library Quarterly, xv* (1951-2), 38-40; Angus McInnes, *Robert Harley, Puritan Politician* (1970), 116-19; Edward Gregg, *Queen Anne* (1980), 299-300.

24. Namier, *Crossroads of Power*, 30 *et seq.*; *The Structure of Politics at the Accession of George III* (2nd edn, 1957), 4-5.

25. Lady Elizabeth C. Cust, *Records of the Cust Family* (3 ser., 1898-1927), II, 147, 151; HMC, *Portland MSS*, III, 536.
26. Holmes, *Politics in the Age of Anne*, 222.
27. See Appendix. The Bank directors were Sir John Cope and John Rudge; the East India Co. directors William Betts and Thomas Heath; the South Sea director Jacob Sawbridge. Unless otherwise stated, information about M.P.s has been drawn from Sedgwick, *House of Commons*, and from draft biographies in the possession of the History of Parliament Trust.
28. HMC, *Buccleuch MSS*, II, 651; Holmes, *Politics in the Age of Anne*, 324.
29. PRO, 30/24/22/1/91 (Shaftesbury MSS): Edward Hooper to Shaftesbury, Nov. 1701.
30. Derek Hirst, 'Court, country and politics before 1629', in *Faction and Parliament: Essays in Early Stuart History,* ed. Kevin Sharpe (1978), 119. See also Conrad Russell, *Parliaments and English Politics 1621-1629* (1979), 5-26.
31. Beaufort MSS (Duke of Beaufort, Badminton House, Gloucestershire), Beaufort letterbook 1710-14 (unfol.): Beaufort to John Manley, 24 Nov. 1711.
32. BL, Loan 29/126: Barker to Oxford, 29 May 1711; HMC, *Portland MSS*, V, 233, 307. See also Holmes, *Politics in the Age of Anne*, 117. According to the sometime Country Whig Sir Richard Onslow 'the most valuable part' of taking office was 'to be serviceable to my King, my country and my friends' (Gloucestershire RO, D340a/C22/31: Onslow to Matthew Ducie Moreton, 16 Dec. 1714).
33. BL, Loan 29/133: Davers to Oxford, 2, 29 Sept. 1712, 12 July 1714; 29/131/13: Corrance to Oxford, 10 June 1711, 29 Oct. 1712; 29/313/10: Etheridge to Oxford, 29 May 1712.
34. Peter Roebuck, 'The county squirearchy and the fight for place in the early eighteenth century', *Yorkshire Archaeological J., xlvi* (1974). 'The elections of 1710,' writes Roebuck, 'produced a situation in which Country-Tory M.P.s such as Kaye expected to wallow in patronage, as they had always accused the Whigs of doing' (103).
35. BL, Add. MS 18986, fos 473, 477: Barker to Sir Richard Haddock, 28 Feb. 1690, to the Navy commissioners, 21 May 1690; Robert Walcott, 'The East India interest in the general election of 1700-1701', *EHR, lxxi* (1956), 226; *Calendar of Treasury Books*, XXVI, 208, 256, 342; XXVII, 125, 188, 223.
36. *CSP Dom.*, *1697*, 513; BL, Add. MS 61461, fos 149-50: [Arthur Maynwaring to the Duchess of Marlborough], 'Wednesday evening' [?21 May 1711]; Berkshire RO, Trumbull MSS, Alphab. 51: T. B[ateman] to [Sir William Trumbull], 19 June 1713. See also 'P.H.', *An Impartial View of the Two Late Parliaments* ... (1711), 48. 'Polesworth' was presumably Sir Humphrey Mackworth.
37. Cruickshanks *et al.*, 'Ten new lists', 69; James, *Letters Illustrative . . .*, II, 434.
38. BL, Add. MS 29584, fos 95-6: Trelawney to Nottingham, 17 Aug. 1702; Scottish RO, GD 220/5/807/2 (Montrose MSS): Mungo Graham to Montrose, 25 Nov. 1710. See also, Hill, *Growth of Parliamentary Parties*, 27-8.
39. Holmes, *Politics in the Age of Anne*, 249, 252; H. T. Dickinson, *Bolingbroke* (1970), 20-1.
40. Colley and Goldie, 'Principles and practice', 246; Colley, *In Defiance of Oligarchy*, 93. See below, p. 57.
41. *The Parliamentary Diary of Narcissus Luttrell, 1691-1693*, ed. Henry Horwitz (1972), 390-1; Horwitz, *Parliament, Policy and Politics*, 107-11.
42. For these lists see Hayton and Jones, *Register of Parliamentary Lists*, 88-92. The figures that they yield can only be approximate, because of various obscurities and deficiencies. In particular it should be noted that the 'base list', Carmarthen's 1690 analysis, as well as classifying Members as Whigs and Tories, places 21 in a third category, presumably as 'doubtfuls'; and that the Grascome

list, since it omits the representatives of the Cinque Ports and of the Welsh constituencies, understates the proportion of 'Court' to 'Country' Whigs.

43. For what follows, see Appendix.

44. Hayton and Jones, *Register of Parliamentary Lists*, 37–50.

45. Anchitell Grey, *Debates of the House of Commons from the Year 1667 to the Year 1694* (10 vols, 1769); Horwitz, *Luttrell Parliamentary Diary*; Bodl., MS Eng. hist. b. 209–10: Sir Richard Cocks's diary and commonplace-book.

46. 'An anonymous parliamentary diary, 1705–6', ed. W. A. Speck, *Camden Miscellany XXIII* (Camden Soc., 4th ser., VII, 1969), 61–6, 79–81, records contributions by the following Country Whigs: John Aislabie, Robert Eyre, Sir John Hawles, Peter King, Sir Richard Onslow, James Stanhope and 'Mr Ward' [? John, M.P. Bletchingley].

47. Holmes, *Politics in the Age of Anne*, 221–3, names the following as Country Whigs in Anne's reign: Lords Hervey, Shaftesbury and Warrington; and in the Commons Sir Michael Biddulph, Sir William Bowes, Sir John Cropley, John Dibble, Richard Edgcumbe, Sir William Ellys, Robert Eyre, Peter Gott, Sir John Guise, William Harris, Sir John Hawles, Henry Henley, (Sir) Thomas Johnson, Peter King, James Lowther, John Morgan, Richard Neville, Sir Richard Onslow, Thomas Onslow, Sir Isaac Rebow, Sir William Robinson, John Rudge, James Stanhope, John Thornaugh, Roger Tuckfield, Richard Vaughan, Daniel Wilson, Edward Wortley Montagu, John Yorke and Thomas Yorke.

48. *Ibid.*, 43, 223, 480; Beaufort MSS, letterbook 1710–14: Beaufort to Morgan, 12 Sept. 1710, 15 Jan. 1712, 11 July 1713; Beaufort to Mr Gwyn, 12 Jan. 1712; *Autobiography of Thomas Raymond and Memoirs of the Family of Guise of Elmore, Gloucestershire*, ed. G. Davies (Camden Soc., 3rd ser., XXVIII, 1917), 138–57, esp. 143–4, 147–9, 151–2.

49. *Ideology and Conspiracy: Aspects of Jacobitism 1689–1759*, ed. Eveline Cruickshanks (1982), 8.

50. Sedgwick, *House of Commons*, I, 440–2, 507; Linda Colley, 'The people above in eighteenth-century Britain', *HJ, xxiv* (1981), 976.

51. J. V. Beckett, 'A back-bench M.P. in the eighteenth-century: Sir James Lowther of Whitehaven', *Parliamentary History, i* (1982).

52. Marjorie Cox, 'Sir Roger Bradshaigh, 3rd baronet, and the electoral management of Wigan, 1695–1747', *Bulletin of the John Rylands Library, xxxvii* (1954), 121–3.

53. *CJ, xvi*, 423; West Sussex RO, Ac. 454/869 (Shillinglee MSS): Clement Corrance to Sir Edward Turnor, 10 June 1709.

54. W. Sussex RO, Ac. 454/969, 911, 1013–15, 1020: Nathaniel Gooding to Sir Edward Turnor, 27 Jan. 1696[-7]; Edward Pratt to Turnor, 2 Mar. 1696[-7]; Theo. Hooke to Turnor, 2, 5, 13 Mar. 1697; John Hooke to Turnor, 6 Mar. 1697.

55. Narcissus Luttrell, *A Brief Historical Relation of State Affairs* (6 vols, 1857), VI, 54, 105; 'Bishop Nicolson's diaries: part VI', ed. R. G. Collingwood, *Transactions of the Cumberland and Westmorland Antiquarian and Archaeological Society*, n.s., *xxxv* (1935), 86; HMC, *Downshire MSS*, I, 842; *The Private Diary of William, First Earl Cowper*, ed. E. C. Hawtrey (1833), 37.

56. *The Wentworth Papers, 1705–1739*, ed. J. J. Cartwright (1883), 106.

57. Holmes, *Politics in the Age of Anne*, 117–18; William Pittis, *The History of the Present Parliament and Convocation* (1711), 9, 177, 235–6; Jonathan Swift, *Journal to Stella*, ed. Harold Williams (2 vols, 1948), II, 492–3, 496, 499, 625, 628; *Wentworth Papers*, 276; Richard Chandler, *The History and Proceedings of the House of Commons from the Restoration to the Present Time* (14 vols, 1742–4), V, 9, 11, 42, 159; *CJ, xvii*, 2, 28, 94, 406, 436. It would seem that Hanmer was in fact granted a secret pension on the Irish establishment in 1712, though probably this was in trust for his friend William Philips, an

impoverished Irish soldier and playwright: see David Hayton, 'Ireland and the English ministers, 1707–16' (D. Phil. thesis, University of Oxford, 1975), 262.

58. HMC, *Portland MSS*, IV, 657; *The Private Correspondence of Sarah Duchess of Marlborough* (2 vols, 1838), II, 11.

59. Pocock, *Works of Harrington*, 142–3; Edmund Ludlow, *A Voyce from the Watch Tower. Part five: 1660–1662*, ed. A. B. Worden (Camden Soc., 4th ser., XXI, 1978), 42; Horwitz, *Parliament, Policy and Politics*, 134.

60. Holmes, *Politics in the Age of Anne*, 223.

61. Kent Archives Office, U. 1590/C9/31 (Stanhope MSS): Sir John Cropley to James Stanhope, 19 Feb. 1706. See also PRO, 30/24/20/281: Cropley to Lord Shaftesbury, Feb. 1705–6, endorsed 'self denying clause' (1).

62. Holmes, *Politics in the Age of Anne*, 133, 141, 203, 223, 341; *Duchess of Marlborough Corresp.*, I, 105; HMC, *Bath MSS*, I, 192; *Portland MSS*, IV, 506, 592.

63. Aubrey Newman, *The Stanhopes of Chevening* (1969), ch. 1, esp. 27–33. See also Boston Public Library, Boston, Mass., MS K.5.5 (unfol.): Stanhope to Sunderland, 15 June, 15 Aug. 1703; Alexander Stanhope to Somerset, 20 July 1705. There is a sour assessment of Stanhope, the reputed 'great patriot', in Alexander Cunningham, *The History of Great Britain from the Revolution in 1688 to the Accession of George I*, trans. William Thomson (2 vols, 1787), I, 461. Cf. Basil Williams, *Stanhope* (1932), 44–5.

64. *CJ, xvi*, 287; G. S. Holmes, 'The attack on "the influence of the Crown", 1702–16', *BIHR, xxxix* (1966), 65. In contrast to his father's, Thomas Onslow's nickname did not suggest staunchness of principle: it was 'Dicky Ducklegs'. For an account of this 'privileged though occasionally unpleasing buffoon', see C. E. Vulliamy, *The Onslow Family 1528–1874. With some account of their times* (1953), 30–4, 48, 50–86.

65. Kenneth A. Spencer Research Library, University of Kansas, MS C163: Sir William Simpson to John Methuen, 27 Mar. 1704[-5] ; E. L. Ellis, 'The Whig Junto, in relation to the development of party politics and party organisation, from its inception to 1714' (D. Phil. thesis, University of Oxford, 1961), Appendix C; Cobbett, *Parl. Hist.*, VII, 536–7.

66. J. H. Plumb, *The Growth of Political Stability in England 1675–1725* (1967), 131.

67. *Private Diary of Earl Cowper*, 11–12.

68. Bodl., MS Locke c. 38, f.1: Onslow to Peter King, 14 Oct. 1705; HMC, *14th Report*, IX, 492; William Coxe, *Memoirs of the Life and Administration of Sir Robert Walpole* (2 vols, 1798), II, 4; HMC, *Downshire MSS*, I, 8; *Private Diary of Earl Cowper*, 37; Speck, 'Anon. parl. diary', 58–65, 67–72; *Duchess of Marlborough Corresp.*, II, 233; P. W. J. Riley, *The Union of England and Scotland: A Study in Anglo-Scottish Politics of the Eighteenth Century* (1978), 166–8, 191; Holmes, 'Influence of the Crown', 54–5.

69. Holmes, 'Influence of the Crown', 57–9.

70. Holmes, *Politics in the Age of Anne*, 340–1.

71. Holmes, 'Influence of the Crown', 53, 59–64; NLS, Wodrow Letters, Quarto S: Charles Morthland to Robert Wodrow, 16 Dec. 1710.

72. For what follows, see Appendix.

73. PRO, 30/24/20/282: Cropley to Shaftesbury, 'self denying clause' (2).

74. Kenneth A. Spencer Research Library, MS C163: Simpson to Methuen, 13 Feb. 1705. See also *The Correspondence of Jonathan Swift*, ed. Harold Williams (5 vols, 1963–5), I, 424: 'the young people in parliament are very eager to have some enquiries made into past managements'.

75. For Shaftesbury see PRO, 30/24/21/216 *et seq.*: MS sketch of his life, by his son, the fourth earl; *Letters from the . . . Earl of Shaftesbury to Robert Molesworth . . .*, ed. John Toland (1721); *Original Letters of John Locke, Algernon*

Sydney and the Third Earl of Shaftesbury, ed. Thomas Forster (2nd edn, 1847); Benjamin Rand, *The Life . . . Letters and Philosophical Regimen of . . . the Third Earl of Shaftesbury* (1900); and the *DNB*. He has been the subject of two recent doctoral theses: Peter Robinson, 'The third Earl of Shaftesbury and the socialization of philosophy' (University of Edinburgh, 1978); and C. J. Cunliffe, 'The third Earl of Shaftesbury . . . his politics and ideas' (University of Oxford, 1981).

76. PRO, 30/24/21/222. See also James, *Letters Illustrative . . .*, I, 189; II, 15.

77. Forster, *Original Letters . . .*, 119–20. The three Dorset M.P.s missing from the standing army list, besides Trenchard, were Thomas Freke, William Jolliffe and Alexander Pitfield; the four missing from the Regency Bill list, besides Cropley and Maurice Ashley, were Freke and Pitfield again, John Burridge and Awnsham Churchill. Maurice Ashley, a difficult man to deal with, was not on particularly good terms with Shaftesbury in 1706, but he was certainly a Country Whig — if anything an even more vehement opponent of the Junto: see PRO, 30/24/20/282, 21/4: Cropley to Shaftesbury, Feb. 1705–6, 'self denying clause' (2), 15 Jan. 1708. Strictly speaking, only he and Cropley can be described as owing their seats to the earl, though Shaftesbury did have some influence at Poole, which Joliffe represented, and possibly also at Dorchester. At any rate Churchill, the publisher, who sat for Dorchester, was known to him and had approached him early in 1705 at his first thought of standing for Parliament (PRO, 30/24/22/2/156: Shaftesbury to Churchill, 29 Jan. 1704–5). Freke, though Shaftesbury probably had little or nothing to do with his election, had been described by him in 1700 as one of his 'Country interest . . . friends' (PRO, 30/24/20/35: Shaftesbury to Freke, 10 Sept. 1700). Information on Shaftesbury's connections and electoral interest has in general been drawn from the Shaftesbury MSS in the PRO.

78. PRO 30/24/20/288, 309–10, 350–1, 338–9, 342–5, 352–7; 30/24/21/41–6, 71–2: Shaftesbury to Furly, 11 Oct. 1706; Somers to Shaftesbury, 7 Jan. 1706–7; Godolphin to Shaftesbury, 23 Dec. 1707; Cropley to Shaftesbury, May, 15 Dec., Dec., 30 Dec. 1707, 15 Apr. 1708, n.d.

79. John Burridge and Maurice Ashley.

80. 'Some advice to the October Club' in *The Prose Works of Jonathan Swift*, ed. Herbert Davis *et al.* (16 vols, 1939–68), VI, 78. Cf. *Letters and Correspondence . . . of . . . Henry St.John, Lord Viscount Bolingbroke . . .* (4 vols, 1798), I, 399.

81. Bodl., MS Ballard 31, f. 145: [William Bishop to Arthur Charlett], 19 May 1715.

82. Anne Manning, *Family Pictures* (1861), 10; Scottish RO, GD 124/15/259/1 (Mar and Kellie MSS): Cleland to James [Erskine], 10 Nov. 1705.

83. Holmes, *Politics in the Age of Anne*, 119.

84. East Suffolk RO, M142(1) (Gurdon MSS), II, 149: Richard Berney to Thornhagh Gurdon, 3 Jan. 1710[-11].

85. C. B. Realey, *The London Journal and its Authors, 1720–1723 (Bulletin of University of Kansas, Humanistic Studies, v, no. 3, 1935)*; Robbins, *Eighteenth-Century Commonwealthman*, 115–24; Sedgwick, *House of Commons*, II, 481; J. P. Kenyon, *Revolution Principles: The Politics of Party 1689–1720* (1977), 198–9; Dickinson, *Liberty and Property*, ch. 5.

86. Robbins, *Eighteenth-Century Commonwealthman*, ch. 4; *Two English Republican Tracts*, 31–3; Anthony Hammond, *The Whole Works of Walter Moyle . . .* (1727), introduction, 19.

87. Pocock, *Politics, Language and Time*, 120–3, 125–7, 136–9; *Macchiavellian Moment*, 427–32; *Works of Harrington*, 136–42; Lois G. Schwoerer, 'The literature of the standing army controversy 1697–1699', *Huntington Library Quarterly*, xxviii (1964–5); *No Standing Armies! The Antiarmy Ideology in Seventeenth-Century England* (Baltimore, 1974), ch. 8.

88. Dickinson, *Liberty and Property*, 112–13, 115; Robert Molesworth, *The Principles of a Real Whig; Contained in a Preface to . . . Hotoman's Franco-Gallia . . .* (1775), preface, 13.

89. Pocock, *Works of Harrington*, 141–3; Ludlow, *Voyce from the Watch Tower*, 17–80.

90. Bodl., MS Rawl. D. 174, fos 41–2, 87–8; D. 386, fos 36, 41, 43, 56, 63–4, 66; D. 738, f. 66; Sir Keith Feiling, *A History of the Tory Party 1640–1714* (1924), 480; E. Suffolk RO, M 142 (1), II, 27, 41: Cook to Thornhagh Gurdon, 19 Jan. 1698[–9], 9 Mar. 1698–9.

91. Grey, *Debates*, X, 354–5. For Hungerford see *Poems on Affairs of State*, ed. G. de F. Lord *et al.* (7 vols, New Haven, Conn., 1938–75), VII, 124–5.

92. Francis Woodhouse, land agent to James Brydges of all people, in asking his employer to intercede for him at the Exchequer and blissfully unaware of any irony, struck the conventional note of world-weary pessimism: 'how far courtiers' words are to be taken', he wrote, referring to Auditor Edward Harley, 'I leave other people to be judge' (Huntingdon Library, Stowe MSS 58, VIII, 263: Woodhouse to Brydges, 16 July 1711). Brydges's reaction is unknown.

93. Colley and Goldie, 'Principles and practice', 246. See also J. R. Jones, 'Parties and parliament', in *idem* (ed.), *The Restored Monarchy 1660–1668* (1979), 65–70.

94. *Swift's Prose Works*, III, 163–4.

95. Grey, *Debates*, VIII, 355–8, 367.

96. Rubini, *Court and Country*, 134. Pocock, *Politics, Language and Time*, 121–3; *Swift's Prose Works*, III, 145–6. See also Henry Maxwell, *An Essay upon an Union of Ireland with England* (Dublin, 1704), 4, 6–8.

97. HLRO, House of Commons Library MS 12, f. 101. That it should be Robert Harley to make this point is especially interesting, given his close connection both with Swift's *Examiners* and earlier with John Toland, presumed editor of Ludlow: see W. A. Speck, '*The Examiner* examined: Swift's Tory pamphleteering', in *Focus: Swift*, ed. C. J. Rawson (1971); Pocock, *Politics, Language and Time*, 122; Ludlow, *Voyce from the Watch Tower*, 22–9, 42; J. A. Downie, *Robert Harley and the Press: Propaganda and Public Opinion in the Age of Swift and Defoe* (1979), 36–7.

98. Horwitz, *Luttrell Parliamentary Diary*, 284; HLRO, House of Commons MS 12, f. 101v. See also Hertfordshire RO, D/EP F98 (Panshanger MSS), fos 6, 11: William Cowper's parliamentary diary, 16, 23 Dec. 1698.

99. HLRO, House of Commons Library MS 12, f. 101.

100. Herts. RO, D/EP F98, fos 5–7: Cowper diary, 16 Dec. 1698.

101. Cobbett, *Parl. Hist.*, VII, 510; Huntington Library, MS LO 7948 (Loudoun MSS): [Charles Cathcart to Loudoun], 15 Feb. 1718. Cf. Colley, *In Defiance of Oligarchy*, 87–8. This argument, adumbrated by Court pamphleteers, had been employed by Charles Montagu in 1699, when he pointed out that the army 'can't be increased without leave of Parl[iament]' (Herts. RO, D/EP F101: William Cowper's 'Notes taken in the Mony-Chair' [as chairman of ways and means]).

102. *Seventeenth-Century England: A Changing Culture. Volume I: Primary Sources*, ed. Ann Hughes (1980), 32; Grey, *Debates*, VIII, 355–8, 367; Schwoerer, *No Standing Armies!*, 139–43.

103. Horwitz, *Luttrell Parliamentary Diary*, 97, 250–7; Grey, *Debates*, X, 252–63; Robert Molesworth, *An Account of Denmark as it was in the Year 1692* (1694), 268. See also Robbins, *Eighteenth-Century Commonwealthman*, 104. The Tory Lord Cornbury had come to similar conclusions about Denmark's 'miserable tyranny' in 1687, though he did not set them down in print: *The Diary of John Evelyn*, ed. E. S. De Beer (6 vols, 1955), IV, 558–9.

104. Horwitz, *Luttrell Parliamentary Diary*, 250, 262.

105. *Ibid.*, 26, 82; Grey, *Debates*, X, 340. See also *ibid*., 264, 313 (Sir Thomas Clarges), 315 (Sir Edward Seymour), 339–40 (Sir Christopher Musgrave, Sir Francis Winnington, Sir John Thompson), 343 (Henry Cornewall). On Tory xenophobia in Anne's reign, see H. T. Dickinson, 'The Tory party's attitude to foreigners: a note on party principles in the age of Anne', *BIHR, xl* (1967).

106. Horwitz, *Luttrell Parliamentary Diary*, 31.

107. Grey, *Debates*, X, 262.

108. Horwitz, *Luttrell Parliamentary Diary*, 26; Grey, *Debates*, X, 271, 313.

109. HLRO, House of Commons Library MS 12, f. 131.

110. Hammond, *Moyle's Works*, introduction, 30–1, 50–1, text, 159, 188–9; Robbins, *Two English Republican Tracts*, 26–8; Pocock, *Macchiavellian Moment*, ch. 13, esp. 436 *et seq.*; Schwoerer, *No Standing Armies!*, 181–2. Cf. Robbins, *Eighteenth-Century Commonwealthman*, 104.

111. *The Political and Commercial Works of Charles D'Avenant . . .*, ed. Sir Charles Whitworth (5 vols, 1771), III, 268. See also Horwitz, *Luttrell Parliamentary Diary*, 439; Bodl., MS Eng. hist. b. 209, f. 92. Tories in 1711 made the same point, attacking William's grants, those to Portland in particular (Niedersächsisches Staatsarchiv, Hannover, Cal. Br. 24 England, 99, fos. 145–6: Kreienberg despatch, 2 Mar. 1711).

112. Whitworth, *D'Avenant's Works*, III, 269–70, 289–90.

113. *Poems on Affairs of State*, ed. G. de F. Lord *et al.*, VI, 639; Luttrell, *Brief Relation*, IV, 14.

114. *To the Honourable the Commons of England in Parliament, a Remedy Against Taxes: Or, the Resumption of Crown Lands and Forfeitures* (n.d.; copy in Lothian MSS [the Marquess of Lothian, Melbourne Hall, Derbyshire], folder marked 'Thomas Coke . . . Parliamentary papers James II–Anne'). My italics. See also 'The Exorbitant Grants of King William the Third examined and questioned . . .' (1703), in *A Collection of Scarce and Valuable Tracts . . .*, ed. Sir Walter Scott (2nd edn, 13 vols, 1809–15), XII, 419.

115. On the Irish land settlement, see J. G. Simms, *The Williamite Confiscation in Ireland, 1690–1703* (1956).

116. Hayton, 'Ireland and the English ministers', ch. 5; David Hayton, 'The beginnings of the "undertaker system" ' in *Penal Era and Golden Age: Essays in Irish History, 1690–1800*, ed. Thomas Bartlett and David Hayton (1979), 42–5.

117. Pocock, *Works of Harrington*, 71–2; Caroline Robbins, 'The "excellent use" of colonies', *Huntington Library Quarterly, xxiii* (1966), 620–6; Robbins, *Two English Republican Tracts*, 27; Blair Worden, 'Classical republicanism and the Puritan revolution', in *History and Imagination: Essays in Honour of H. R. Trevor-Roper*, ed. Hugh Lloyd-Jones, Valerie Pearl and Blair Worden (1981), 196–9. See also Molesworth, *Principles of a Real Whig*, 14.

118. See for example, John Trenchard, *A Letter from a Soldier to the Commons of England, Occasioned by an Address now Carrying on by the Protestants in Ireland . . .* (1702), *passim; The Several Addresses of Some Irish Folks to the King and the House of Commons* (n.d.), 7. Cf. *Some Few Remarks upon a Pamphlet Intitul'd, a Letter from a Soldier . . .* (n.d.), 3; *A Letter from a Soldier, Being some Remarks upon a Late Scandalous Pamphlet; Entituled, An Address of Some Irish Folks* (1702), 5.

119. *The Several Addresses of Some Irish . . . Folks*, 2, 5–7.

120. *Ibid.*, 2–3, 5; *To the Honourable the Commons of England in Parliament, a Remedy Against Taxes . . . .*

121. *CJ, xiii*, 394; *The Journals of the House of Commons of the Kingdom of Ireland* (19 vols, Dublin, 1753–76), III, 64–7. In the English House of Commons Molesworth had been a vigorous defender of Irish interests (Bolton MSS [Lord Bolton, Bolton Hall, Wensley, Yorkshire], D/16: Ben Overton to Lord Winchester, 3 May 1698).

122. Hammond, *Moyle's Works*, introduction, 19–20.
123. James, *Letters Illustrative . . .*, II, 356, 406, 409–12, 439–40; Bodl., MS Eng. hist. b. 209, fos 92, 84 (reverse foliation); b. 210, fos 3, 4, 10; Cobbett, *Parl. Hist.*, V, 1204–14; *CJ, xiii*, 65–6.
124. Cobbett, *Parl. Hist.*, V, 1204–14.
125. *The Whigs' Thirty-Two Queries, and as Many of the Tories' in Answer to Them . . .* (1701), 8. Cf. *The Secret History of the Trust; with Some Reflections upon the Letter from a Soldier. In a familiar Discourse between J. Truncheon Esq. and Mr. Inquisitive* (1702), 4, in which Truncheon (Trenchard) is made to admit: 'Most certainly the Tories were a broken party, till I cemented 'em. I did not only write my book against the army for their service, but my first report.'
126. Trenchard, *Letter from a Soldier*, 16, 20. It was alleged that he was also the author of the anonymous, and intemperate, satire *An Address of Some Irish Folks: A Letter from a Soldier, Being some Remarks upon . . . An Address of Some Irish Folks*, 2, 16.
127. The Irish Whigs were Henry Langford and James Hamilton of Tullymore (replaced after his death by James Hooper). The other trustees were Francis Annesley, John Baggs, William Fellowes, Thomas Harrison, John Isham, Sir Henry Sheres and Sir Cyril Wyche. See Simms, *Williamite Confiscation*, 98–9, 118; for Rawlins, J. A. Downie, 'William Stephens and the *Letter to the Author of the Memorial of the State of England* reconsidered', *BIHR, l* (1977), 253–9; and for Cary, the *DNB*.
128. For Nutley, see F. E. Ball, *The Judges in Ireland 1221–1921* (2 vols, 1926), II, 39, 72.
129. I hope to publish a fuller account of this episode, in which the question of pro-Catholic bias and other political implications of the trustees' activities will be explored.
130. Lothian MSS, Correspondence: Burdett Jodrell to [Thomas Coke], 27 Oct. 1702.
131. Pocock, *Politics, Language and Time*, 124–5; Dickinson, *Liberty and Property*, 104; BL, Lansdowne MS 773, f. 57: Davenant to his son Henry, 22 Sept. 1704. For Davenant, see D. A. G. Waddell, 'The Career and Writings of Charles Davenant . . .' (D. Phil. thesis, University of Oxford, 1954), summarized in 'Charles Davenant . . . a biographical sketch', *Economic History Rev.*, 2nd ser., *xi* (1958–9); Pocock, *Macchiavellian Moment*, ch. 13.
132. Waddell, thesis, 23–38, 82–4, 107–9, 112–14, 127–8, 134 n. 3; Whitworth, *D'Avenant's Works*, I, 394 *et seq.* Hatred of the Dutch became in Anne's reign a hallmark of high Toryism: e.g. *March and October, a Dialogue* (1712), 5.
133. Waddell, thesis, 280–3, 289–95; Horwitz, *Parliament, Policy and Politics*, 297.
134. For Maxwell, the reputed author of *Anguis in Herba* (1702), opposing any peace with Louis XIV, see Robbins, *Eighteenth-Century Commonwealthman*, 147–9, 416–17. This very point was made by John Toland in *The Art of Governing by Partys . . .* (1701), 53–4.
135. *Letter to Sir William Wyndham*, quoted in Geoffrey Holmes and W. A. Speck, *The Divided Society: Party Conflict in England 1694–1716* (1967), 141; Scottish RO, GD 220/5/808/15, Mungo Graham to Montrose, 6 Feb. 1711.
136. O'Gorman, *Rise of Party*, 495.

Appendix   The identification of Country Whigs
from House of Commons division lists

As we have seen, for three of the most notable occasions in this period in which
Whigs in the Commons split from the rest of the party on 'Court' against 'Country'
issues – the Disbanding Bill (1699), the place clause in the Regency Bill (1706)
and the Septennial Bill (1716) – a record survives in the form of a contemporary
division list. What follows is an attempt to isolate the Country Whigs in these votes.
Since both the Disbanding Bill and Regency Bill lists give only the Court side, I have
identified all the missing Whigs who could have been present at each division. In the
case of the Disbanding Bill we can take the process a little further, because of the
existence of two lists of the 'Country party' in the 1698–9 session, one of which is
almost certainly a forecast of the opposition to the bill. However, it must be noted
that two Whigs known for certain to have voted against, Lord Hartington and
Thomas Pelham, were neither of them identified as opponents in these 'Country
party' lists. Furthermore, we should keep in mind that all three of the division lists
are published 'black lists' (in the case of the Septennial Bill, a combined 'white' and
'black list', since both sides in the vote are given), a genre of list especially vulnerable
to error. In identifying Members as Whigs or Tories I have made use of information
from a wide variety of sources, in particular the other parliamentary lists of the
period, enumerated and described in Hayton and Jones, *Register of Parliamentary
Lists*, and the biographies and constituency articles prepared for the History of
Parliament Trust – some, for the period 1715–54, already published, others, for
the period 1690–1715, still in draft. Finally, it should be noted that the names of
Members appearing on more than one of the lists below have been italicized.

1. Whigs absent from the Court side in the division on the Disbanding Bill, 18 Jan. 1699

Known Whigs who could have been present but whose names do not occur on any of
the available four lists of supporters of the standing army on 18 Jan. 1699. These
lists are:

1. BL, Add. MS 28091, f. 167, printed in Andrew Browning, *Thomas Osborne,
    Earl of Danby and Duke of Leeds, 1632–1713* (3 vols, 1944–51), III, 213–17.
2. Newberry Library, Chicago, Case 6a 160 no. 70: *A List of the Members of the
    Last House of Commons, Convened First to Sit on the 27th of September 1698
    who Voted for a Standing Army* [1701] .
3. National Library of Wales, Carreg-Llwyd MS II, 74.
4. Pepys Library, Magdalene College, Cambridge, PL 2179, pp. 71–4.

The superior letters [a] and [b] denote that the Member figured on either of the two lists
indicating supporters of the Country party at the beginning of the 1698–9 session:

[a]An analysis of Court and Country parties in the new House of Commons elected in
1698, as compared with the preceding Parliament, the original of which is to be
found in BL, Loan 29/35, bundle 12. This list is printed by Henry Horwitz, 'Parties,
connections and parliamentary politics 1689–1714: review and revision', *J. British
Studies, vi* (1966), 62–9, who suggested there and in *Parliament, Policy and Politics
in the Reign of William III* (1977), 339, that it is 'perhaps' a forecast for the standing
army issue.

[b]A list of the Country party early in the session, which I identify as a forecast of
the opposition to the standing army: BL, Egerton MS 3359, fos 35–6. See David

Hayton, 'The Country party in the House of Commons, 1698-9', *Parliamentary History* (forthcoming).

John AISLABIE[b] (Ripon 1695-1702, 1705-21, Northallerton 1702-5)

Sir Thomas ALSTON, 3 bt (Bedford 1698-1700)

Edward ASHE (Heytesbury 1695-1747)

William ASHE (Heytesbury 1668-81, 1685-1701, Wilts. 1701-2)

Sir Henry ASHURST, 1 bt (Truro 1681, 1689-95, 1698-1700, Wilton 1701-2)

Henry ASHURST (Preston 1698-1702)

Sir Samuel BARNARDISTON, 1 bt[ab] (Suffolk 1674-81, 1690-1702)

Samuel BARNARDISTON[ab] (Ipswich 1698-1700)

Thomas BERE (Tiverton 1690-1710, 1715-25)

Hugh BETHELL (Hedon 1695-1700)

Sir Michael BIDDULPH, 2 bt (Lichfield 1679-81, 1689-90, 1695-1700, 1701-5, 1708-10)

Jacob des BOUVERIE[b] (Hythe 1695-1700, 1713-22)

William BROMLEY[b] (Worcester 1685-1700, Worcs. 1701-2, 1705-7)

Edward BULLOCK[ab] (Essex 1698-1700, Colchester 1705)[1]

Reynolds CALTHORPE[b] (Hindon 1698-1701, 1701-2, 1705-8, 1709-10, 1715-20)

Lawrence CARTER[a] (Leicester 1698-1702, 1722-6, Bere Alston 1710-22)

William CAVENDISH, marquess of Hartington (Derbys. 1695-1701, Castle Rising 1702, Yorks. 1702-7)[2]

John CHOLMLEY (Southwark 1698-1702, 1702-11)

Sir Robert CLAYTON[ab] (London 1679-81, 1689-90, 1695-8, 1701-2, 1705-7, Bletchingley 1690-5, 1698-1700, 1702-5)

Charles COCKS (Worcester 1694-5, Droitwich 1695-1708)[3]

Sir Richard COCKS, 2 bt (Glos. 1698-1702)[4]

Hon. Spencer COMPTON (Eye 1698-1710, E. Grinstead 1713-15, Sussex 1715-28)

John COOKE (Midhurst 1681, Arundel 1694-5, 1698-1702)

Sir Robert COTTON, 1 bt[ab] (Cheshire 1680-1, 1689-1702)

Sir William COWPER, 2 bt (Hertford 1680-1, 1689-1700)

William COWPER (Hertford 1695-1700, Bere Alston 1701-5)[5]

Courtenay CROKER (Plympton Erle 1695-1702)

Sir Rushout CULLEN, 3 bt (Cambs. 1697-1710)

Sir Thomas DAY (Bristol 1695-1700)[6]

Richard DOWDESWELL (Tewkesbury 1685–1710)

Sir William ELLYS, 2 bt[a?b] (Grantham 1679–81, 1689–1713)[7]

George ENGLAND[ab] (Gt Yarmouth 1680–1, 1689–1701)

John EYRE (Downton 1698–1701, 1705–15)

Robert EYRE[ab] (Salisbury 1698–1710)[8]

Thomas, Ld FAIRFAX (Malton 1685–7, Yorks. 1689–1702, 1707)

Thomas FREKE (Cricklade 1685, 1689–90, Weymouth 1691–1700, Lyme Regis 1705–10)

Peter GOTT (Hastings 1690–5, 1698–1701, Suss. 1708–10, Lewes 1710–12)

William HARRIS[ab] (St Ives 1690–5, Okehampton 1698–1702, 1708–9)[9]

Sir Charles HOTHAM, 4 bt (Scarborough 1695–1702, Beverley 1702–23)

Sir Edward HUNGERFORD[ab] (Chippenham 1659, 1660, 1661, 1661–81, Shoreham 1685–95, Steyning 1695–1701, 1702–5)[10]

Sir Edward HUSSEY, 3 bt[ab] (Lincoln 1689–95, 1698–1700, 1701–5)[11]

Arthur INGRAM, 3 viscount Irwin (Scarborough 1693–1701, Yorks. 1701–2)

Thomas JERVOISE (Stockbridge 1691–5, Hants 1698–1702, 1705–8, 1709–10, Plympton Erle 1702–3, Hindon 1704–5)

William JOLLIFFE[ab] (Poole 1698–1705)

Sir Stephen LENNARD, 2 bt[ab] (Winchelsea 1681, Kent 1698–1700, 1708–9)[12]

Robert MICHELL (Petersfield 1689–1700, 1701–5)

Charles MOMPESSON (Old Sarum 1698–1705, 1705–8, Wilton 1708–13)

Edward MONTAGU (Chippenham 1698–1700)[13]

John MORICE[ab] (Newport 1690–8, Saltash 1698–1700)

Foot ONSLOW (Guildford 1689–1700)

Sir Richard ONSLOW, 3 bt (Guildford 1679–81, 1685–7, Surrey 1689–1710, 1713–15, St Mawes 1710–13)[14]

Arthur OWEN[a] (Pembs. 1695–1705, 1715–27, Pembroke bor. 1708–12)[15]

Thomas PAPILLON (Dover 1674–81, 1689–95, London 1695–1700)

Charles, Ld PASTON (Thetford 1699–1700)[16]

Thomas PELHAM (E. Grinstead 1678–81, Lewes 1680–1, 1685–1702, Suss. 1702–5)[17]

Alexander PITFIELD[ab] (Bridport 1698–1708)

Carew RALEIGH[a] (Downton 1698–1702)

Hon. Russell ROBARTES[b] (Bodmin 1693–1702, 1708–13, Lostwithiel 1702–8)

John RUDGE[ab] (Evesham 1698–1701, 1702–34)

Francis ST JOHN[b] (Tewkesbury 1654–5, Peterborough 1656–8, 1659, 1679–81, 1698–1700)

Sir Richard SANDFORD, 3 bt (Westmld 1695–1700, 1701–2, Morpeth 1701, 1705–13, Appleby 1713–23)

Sir Clowdisley SHOVEL (Rochester 1695–1701, 1705–7)

Philip TAYLOR (Weymouth 1698–1700)

Sir William THOMAS, 1 bt (Seaford 1661–81, 1685–7, 1701, Sussex 1681, 1689–1700, 1701–6)

John THURBARNE[ab] (Sandwich 1679–81, 1689–95, 1698–1700)

Richard TOPHAM[a] (Windsor 1698–1713)

Thomas TRENCHARD (Dorchester 1689–90, 1690–5, 1701, Wareham 1695–1700, Dorset 1701–2)

Thomas TURGIS[ab] (Gatton 1659, 1660–81, 1685–1702)

Sir Charles TURNER (King's Lynn 1695–1738)[18]

Richard VAUGHAN[a] (Carmarthen 1685–1724)

Robert WALPOLE (Castle Rising 1689–1700)[19]

William WALSH (Worcs. 1698–1701, 1702–5, Richmond 1705–8)[20]

Sir Michael WARTON[b] (Boroughbridge 1675–9, Hull 1680–1, Beverley 1689–1702, 1708–22)

Ralph WARTON[a] (Beverley 1695–1701)

George WHICHCOT[a] (Lincs. 1698–1700, 1705–10)

Walter WHITE (Chippenham 1695–1702, 1705)[21]

Sir John WOLSTENHOLME, 3 bt (Middx 1695–1700, 1705–9)

James WORSLEY (Newtown I.o.W. 1695–1701, 1705–22, 1727–9, 1734–41)[22]

Francis WORTLEY MONTAGU (Huntingdon 1697–1702)

Hon. Sidney WORTLEY MONTAGU (Huntingdon 1679–81, 1689–95, 1713–22, Camelford 1696–8, Peterborough 1698–1710, 1722–7)

Thomas YORKE (Richmond 1689–90, 1695–1710, 1713–16)

NOTES

1. Included on the basis of his classification as a Whig in 1705 and his vote for John Smith in the Speakership division of 25 Oct. 1705: no evidence of his party affiliation in the 1698–1700 Parliament.
2. Recorded as having voted against the bill: *CSP Dom. 1699–1700*, 28.
3. A 'Mr Cox' (either Charles Cocks, Charles Cox M.P. Southwark or Charles Coxe M.P. Cirencester) was appointed to a committee on 17 Jan. 1699: *CJ*, *xii*, 424. Being named to a committee, though an indication of probable attendance, is not proof. It was possible to be nominated in absentia.
4. Cocks had spoken earlier against the Disbanding Bill: Bodl., MS Eng. hist. b.

209, f. 93v: 'My first speech in Parliament spoken the 4th of Jan. 1698[–9] upon disbanding the army'; HLRO, House of Commons Library MS 12, f. 109. He was appointed to a committee on the day of the division: *CJ, xii,* 425.

5. Cowper's narrative of events in the Commons during the 1698–9 session (Herts. RO, D/EP F98, fos 3–18), though generally an objective and almost impersonal account, provides several hints that his position may have been nearer the opposition than the Court (fos 6–7, 11, 12). It is possible, however, that he was absent from the House on 18 Jan., since he inserts into his description of the crucial debate the disclaimer 'as I was informed' (f. 15). Later in the narrative he explains his failure to 'observe' a sitting of the Committee of the Whole House on the affairs of the Admiralty with the phrase 'it being term time' (f. 17). Cowper was of course a practising lawyer.

6. Given a month's leave of absence on 12 Jan. 1699: *CJ, xii,* 396.

7. Appointed to a committee on 18 Jan.: *ibid.,* 425.

8. A 'Mr Eyres' (either John, Robert or Gervase Eyre M.P. Notts.) was named to a committee on 18 Jan.: *ibid.,* 425. For Robert Eyre's support of the 1706 place clause in its early stages, see above, p. 50.

9. Difficult to classify by party. Even a contemporary wrote, 'I cannot tell what to make of him' (quoted in Holmes, *Politics in the Age of Anne,* 223).

10. Appointed to committees on 17 and 19 Jan.: *CJ, xii,* 424, 444.

11. Apparently an opponent of the standing army at this time: see Herts. RO, D/EP F101, fos 16v, 17.

12. Appointed to a committee on 17 Jan.: *CJ, xii,* 424.

13. But see 'Wiltshire politicians (c. 1700)', ed. Marquess of Lansdowne, *Wiltshire Archaeological and Natural History Magazine, xlvi* (1932–4), 73.

14. Seconded the motion to pass the bill: *Correspondence of the Family of Hatton* . . ., ed. E. M. Thompson (2 vols, Camden Soc., n.s., XXII–XXIII, 1878), II, 238. See also De Beer, *Diary of John Evelyn,* V, 311.

15. Given leave of absence on 16 Jan. 1699, 'his father being very ill': *CJ, xii,* 409.

16. Returned at a by-election only on 16 Jan.

17. Voted against the bill: *CSP Dom., 1699–1700,* 28.

18. A possible absentee, as he had been from the divisions on guineas and the Fenwick Attainder Bill in 1696. See also *CJ, xii,* 92.

19. Probably absent. He had suffered from chronic ill health since at least 1691, which had severely restricted his attendance at the House: see J. H. Plumb, *Men and Places* (1963), 136–63, esp. 146; *CJ, x,* 553, 559; *xi,* 109, 542; *xii,* 195; Cambridge UL, Cholmondeley (Houghton) MSS, Corresp.: Walpole to John Relfe, 5 Feb. 1695; Lord Mordaunt to Walpole, 28 Nov. 1699; HMC, *House of Lords MSS,* n.s., I, 430, 432. He was indeed granted leave of absence on health grounds on 1 Feb. 1699 (*CJ, xii,* 467).

20. Named to a committee on 19 Jan.: *CJ, xii,* 444.

21. Probably absent: see Lansdowne, 'Wiltshire politicians', 72–3.

22. A record of absenteeism: see *CJ, xi,* 523, 724; *xii,* 56. With some hesitation I have counted Worsley as a Whig in 1699, though in Anne's reign he seems better described as a 'non-party placeman' (Holmes, *Politics in the Age of Anne,* 373), and under George I he appears as an opposition Tory (Sedgwick, *House of Commons,* II, 554).

2. Whigs absent from the Court side in a division on the place clause of the Regency Bill, c. 18 Feb. 1706

Known Whigs who could have been present but whose names are missing from the list of Court supporters in a division on the place clause, almost certainly one of the divisions on 18 February 1706: *A List of Moderate Patriots, who in the Second [sic] Session of the Last Parliament Voted for the Repeal of a Clause in an Act Pass'd in the 13th and 14th of His Late Majesty King William . . . Intituled 'An Act for the Further Limitation of the Crown, and better Securing the Rights and Liberties of the Subject'* . . . (1708), printed in R. R. Walcott, 'Division lists of the House of Commons, 1689-1715', *BIHR, xiv* (1936-7), 30-3. [Names of Members appearing on more than one of the lists given here have been italicized.]

John AISLABIE[1]

Hon. Maurice ASHLEY (Weymouth 1695-8, 1701, 1705-13, Wilts. 1701-2)

Sir John AUBREY, 3 bt (Cardiff 1706-10)[2]

George BALCH (Bridgwater 1701-10)[3]

Samuel BARKER (Cricklade 1702-8)

Edward BAYNTUN (Calne 1705-10)

Henry BENTINCK, viscount Woodstock (Southampton 1705-8, Hants 1708-9)[4]

Sir William BOWES (Co. Durham 1680-1, 1695-8, 1702-7)

Edmund BRAY (Tewkesbury 1701-8, Glos. 1720-2)

John BURRIDGE (Lyme Regis 1689-95, 1701-10)

James BUTLER (Arundel 1705-8, Sussex 1715-22, 1728-41)

William CARR (Newcastle-upon-Tyne 1690-1710)

Richard CHAUNDLER (Hants 1701-2, 1705-8, St Ives 1702, Lymington 1708-10, 1715-22)

Awnsham CHURCHILL (Dorchester 1705-10)

Edward CLARKE (Taunton 1690-1710)

Maynard COLCHESTER (Glos. 1701-8)

Sir Thomas COLEPEPER, 3 bt (Maidstone 1705-13, 1715-23)

Sir John COPE (Plympton Erle 1705-8, Tavistock 1708-27, Hants 1727-34, Lymington 1734-41)

Sir Robert CORBET, 4 bt (Salop 1705-10, 1715-22)

Sir John CROPLEY, 2 bt (Shaftesbury 1701-10)[5]

Sir John DELAVAL, 3 bt (Morpeth 1701-5, Northumb. 1705-8)

Sir Edmund DENTON, 1 bt (Buckingham 1698-1708, Bucks. 1708-13)

John DIBBLE (Okehampton 1705-13)

John DRYDEN (Hunts. 1690-5, 1699-1708)[6]

Edmund DUMMER (Arundel 1695–8, 1701, 1702–8)[7]

Edmund DUNCH (Cricklade 1701–2, 1705–13, Boroughbridge 1713–15, Wallingford 1715–19)

Richard EDGCUMBE (Corn. 1701, St Germans 1701–2, Plympton Erle 1702–34, 1741–2, Lostwithiel 1734–41)

Sir William ELLYS, 2 bt[8]

George EVELYN (Bletchingley 1705–24)

Thomas FREKE

Sir Henry FURNESE, 1 bt (Bramber 1698–9, Sandwich 1701, 1701–12)

Roger GALE (Northallerton 1705–13)[9]

Nathaniel GOULD (Shoreham 1701–8, 1710–28)

John HANBURY (Gloucester 1701–2, 1702–8, Monmouths. 1720–34)[10]

Stephen HARVEY (Reigate 1698–1707)[11]

Sir John HAWLES (Old Sarum 1689–90, Wilton 1695–8, 1702–5, Mitchell and Bere Alston 1698–1700, Truro 1701, St Ives 1701–2, Stockbridge 1705–10)[12]

Sir Edward IRBY, 1 bt (Boston 1702–8)

Thomas JOHNSON (Liverpool 1701–23)[13]

Peter KING (Bere Alston 1701–15)[14]

Sir Henry LIDDELL, 3 bt (Durham 1689–90, 1695–8, Newcastle-upon-Tyne 1701–5, 1706–10)[15]

Robert LOWTHER (Westmld 1705–8)

Sir Philip MONOUX, 3 bt (Bedford 1705–7)[16]

John MORGAN (Monmouths. 1701–20)[17]

John MOYSER (Beverley 1705–8)

Grey NEVILLE (Abingdon 1705–8, Wallingford 1708–10, Berwick 1715–23)

Sir Richard ONSLOW, 3 bt[18]

Thomas ONSLOW (Gatton 1702–5, Chichester 1705–8, Bletchingley 1708–15, Surr. 1715–17)

Alexander PITFIELD

Nicholas POLLEXFEN (Gt Bedwyn 1705–7, 1707–8)

Charles POWLETT, marquess of Winchester (Lymington 1705–8, Hants 1708–10, Carmarthens. 1715–17)

Sir Isaac REBOW (Colchester 1689–90, 1692–1702, 1702–14, 1715–22)

Sir William RICH, 2 bt (Reading 1689–98, 1705–8, Gloucester 1698–1700)

Sir William ROBINSON, 1 bt (Northallerton 1689–95, York 1698–1722)[19]

John RUDGE

Hon. James SAUNDERSON (Newark 1698–1700, 1701–10)[20]

Algernon SEYMOUR, earl of Hertford (Marlborough 1705–8, Northumb. 1708–22)

Edward STRODE (Ilchester 1705–8)[21]

Sir William THOMAS, 1 bt[22]

Richard VAUGHAN[23]

John WARD (Bletchingley 1701–8, Reigate 1710–13, Ludgershall 1714–15, Weymouth 1722–6)[24]

Hon. Thomas WATSON WENTWORTH (Bossiney 1701, Higham Ferrers 1703–13, 1722–3, Malton 1713–22)

Sir Thomas WEBSTER, 1 bt (Colchester 1705–11, 1713–14, 1722–7)[25]

Samuel WESTON (Poole 1705–8)[26]

William WHITMORE (Bridgnorth 1705–10, 1713–25)

John WICKER (Horsham 1701–5, 1708–13, Shoreham 1705–8)

Edward WORTLEY MONTAGU (Huntingdon 1705–13, 1722–34, Westminster 1715–22, Peterborough 1734–61)

Thomas WYLDE (Worcester 1701–27)[27]

Thomas YORKE

NOTES

1. For his speeches in favour of the clause see Speck, 'Anon. parl. diary', 63, 64, 79, 81. According to Sir John Cropley these earned widespread admiration: Kent Archives Office, U.1590/C9/31: Cropley to James Stanhope, 19 Feb. 1706.
2. Only returned at a by-election on 1 Feb. 1706.
3. Given leave of absence on 11 Jan. 1706, 'his family being ill': *CJ, xv*, 84.
4. Present that day: *CJ, xv*, 160.
5. See above, pp. 52, 54.
6. For his affiliation to 'the Country party' in November 1699 and his expected opposition then to any 'endeavour to keep up a standing army', see *The Letters of John Dryden*, ed. C. E. Ward, (Durham, N. Carolina, 1942), 124.
7. Apparently present on 19 Feb.: Snyder, 'Party configurations', 48.
8. 'Firm to the last' in support of 'the clause': Kent Archives Office, U.1590/C9/31: Cropley to Stanhope, 19 Feb. 1706.
9. Returned at a by-election only on 3 Dec. 1705.
10. Given a month's leave of absence on 9 Jan. 1706: *CJ, xv*, 78.
11. A 'Mr Harvey' (either Stephen, Edward Harvey M.P. Clitheroe or William Harvey M.P. Appleby) was named to a committee on 18 Feb.: *CJ, xv*, 159. In Stephen Harvey's case failure to appear on the list of Court supporters may be explained in another way than by his presence on the other side of the division or absence from the House. He died on 24 May 1707, before the list was published, and it was therefore unnecessary to blacklist him for the 1708 election. The lists did, however, mark three Members as 'deceased' or 'defunct' and included another (Thomas Dore) who had died before even the division took place.

12. He had spoken several times in support of the clause: Speck, 'Anon. parl. diary', 64, 66, 80. See also *Private Diary of Earl Cowper*, 37.

13. A 'Mr Johnson' (Thomas or William M.P. Aldeburgh) was appointed to a committee on 19 Feb.: *CJ*, xv, 160. See also *The Norris Papers*, ed. Thomas Heywood (Chetham Soc., IX, 1846), 147: Thomas Johnson to Richard Norris, London, 18 Feb.: 'The Lords have got their end relating to the Regency Bill — the expedient is a jest as near as I can take it'.

14. See above, pp. 50, 52.

15. Returned at a by-election only on 2 Jan. 1706.

16. Monoux had died on 25 Nov. 1707 and may for this reason have been omitted from the division list. See the parallel case of Stephen Harvey (n. 11, above).

17. A 'Mr Morgan' (John or Anthony Morgan M.P. Yarmouth, I.o.W.) was granted leave of absence for a month on 5 Feb. 1706: *CJ*, xv, 128.

18. Apparently present on 19 Feb.: Snyder, 'Party configurations', 49.

19. But according to Cropley he 'fainted at last in the pursuit': Kent Archives Office, U.1590/C9/31: to Stanhope, 19 Feb. 1706. See above, pp. 50, 52.

20. A possible absentee, as he had been in the division on the Speaker, 25 Oct. 1705.

21. Named on 4 Feb. to the Commons committee to draw up reasons for insisting on their amendments: *CJ*, xv, 128.

22. He died on 18 Nov. 1706, aged 65, and may thus have been either absent through ill health at the time of the division or, like Stephen Harvey and Sir Philip Monoux (above, nn. 11, 16), beyond being hurt by a 'black list' published some two years later.

23. A 'Mr Richard Vaughan' (either the M.P. for Carmarthen or his namesake for Merioneth) was allowed a month's leave of absence on 8 Jan. 1706: *CJ*, xv, 77.

24. A 'Mr Ward' (either John M.P. Bletchingley or John M.P. Newton) was named to a committee on 18 Feb.: *CJ*, xv, 159. For the speeches of 'Ward' on the place clause, see Speck, 'Anon. parl. diary', 62, 63.

25. Appointed to a committee on 19 Feb.: *CJ*, xv, 160.

26. He had been given leave of absence for a month on 9 Feb.: *CJ*, xv, 138. In December 1707 Robert Molesworth recalled with some bitterness that both Weston and his colleague at Poole, Sir William Phippard, who had supported the Court in this division, had acted as 'the Juncta's' Whigs and not as 'true Whigs' in 'our famous place clause': PRO, 30/24/20/357: Cropley to Shaftesbury, 30 Dec. 1707. By this time Shaftesbury was also describing both men contemptuously as 'mercenary tools' and was working for the election of an alternative Whig candidate (his brother-in-law) for the borough: PRO, 30/24/22/1159-60; 30/24/21/26: Shaftesbury to Edward Hooper, '1708/7'; Cropley to Shaftesbury, 1707–8.

27. He had been given three weeks' leave of absence on 21 Dec. 1705: *CJ*, xv, 74.

3.   Whigs voting against the Septennial Bill, April 1716

Whigs included as voting against the bill in the three available division lists (described in Romney Sedgwick (ed.), *The House of Commons 1715–54* (2 vols, 1970), I, 126–8). All three lists claim to record the division on 24 April on committing the bill, though the figures do not fit. The lists are:

1. *An Exact and Correct List of the Members of the House of Commons who Voted For and Against the Bill for Repealing the Triennial-Act, 24, April 1716. Also of the Absent Members; which makes this a Complete List* (1716).

2. *A Guide to the Electors of Great Britain, being Lists of all those Members in the Last Parliament who Voted For, and Against such Bills as were of*

> *Importance either to the Prerogatives of the Crown, or to the Privilege of the People* ... (1722).

3. Richard Chandler, *The History and Proceedings of the House of Commons* ... (14 vols, 1742–4), XII, Addenda, 73–92.

My calculation of the number of Whigs in opposition on this issue, in all 33, differs from that in the *History of Parliament* volumes, which gives the total as 43 (I, 81). I have re-classified the following 'Whigs': John Bromley; Thomas Catesby, Lord Paget; Joseph Earle; Daniel, Lord Finch; Peter Godfrey; Archibald Hutcheson; Thomas King; Richard Reynell; Samuel Shepheard and Richard Sutton. The original notes on which the *History of Parliament* calculations were based were made available to me by Dr Eveline Cruickshanks. [Names of members appearing in more than one of the lists given here have been italicized.]

William BETTS (Weymouth 1710–11, 1711, 1713–14, 1715–30)

Hon. Langham BOOTH (Cheshire 1705–10, 1715–22, Liverpool 1723–4)

James BUTLER

Reynolds CALTHORPE

Arthur CHAMPERNOWNE (Totnes 1715–17)

Sir Robert CHAPLIN, 1 bt (Grimsby 1715–21)

Walter CHETWYND (Lichfield 1715–18, 1718–31)

Richard CHISWELL (Calne 1715–22)

Richard COFFIN (Camelford 1715–22, 1727–34)

Sir John COPE

William DELAUNE (Kent 1715–22)

Thomas DE GREY (Thetford 1708–10, Norfolk 1715–27)

Sir Hervey ELWES, 2 bt (Sudbury 1706–10, 1713–22)

Hon. John FANE (Hythe 1708–11, 1715–22, 1727–34)

Thomas HEATH (Haslemere 1704–5, Harwich 1714, 1715–22)

John HEDWORTH (Co. Durham 1713–47)

Hon. Arthur INGRAM (Horsham 1715–21)

Anthony LECHMERE (Bewdley 1710, Tewkesbury 1714–17)

Nicholas LECHMERE (Appleby 1708–10, Cockermouth 1710–17, Tewkesbury 1717–21)

Sir Thomas LEE, 3 bt (Wycombe 1710–22, Bucks. 1722–7, 1729–41)

Thomas LEWIS (Monmouths. 1713, 1715–22)

James LOWTHER (Carlisle 1694–1702, Cumb. 1708–22, 1727–55, Appleby 1723–7)

Samuel PARGITER FULLER (Petersfield 1715–22)

Sir John ROGERS, 2 bt (Plymouth 1713–22)

John RUDGE

Sir John RUSHOUT, 4 bt (Malmesbury 1713–22, Evesham 1722–68)

Jacob SAWBRIDGE (Cricklade 1715–21)

Thomas SMITH (Milborne Port 1709–10, E. Looe 1710–13, Eye 1715–22, Tregony 1727–8)

Thomas STEPHENS (Glos. 1713–20)

John Morley TREVOR (Sussex 1705–8, Lewes 1712–19)

Joshua WARD (Marlborough 1715–17)

Hon. Thomas WATSON WENTWORTH

Thomas WESTERN (Sudbury 1715–22)

3 *Ashby* v. *White*: the case of the men of Aylesbury, 1701-4

Eveline Cruickshanks

The appellate jurisdiction of the House of Lords as a means of expanding its judicial authority was a perennial source of conflict between the two Houses of Parliament, and *Ashby* v. *White* provides one of the most spectacular examples of it.

Even more important from the political point of view is that the case was part of a deliberate campaign waged by the Junto lords, Sunderland, Wharton and Halifax, to make use of the Whig majority in the upper House to thwart any Tory majority in the Commons. It was carefully stage-managed to give a populist look to an hereditary body appealing to the country over the heads of its elected representatives. For instance, when the Parliament which met in February 1701 produced a small Tory majority, the Kentish petition presented in May pressed for the speedy voting of supplies to enable King William to support his allies against the French before it was too late. This petition was voted 'scandalous, insolent and seditious' and its signatories ordered to be taken into custody for breach of the Commons' privilege. The great Tory leader Sir Edward Seymour regarded it as having been financed, as well as inspired, by the Junto lords. In the same Parliament the House of Lords foiled the Commons' impeachments of William's ministers by acquitting Somers and Orford and discharging Halifax, further challenging the Commons by having their reasons for doing so printed for the use of the public.[1] The large Tory majority in the 1702 Parliament saw two cherished occasional conformity bills — promoted in 1702 and 1703 by Seymour, William Bromley and Sir John Pakington — brought to nought in the Lords by the efforts of Sunderland, Wharton and Halifax secretly assisted by Marlborough and Godolphin, who were anxious for the continuance of moderate government and the regular grant of supplies for the war against France.[2]

The immediate cause of the struggle between the two Houses over *Ashby* v. *White* was the conflict of electoral interests at Aylesbury between Sir John Pakington, the high Tory lord of the manor, and Thomas, 5th Baron Wharton, both of whom were attempting to dominate the 200–300 odd householders, not receiving alms, who formed the local electorate.[3] The story presents throughout a curious mixture of high constitutional issues and sheer farce. Central to the whole issue was a charity founded by John Bedford in 1494 for the uses of the poor of Aylesbury, and governed by nine trustees. Its administration had fallen into the hands of Dissenters during the Interregnum, and in 1685 eight out of the nine trustees were still described as 'fanatics', who evaded the provisions of the Corporations Acts and managed to control about 100 voters either through pressure on tenants of Bedford charity houses or through the distribution of poor relief out of the charity.[4] This asset was exploited to the full by Wharton, whose family held large Buckinghamshire estates and who soon earned the reputation of being the most skilled electoral manager of his time.

At a by-election in April 1691 Wharton secured the return of his own electoral agent in the county, Simon Mayne, despite opposition from James Herbert, the Tory son-in-law of Lord Carmarthen, then chief minister.[5] The son of a regicide, Mayne had been accused of involvement in the Rye House Plot of 1683 and was appointed a commissioner of victualling after the Revolution. Before the 1695 election, Wharton as *custos rotulorum* of the county attended the assizes with Simon Mayne and their friends on the Bench when, by dint of a threat to move the assizes from Aylesbury to Buckingham,[6] two of Pakington's constables were removed and replaced as returning officers by Wharton's nominees. This as well as a good deal of treating at the 1695 election did much to restore the Mayne interest at Aylesbury which was said to have been 'much abated there, by reason of his being so fierce against the poor men fishing in the rivers and their going after hare and partridge and there is some sixteen score electors, and the poorest of them has as good a voice as the richest'.[7]

Herbert attended the election in the company of his kinsmen the Earls of Carnarvon and Abingdon, as well as that of Carmarthen himself. Mayne was again returned through the assistance of the trustees of the Bedford Charity, who were accused of having used their power, 'to affright poor labourers out of their voices'. Herbert gained the seat on petition, however, in January 1696.

At the general election of 1698, when the Bedford Charity men offered their votes for Mayne and his partner Robert Dormer, a Whig lawyer and a protégé of Wharton's, Pakington's constables refused to accept them. Among the Bedford Charity votes disallowed at the poll were those of John Oviat, Henry Basse and Daniel Horne, later three of the principal actors in *Ashby* v. *White*. Another voter objected to as a Bedford Charity man was John Pate, perhaps either John Paty or John Paton, two of the Aylesbury men in the case. Matthew Ashby himself had his vote rejected as a poor hostler who had been warned out of the town lest he should become a charge on the parish. Involved in this election on Mayne's side was yet another of the *dramatis personae* in the case: Robert Mead, a local attorney and a

Dissenter connected with Wharton.[8] Mayne and Dormer, who had been
defeated, petitioned but the elections committee and the House of Commons ruled against them, resolving that the Bedford Charity men and
other paupers were not eligible to vote. Mayne was defeated by James
Herbert in January 1701. This time he did not petition, presumably
expecting no joy out of that Tory House of Commons. Instead, Matthew
Ashby, the hostler of the 1698 election now established in the borough
as a cobbler but with an income agreed to be less than £4 a year, began an
action at the county assizes against William White and the other three
constables of Aylesbury for depriving him of his vote at that election.
He was awarded £5 damages.[9] From this modest beginning was to grow
one of the most expensive, bitterly contested and constitutionally important cases of the eighteenth century.

Square behind Ashby, providing the ablest and most expensive legal
advice, stood Wharton. Throughout the case, the Commons took the
view that Ashby was but a puppet being manipulated by that lord. This
was confirmed by Wharton's friend and biographer Richard Steele, who
wrote:

> Nothing was ever managed with more vigour and address than the
> Aylesbury business, the case of *Ashby* and *White*. The borough of
> Aylesbury is of itself very well inclined to the English [i.e. Whig]
> interest, but Sir John Pakington having the naming of the constables,
> several of the poor inhabitants have for many years past been
> influenced by the lord of the manor to vote for persons that were
> either Jacobites or rank Tories. Among the rest, one of Jeffrey's
> Western clerks, who attended and served him in that notorious
> butchery [?Simon Harcourt] has crept in by the arbitrary manage-
> ment of the constables, which to prevent the Lord Wharton resolved
> to have the matter determined by law, and it was chiefly at his
> expence and by his direction that the cause of *Ashby* and *White* was
> carried on.[10]

What was being tested at law was a clause in the Act of 7 and 8 Wm III
cap. 25 (1696) for further regulating parliamentary elections and preventing irregular proceedings on the part of sheriffs and other returning
officers, some of whom had 'greatly injured and abused' freeholders and
other electors as well as the persons elected by them. The clause provided
that a returning officer in breach of this act 'shall forfeit to every part so
aggrieved the sum of £500 to be recovered by him or them . . . together
with the full costs of suit and for which he or they may sue by action of
debt, bill, plaint or information in any of His Majesty's courts at Westminster'. There had been a previous testing of the water under this act over
the Liskeard election of August 1698, when the defeated candidate John
Buller (M.P. Lostwithiel in January 1701) wished to sue the mayor of
Liskeard for £500 damages for a false return. Another similarity was that

the mayor had rejected voters for Buller because they were paupers. Buller took legal advice from Nicholas Hooper, a serjeant-at-law (M.P. Barnstaple 1695–1715), who advised him not to petition the House of Commons — because once he had done so that House would never allow proceedings at law until after the petition had been decided — but to avoid delays by starting an action immediately. Buller's agent at Liskeard, Emanuel Pyper (M.P. Liskeard 1690–5), disagreed, arguing that if Buller did not petition within eight days after the meeting of Parliament he would be totally excluded from the House and from obtaining damages under that act because he had wilfully refused to take his case to the 'proper place'. Buller went on regardless and on 13 March 1699 there was a complaint made to the Commons that Buller had brought an action for £500 damages against the mayor of Liskeard for a false return without having petitioned the House against it. This was voted a breach of privilege and Buller lost out on both fronts.[11]

Mayne stood for Aylesbury in December 1701, was defeated, but again did not petition. Pakington was returned unopposed with James Herbert in 1702. Meanwhile, White and the other constables had begun an appeal (presumably with financial help from Pakington) against the damages awarded to Ashby in 1701. *Ashby* v. *White* came before the Queen's Bench in the autumn of 1703. Lord Chief Justice Holt, a Whig, argued strongly in Ashby's favour, declaring that a qualification of £4 a year was necessary to serve on a jury but not to be a voter at Aylesbury, where anyone who had a freehold had the right to vote irrespective of its value. To the objection that no such action had ever been brought before, Holt retorted that this was no reason why the claim should not be good in law.[12] On the other hand, the other three judges gave it as their opinion that the reason no such case had ever been brought before — notwithstanding the many cases of controverted elections — was that the determination of the right of election concerned the House of Commons alone, and by a majority of three to one they ruled that 'no such action did by law lie against the defendants'.[13]

All the members of the House of Lords at this time decided legal cases, and Wharton had used the Whig majority in the Lords to good effect in a case involving himself.[14] His next move was to apply to Nottingham, the secretary of state, for a writ of error in Ashby's name to reverse the Queen's Bench judgment. It was granted.[15] The writ was heard in the Lords on 14 January 1704, when Chief Justice Trevor strongly insisted on the authority of the House of Commons to judge its elections — from which he inferred 'that the Commons only could judge who were the electors' and that therefore 'this matter was triable by them and by them only'; he concluded that if two independent jurisdictions had the same cause brought before them, it would lead to contrary judgments and great problems in the execution of those judgments. Holt, on the other hand, argued that 'a right of voting in an election was the greatest of all the rights of an Englishman since by that he was represented in Parliament' but that the House of Commons could give no relief nor any monetary damages to an elector who had been wronged.

Witnesses were then heard on Ashby's side. After a debate lasting till nine o'clock at night, reversal was carried by 55 votes to 16 with 13 dissentients. The Lords then resolved that

> by the known laws of this kingdom, every freeholder, or other person, having a right to give his vote at the election of members to serve in Parliament, and being wilfully denied or hindered so to do by the officer who ought to receive the same, may maintain an action in the Queen's courts against such officer, to assert his right, and recover damages for the injury.[16]

The House of Lords' judgment, the Dutch envoy commented, caused a sensation in the country as this was a blow to the Commons on their most sensitive point.[17] The right of determining their own elections had been one of the greatest gains ever made by the House of Commons.[18] The verdict was in blatant disregard of the custom of Parliament as, in practice, the Commons through the elections committee or at the bar of the House decided on the qualification of any voter or particular sets of voters, in the course of hearing the merits of an election and deciding which candidate had been duly elected. The Lords' ruling would have made a man's right to vote a piece of property, whereas, in theory at least, a vote could not be bought or sold — and indeed Members of Parliament could be unseated if bribery could be proved against them at an election. Ultimately, the Lords' decision would have transferred the final determination of a parliamentary election from the lower House to the upper.

On 17 January the House of Commons was informed of an 'extraordinary judgment' given in the Lords which closely concerned its privileges. A committee was appointed, with Ralph Freman in the chair, to search the Queen's Bench records and the Lords' Journals concerning the *Ashby* v. *White* case, while another, headed by John Brewer, was to search for precedents in the case of *Barnardiston* v. *Soames*, one in which the Lords had admitted the sole right of the Commons to judge their own elections.[19] On 21 January, having received both reports, the Speaker, Robert Harley, urged caution and careful deliberation over a matter of such great consequence and one which involved the 'ancient usage and custom of Parliament'. Consideration was deferred to a Committee of the Whole House, with Freman in the chair, on the 25th. So successful was the Junto management of the Whig M.P.s that the Commons split on party lines in this debate, with the Whigs supporting the Lords' verdict against the rights and privileges of their own House. Brewer opened the debate by remarking that the case was

> a matter of the last consequence to the privileges of the House of Commons, which I think are dangerously invaded by the Lords

pretence of juricature over them . . . for by law and usage of parliament, the House of Commons have heard and determined the right
of their own elections, and consequently and necessarily the right
of electors to vote; and for this purpose at the opening of all parliaments a committee of elections is nominated of members of our
own, to hear and determine of such right of elections, to whom
petitions (after presented to the House) are referred; and if any
elector had been refused his vote in the country he is, notwithstanding, allowed his vote here in case he had right; and it shall avail the
candidate as much as if the vote had been received below . . . But it
may be objected, that no single petitioner will be received by the
House: in answer to this, I say he may: and I have known petitions
touching elections preferred by very few persons, and by the same
reason may by one: I am sure we have no order of the House against
it; and if gentlemen object, that no single petition of this nature
was ever received, if they will show me when it was offered, I will
show them when it was received; I believe they cannot show me it
was ever refused.

Though agreeing that the Commons awarded no pecuniary damages to
voters, he pointed out that offending returning officers were punished by
the House, concluding that 'a great man' was making use of 'that poor
fellow' 'in order to enlarge a jurisdiction'.[20] Sir Thomas Powys, a leading
Tory M.P., who had acted as counsel for White in the case before the
Lords, said he had done everything in his power to defend the right and
privileges of the House of Commons and that if five or even one of the
electors 'of this sorry town of Aylesbury' had petitioned they would have
been done justice, since returning officers were accountable to the Commons for their conduct at elections. Like all Tory speakers in this debate,
Powys conveniently ignored the fact that the Commons' decisions in
election cases were decided along party lines! Sir John Hawles on the other
hand, a Junto Whig and formerly solicitor-general, felt no awkwardness
in arguing in favour of the Lords decision.

At this point Sir Edward Seymour weighed in thus:

I cannot but take notice that this is an action without any precedent to warrant this proceeding: and I believe it might have remained so still (for I do not think there was virtue enough in the
cobbler of Aylesbury, nor had he purse enough) if a lord had not
acted that part. For my part, sir, I do not think this to be the
single instance of the House of Lords we have reason to complain
of: I think in a great measure, by their proceedings, that they seem
to hold forth, that the axe is laid at the root and that they have a
dislike of the House of Commons and endeavour to be rid of them.

The Marquess of Hartington, son of the Duke of Devonshire and a leading Junto supporter, answered him:

> as long as I sit here and as long as I live, I shall be as tender of the privileges of the House as any body. I think it is upon the due balance of both Houses, that the safety of the whole consist; and I must confess, I think the liberty of a cobbler ought to be as much regarded as of anybody else; and that is the happiness of our constitution.

William Lowndes, the secretary to the Treasury, observed that the law courts never did have the power to meddle in parliamentary elections, while Sir Simon Harcourt, the Tory solicitor-general, argued that the real question at issue was whether or not the Commons of England had the sole right of determining their own elections.[21] Robert Dormer countered this by saying the issue was whether or not 'a freeholder, or a freeman, who hath the right to give his vote for his representatives in Parliament may arbitrarily and maliciously be deprived of that privilege without any redress whatsoever?'. He then pointed out that Pakington himself had sued and received considerable damages from the Bishop of Worcester over a Worcestershire election.[22] Sir Joseph Jekyll, another Whig, said the case did not depend on the law of Parliament but on 'common law', conveniently ignoring the fact that the franchise was decided by the Commons, who were free to alter it at any time. He was reproved by Speaker Harley who replied that deciding the right of election belonged to the House of Commons alone and that no other court could take cognizance of it except where otherwise provided for by statute.[23] Sir Humphrey Mackworth, a prominent Tory speaker, declared:

> the question is this, whether an elector is entitled to an action at common law against an officer, for recovery of damages, in case his vote which he offered, be not taken down in writing, and entered on the poll? Or, whether the House of Commons have the sole privilege of examining and determining the right of qualification of every elector to give his vote, and adjudge of the behaviour of every sheriff and other officer, in taking the poll on the election of members to serve in parliament? I am of opinion, with great submission to better judgment, that the House of Commons have a sole right to judicature in these cases, and that the elector is not entitled to an action at common law ... If an action lies and upon a judgment on that action a writ of error lies in the House of Peers, the Lords will be the sole judges at last who have the votes to choose a House of Commons .... This will be the way to destroy all checks, and to make the House of Commons dependent on the Lords.[24]

Peter King, a leading member of the Junto, tried to speak in favour of the verdict on the writ of error but was interrupted with shouts, while Sir

Thomas Littleton, attempting to come to his rescue in arguing that the
Lords decision had not interfered with the rights of the Commons, was cut
short by cries of 'No', 'No'. Nicholas Hooper, the Tory involved in the
Liskeard case, declared that, once this jurisdiction was conceded to the
Lords, Members of Parliament would have to apply to them before they
could sit in this House. A clause that the decision of 'the qualification of
any elector' belonged to the Commons alone was carried by 215 votes to
97.[25] The committee of the whole House then resolved that

> according to the known law and usage of Parliament, neither the
> qualification of any elector, or the right of any person elected,
> is cognizable or determinable elsewhere than before the Commons
> of England in Parliament assembled, except in such cases as are
> specially provided for by act of Parliament. . .

> [and that] the examining and determining the qualification or right
> of any elector, or any person elected to serve in any parliament, in
> any court of law or elsewhere than before the Commons of England
> in Parliament assembled, except in such cases as are specifically
> provided for by act of Parliament will expose all mayors, bailiffs
> and other officers, who are obliged to take the poll, and make a
> return thereupon, to multiplicity of actions, vexations, suits, and
> insupportable expenses, and will subject them to different and
> independent jurisdictions, and inconsistent determinations in the
> same case, without relief.

Finally, it was voted that any attorneys, solicitors, counsellors or serjeants-
at-law who acted on any suits on the same grounds as *Ashby* v. *White*
would be guilty 'of a high breach of the privilege of the House'.[26] The
debate had lasted until ten o'clock at night.[27]

Next day, 26 January, the Commons considered the committee's
resolutions. Hartington objected that they would allow returning officers
to behave as they pleased and he was supported by Sir William Strickland,
a Junto Whig, who declared that the right of voting was a 'birthright' of
the people of England and was as much a freehold as any estate. To this,
Henry St John, who like Harley was throughout vigorous in defence of
the rights of the lower House, retorted that the liberties of the people
could find no safer guardians than the Commons. The committee's resolutions were then voted without a division. Ashby was declared guilty of a
breach of privilege but no order was made to take him into the custody of
the House, as was usual in such cases.[28]

Hearing this, the Lords prepared a long representation of the whole
Aylesbury case, in which Lord Chief Justice Holt was said to have had the
chief hand.[29] The report was made by Lord Townshend on 27 March,
when Wharton carried a motion that the proceedings of the other House constituted a 'usurpation' of a jurisdiction to which the Commons had no sort

of claim.[30] The report was accepted, and with no dissentients the House voted that

> by the known laws of this kingdom, every freeholder, or other person, having a right to give his vote at the election of Members to serve in Parliament, and being wilfully denied, or hindered so to do by the officer, who ought to receive the same, may maintain an action in the Queen's courts against such officer, to assert his right, and recover damages for the injury . . .

> that the asserting that a person having right to give his vote at an election, and being hindered so to do by the officer, who ought to take the same, if without remedy for such wrong by the ordinary course of law, is destructive of the property of the subjects against the freedom of elections, and manifestly tends to encourage corruption and partiality in officers, who are to make returns to Parliament, and to subject freeholders, and other electors, to their arbitrary will and pleasure . . .

> that the declaring Matthew Ashby guilty of a breach of privilege of the House of Commons, for presenting an action against the constables of Aylesbury, for not receiving his vote at an election, after he had in the known and proper methods of law, obtained a judgment in Parliament for recovery of his damages, is an unprecedented attempt upon the judicature of Parliament, and is in effect to subject the law of England to the votes of the House of Commons . . .

> that the deterring electors from prosecuting actions in the ordinary course of law, where they are deprived of their right of voting and terrifying attornies, solicitors, counsellors and serjeants at law from soliciting, prosecuting, and pleading in such cases, by voting their so doing to be a breach of privilege of the House of Commons, is a manifest assuming a power to control the law, to hinder the course of justice, and subject the property of Englishmen to the arbitrary votes of the House of Commons.

These resolutions were ordered to be printed and to be sent to the sheriffs in each county.[31]

The two Houses were now set on a collision course. James Vernon, writing to Shrewsbury, commented that the Commons would not have time to reply to the printed Lords case before the prorogation, but that they were unlikely to drop the case once Parliament reassembled, adding that this made it 'very problematical whether in this state there should be a new Parliament or not; and how animosities that are arisen so high can be composed. Some fear my Lord Treasurer [Godolphin] may think it so difficult as not to care to hold his staff any longer.'[32] On 3 April the lower House 'were very busy in directing their Speaker to address himself to the Throne and protest in the name of the Commons of England against some of the Lords proceedings', when Black Rod came to the door to summon them to attend the queen in the House of Lords for the pro-rogation, whereupon they 'quietly though discontentedly' dispersed.[33]

During the recess the propaganda war between the two Houses of Parliament hotted up. In their published report of the *Ashby* v. *White* case the Lords depicted themselves as the defenders of the rights and liberties of individual voters. According to the pro-Whig Dutch envoy, it made a good impression in the country at large and gained the Lords great popularity.[34] After bestowing much praise on Ashby's 'true English spirit', the upper House conceded that the Commons could exclude a 'usurper' while considering the merits of an election, but insisted that the right of election was a 'freehold' and as such actionable at law. (The impossibility of considering the right of election separately from the question of which candidate was elected under the existing Commons procedure was ignored!) The realities of political life were also brushed aside when, to the objection that no such case had ever been brought before, their lordships replied that this was probably because few voters had been wrongly deprived of their votes before![35]

A reply on the Commons' behalf was contained in a pamphlet entitled *Free Parliaments.* Signed by Sir Humphrey Mackworth (but also ascribed to Robert Harley), it made a great stir.[36] Proclaiming that a free Parlia-ment was and had ever been 'the great bulwark of the rights and liberties of the people', its author asserted that electors as well as elected could best seek redress from the House of Commons. It condemned the Lords' ver-dict as a 'new invention' which would lead to such a multiplicity of actions and such conflict of jurisdictions that no election would ever be settled. The sole right of judging the qualifications of the electors as well as of the elected belonged to the House of Commons. Unlike the peers, the commons of England were too numerous to meet and debate in person, and this was the reason for choosing the House of Commons as their representatives. The Lords claimed the exclusive right of deciding the qualification of their own members, yet they sought to invade the Com-mons' right to do so. An elected House rather than a hereditary one was the true defender of the rights and liberties of the people. The Lords were seeking to alter both the custom of Parliament and the constitution. The pamphlet also pointed out that in practice the right of election could not be tried separately from the right of the electors.

A rejoinder followed in the shape of a pamphlet called *The Ancient and Fundamental Right of English Parliaments.*[37] It began with an attack on Mackworth who, after 'blowing the trumpet of peace last year, when war was at the door'[38] and supporting the Occasional Conformity Bill, now posed as the champion 'of so brave a cause as liberty'. After many exam-ples drawn from 'Saxon Parliaments', Matthew Paris, the reigns of the

Plantagenets, but never getting beyond Lord Chief Justice Coke, the writer argued that the Commons should not be the sole judge of their own cases without appeal and that the House of Lords, acting in its judicial capacity, was always impartial. The whole was laced with legal precedents on common law as relating to freeholds. More sensibly, he pointed out that the Lords could not 'claim a privilege of being sole judges of their own rights and of the qualification of their own members' since it was the prerogative of the Crown to create a peer,

> nor when he is legally made, either by creation or writ, can they judge of his qualification, no other than as to the validity of his patent, which is never disputed when lawfully granted; and all barons by inheritance claim the privilege of peers as their birthright; so that there is no such thing as judging of the qualification of their Members as the House of Commons do. For they neither deny the prerogative of the Crown to constitute and create as many as she pleases; nor do they pretend to a power to elect in, who they have a mind to, or call by writ any of their House, but who the Crown appoints.

In conclusion he urged Mackworth to 'go off the stage with applause of all parties that contend for peace and quietness'.

When Parliament reassembled for the third session in October 1704, its greatest preoccupation was the tacking of the third Occasional Conformity Bill to the supply, a device to prevent the House of Lords from rejecting it. This was defeated in the Commons on 28 November through the efforts of Robert Harley, who now combined the Speakership with being secretary of state (in which office he had succeeded Nottingham), acting in close collaboration with Godolphin.[39] However, a complaint was made to the Commons on 21 November that during the recess Robert Mead had proceeded in the case of *Ashby* v. *White*. Mead had deliberately flouted the authority of the lower House by entering the reversal of the judgment on his own hand, boasting he would do it openly, even before the very eyes of Sir Thomas Powys and Sir Edward Seymour. Two days later it was reported that several more actions against William White and the other constables had been started at the Buckinghamshire assizes, in the name of five more voters of Aylesbury whose votes had been refused by White: John Paty, John Oviat, John Paton jun., Henry Basse and Daniel Horne. Three of them (Paton, Paty and Oviate) could not sign their own names and three (Oviat, Horne and Basse) were or had been Bedford Charity men.

Mead and the five men of Aylesbury were summoned to attend the House.[40] This coincided with a by-election at Aylesbury, before which Pakington asked the sheriff to turn out Wharton's bailiff for Ashingdon Hundred and to replace him with a nominee of his own, in order to assist the election of 'an honest gentleman' in the place of James Herbert who

had died.[41] Sir George Parker, a Tory, was returned with Pakington's
support, defeating Mayne. On 5 December it was reported that a copy of
the order of the House had been left at Mead's chamber in Thavies Inn,
but that he would not attend. Paty, Oviat, Paton, Basse and Horne were
then examined at the bar of the House, after which all five as well as Mead
were ordered into the custody of the serjeant-at-arms for breach of privilege, and were taken to Newgate.[42] Wharton, who had borne the whole
expense of these actions, paid for the keep of the men of Aylesbury in
Newgate and gave them clothes as well as money. There they were visited
by leading Junto Whigs and feasted like aldermen, much in the same
fashion as Titus Oates had been in 1689 and John Wilkes was to be in the
reign of George III.[43] The whole controversy began anew, so that Sir
Simon Harcourt complained of being 'very much pestered with the Ayles-
burians this Christmas'.[44] On 2 February 1705 the five men of Aylesbury
accompanied by the keeper of Newgate were summoned before the Commons and examined for some hours, being particularly closely questioned
about Wharton's part in the Aylesbury election; but 'one and all' they
refused to answer the Speaker or say anything, whereupon they were taken
back to Newgate.[45] Steele thought that 'the fellows behaved themselves
with great cunning and resolution'.[46]

Wharton, meanwhile, was not content to leave matters as they were.
On 12 February 1705 four distinguished Whig lawyers, all of them Junto
Whigs connected with him, appeared as counsel for the men of Aylesbury
before Queen's Bench in an application for a writ of Habeas Corpus. They
were Francis Page (M.P. Huntingdon 1708–10) who pleaded that that
court could 'bail all persons who by the laws of England were bailable';
James Montagu (Halifax's brother, M.P. Carlisle 1705–13, made solicitor-
general in 1707) who argued that 'it did not appear that the prisoners
were any ways related to the House of Commons either as Members or
officers'; Nicholas Lechmere (returned by Wharton at Appleby in 1708),
who invoked Magna Carta, 'which I take to be directly concerned in this
question that says no freeman is to be disseised of his freehold or liberties
or free custom, unless by the lawful judgment of his peers, or by the law
of the land'; and Alexander Denton (who became Wharton's secretary
next year and was M.P. Buckingham 1708–10), who objected that the
men had had no notice of the vote or declaration of the House of
Commons. Three of the Queen's Bench judges were of the opinion that
the prisoners were not entitled to bail on a commitment of the House of
Commons. Justice Powell argued that this was no perpetual imprisonment
since there was no perpetual Parliament. Justice Gould said it would
be impossible for the Bench to judge of the privileges of the House
of Commons since 'there are no printed books of their privileges nor
is there any means by which we can attain to the knowledge of them'.
Once again, Lord Chief Justice Holt differed from the rest, arguing that
the prisoners should be discharged as 'neither of the Houses of Parliament,

separately or jointly have any power to dispose of the liberty or property of the subject'.[47]

The upshot was that the men of Aylesbury were remanded to Newgate. The Commons were further provoked, however, when they learnt that John Paty and John Oviat had petitioned the queen for a writ of error in order to bring the Queen's Bench judgment before the House of Lords. An address to the queen was resolved, reasserting the rights of the Commons to commit for breach of privilege, commitments which were not 'examinable in any other court whatsoever' so that no writ of error could or did lie in this case. The queen was reminded of the zeal they had shown in her service and their steady voting of supplies. The House then also resolved that whoever had 'abetted, promoted, countenanced' and endeavoured to prosecute the writs of error were 'disturbers of the peace of the kingdom and guilty of fomenting differences between the Houses.'[48] The petition of the Aylesbury men for a writ of error was referred to Robert Harley, who decided to consult all the judges — a move, commented the Dutch envoy, designed to play for time.[49] Summoned before the queen and the Cabinet to pronounce on whether a writ of error entered in the House of Lords on a Queen's Bench judgment was a matter of right or a matter for the queen to grant or refuse as she saw fit, nine of the eleven judges attending ruled that a writ of error was a matter of right. On 26 February Sir Charles Hedges, the other secretary of state, reported the queen's reply. She expressed her concern at their opinion that the granting of writs of error would be a breach of their privileges, of which she was 'as tender as of her own prerogative', and assured the House she would duly 'weigh and consider' what was proper for her to do in a matter of such great concern. It was 6 p.m. Lord Dysart then reported from the committee to consider what persons had been concerned in the legal proceedings on behalf of the men of Aylesbury. Francis Page was named first and was voted guilty of a breach of privilege by 135 votes to 79, after which James Montagu, Nicholas Lechmere and Alexander Denton were declared guilty without a division and ordered into the custody of the serjeant-at-arms.[50] The debate had lasted until midnight, and St John was said to have been one of those 'most warm' in favour of these resolutions.[51]

Lest the Aylesbury men be given a Habeas Corpus, they were removed from Newgate into the serjeant-at-arms's own custody at midnight in, wrote Boyer, 'such circumstances of severity and terror, as have been seldom exercised towards the greatest offenders'.[52] The same day, the House of Lords had received a petition from the men of Aylesbury asking for the protection of that House for their counsel and agents in the proceedings relating to the writs of error. This was granted to the four counsel as well as two attorneys, with orders to keepers of prisons and serjeants-at-arms to be 'strictly prohibited from arresting, imprisoning or otherwise detaining or molesting them'.[53] The next day (27th) the serjeant-at-arms reported to the House of Commons that the men of Aylesbury were still safely in his custody; that in seeking to arrest James Montagu he had been shown a protection from the House of Lords; that Lechmere had escaped out of his chamber by a back window with the help of sheets and a rope; that he had been able to arrest one of the attorneys concerned but not the other; and that Page and Denton could not be found. A committee was then appointed to search the Lords' Journals concerning the lawyers involved.[54] The Junto Whigs generally were reported to have been so angry at Robert Harley's conduct on this occasion that they decided John Smith should replace him as Speaker in the next Parliament.[55]

On the same day the Lords considered the petitions of the men of Aylesbury and, after a debate, resolved

> That the House of Commons, in committing to Newgate Daniel Horne, Henry Basse, John Paton junior, John Paty and John Oviat for commencing and prosecuting an action at common law against the late constables of Aylesbury for not allowing their votes in election of Members to serve in Parliament, upon pretence that their so doing was contrary to a declaration, a contempt of the jurisdiction and a breach of the privilege, of that House, have assumed to themselves alone a legislative authority by pretending to attribute the force of a law to their declaration, have claimed a jurisdiction not warranted by the constitution and have assumed a new privilege, to which they can shew no title by the law and custom of Parliament; and have thereby, as far as in them lies, subjected the rights of Englishmen and the freedom of their persons to the arbitrary votes of the House of Commons.

After a further debate they voted

> That every Englishman who is imprisoned, by any authority whatsoever, has an undoubted right, by his agents or friends, to apply for and obtain a writ of Habeas Corpus, in order to procure his liberty by due course of law. . .

> [They resolved] That a writ of error is not a writ of grace, but of right, and ought not to be denied to the subject, when duly applied for, though at the request of either House of Parliament; the denial thereof being an obstruction of justice, contrary to *Magna Carta*.

A committee was appointed to draw up the subject matter for a conference with the Commons on these resolutions.[56] The conference, managed by Sunderland for the Lords and Hartington for the Commons, reached no solution, the Commons complaining that the Lords had 'anticipated all debates'.[57] On 6 March the serjeant-at-arms acquainted the House that a writ of Habeas Corpus for James Montagu had been brought

before the lord keeper (Sir Nathan Wright). While he was speaking he had
notice that another such writ had been served upon his deputy on behalf
of Alexander Denton, then also in custody. The House resolved that a
person committed by the House of Commons was not bailable under the
Habeas Corpus Act of 31 Car. II cap. 2 (1679), but came to no decision
on what action to take, except for desiring a further conference with the
Lords. William Bromley, reporting the same day on the reasons to be
offered at such a conference, protested at the 'manifest invasion' of the
Commons' privileges by the Lords adding that they were seeking to enlarge
their own jurisdiction under colour of defending the rights of the people
and the liberties of their persons. The custom of Parliament had been
flouted. The privileges of the House of Commons, the report went on,

> were with great licentiousness of speech denied and insulted in
> public court, not with any hope or prospect of relief for the pri-
> soners (who, in this whole proceeding, have apparently been only
> the tools of some ill-designing persons that are contriving every
> way to disturb the freedom of the Commons elections) but in order
> to vent these new doctrines against the Commons of England and
> with a design to overthrow their fundamental right . . . .

> And the Commons cannot but see how your Lordships are con-
> triving by all methods to bring the determination of liberty and
> property into the bottomless and insatiable gulf of your Lordships
> judicature, which would swallow up both the prerogative of the
> Crown and the rights and liberties of the people.[58]

Boyer, who like all Whigs took the Lords' side, described these reasons
as 'injurious invectives', mere provocation in order to break off all co-
operation between the two Houses.[59] On 13 March Bromley reported the
further conference, which was managed for the Lords by Sunderland, the
Bishop of Salisbury, Halifax, Wharton, Devonshire and Ferrers. All were
Junto Whigs but the last, a Tory, had co-operated with Wharton to defeat
the Occasional Conformity Bills.[60] The managers for the Commons were
William Bromley, Sir Thomas Powys, Sir Humphrey Mackworth, Henry
Poley, John Comyns, John Brewer, John Ward (probably M.P. for
Newton) and Sir John Hawles, all of whom but the last were Tories.

The conference resulted in yet another stalemate. The Commons
accused the Lords of deliberately holding up the money bills in order to
bring pressure to bear over the *Ashby* v. *White* case. The Lords maintained
that if the Commons had their way they would be able to get anyone they
pleased declared duly elected by excluding the votes of the opposite party,
much as the Tory constables of Aylesbury had excluded Whig voters.[61]
(This was, of course, what happened in practice already.) The Commons
ordered that all their proceedings on the Aylesbury case, together with
the reports of their conferences with the Lords, be printed. The Lords

countered with a representation and address to be presented to the queen
by the Duke of Bolton, a strong Whig. In this the Lords accused the
Commons of breaches of the custom of Parliament through the practice
of tacking contentious measures to money bills, and thus sought to put

> the Crown and the Lords under that unhappy necessity, either to
> agree to a law they might think prejudicial to the public or to lose
> the money, which perhaps, at that time, was absolutely necessary
> to the saving of the kingdom. By this method they assume to them-
> selves the whole legislative authority, taking in effect the negative
> voice from the Crown and depriving the Lords of the right of
> deliberating upon what is for the good of the kingdom.[62]

These disputes sparked off yet another pamphlet war. Boyer attacked
unrestricted commitments by the House of Commons whom he compared
to 'the Thirty Tyrants of Athens', arguing that lawyers were able to act on
behalf of their clients even against the Crown but were not able to do so
against the Commons without being imprisoned. These, he said, were the
methods 'of the Inquisition, the very name of which ought to strike all
Englishmen and Protestants with horror'.[63] On the Commons' side,
A Defence of Liberty and Property maintained that they were defending
'the old standing law of parliament' against dangerous innovations proposed by the Lords, and that electors could apply to their representatives
for relief 'and not to be drawn in and made instruments and tools to subvert the constitution and oppose the just rights of the Commons of
Athens'. The Commons had shown forbearance by not committing Ashby,
who might have been ignorant of the law of Parliament, but the five men
of Aylesbury had refused to petition the Commons and had been punished
because they had knowingly offended. It concluded that deciding the right
of election was vital to the Commons:

> The Lords say that the Commons can have no jurisdiction over the
> rights of those to whom they owe their being, the electors, therefore
> it should be absolutely necessary they should have the sole judica-
> ture of their rights as far as relates thereunto, that is, to determine
> who are and who are not qualified to vote in every election or else
> the Commons can have no secure being at all, but the judges or the
> Lords may make a House of Commons and consequently destroy the
> very being of a Free Parliament. . .

> The Commons are not contending for a small thing, but for their All
> and hope they may be able to satisfy the Lords without signing and
> sealing their own ruin.[64]

Another defender of the Commons pointed out that debtors for substantial sums were never granted bail: were the rights of the Commons
of England held any cheaper?

Are not the House of Commons as much to be trusted with the liberty of an offender as a single judge? Are not they entrusted with all our rights and privileges? Are not they a part of the high court of Parliament? Are not they by the Law of Parliament, sole judges of their own privileges, exclusive of the Lords themselves? And shall the inferior courts be admitted to control their judgments? Will the people rather choose to trust their liberties in the hands of persons not chosen by them, than on those who are? . . . .

All the good laws from *Magna Charta* to this day, which have been obtained by the Commons at the expence of so many millions of money will be made precarious on the judgment of the Lords; nay even the prerogatives of the Crown, as well as the rights of the people will be swallowed up (as the Commons have observed) in the bottomless gulf of their Lordships' judicature.[65]

On 14 March 1705 the Duke of Bolton informed the House of Lords that the queen would receive their representation and address on the Aylesbury men at 12 o'clock that day. When she did so she told them that she would have granted the writ of error desired in their address, but that she found 'an absolute necessity of putting an immediate end to this session' which prevented her from proceeding in the matter. At four o'clock that afternoon she prorogued Parliament. Immediately afterwards, Montagu, Denton, Harris (one of the attornies) and the five Aylesbury men were released from the custody of the serjeant-at-arms. Parliament was dissolved on 5 April.[66]

The Whigs won a majority at the general election of 1705, so that when the new Parliament met John Smith replaced Harley as Speaker. The *Ashby* v. *White* case was not raised again. The right of the House of Commons to determine the qualification of electors at parliamentary elections, together with which persons were duly elected as M.P.s, was left unchallenged. It is difficult to believe that Wharton's real objective had been to make every single vote cast at every single election actionable at law, since this would have thrown the whole electoral system into chaos. Richard Steele suggests that his object was only to break Pakington's interest at Aylesbury. This he did achieve in two Parliaments. At the 1705 election the precept was sent to constables appointed by him and not by the lord of the manor, with the result that Pakington and his friend and nominee Simon Harcourt were defeated, and petitioned the Whig House of Commons without success. Wharton again carried both Members at the 1708 election, but in 1710 he had the 'great mortification' to find Pakington regaining both seats for his candidates.[67]

NOTES

1. *CJ, xiii,* 518; Narcissus Luttrell, *Brief Relation of State Affairs* (6 vols, 1857), V, 47, 49, 50, 51, 60, 62, 63, 67; Bodl., MS Eng. hist. b. 120, f. 84v: Diary of Sir Richard Cocks; Henry Horwitz, *Parliament, Policy and Politics in the Reign of William III* (1977), 291–2.

2. H. L. Snyder, 'The defeat of the Occasional Conformity Bill and the Tack', *BIHR, xli* (1968), 172–92; W. Pittis, *The Proceedings of both Houses of Parliament in the Years 1702, 1703, 1704 upon the bill to prevent Occasional Conformity* (1710).

3. BL, Stowe MS 304, fos 206–10: 'The Case of James Herbert sitting Member, Aylesbury *v.* Simon Mayne, petitioner'.

4. Buckinghamshire RO, 165/24: 'The state of the borough of Aylesbury, co. Bucks, December 1685'.

5. BL, Verney MSS microfilm reel 45: John Verney to Sir Richard Verney, Aylesbury, 14 April 1691.

6. This was done by the Grenvilles in 1748: see *The House of Commons, 1715–1754,* ed. Romney Sedgwick (2 vols, 1970), I, 197.

7. BL, Stowe MS 304, fos 206–10; BL, Verney MSS microfilm reel 48: Sir Richard Verney to John Verney, Claydon, 15 Sept. 1695.

8. *CJ, xii,* 487–90. Unfortunately no records of the Bedford Charity have survived before 1750.

9. T. B. Howell, *A Complete Collection of State Trials,* (34 vols, 1816–28), XIV, 780; *Memoirs of the Life of the Most Noble Thomas late Marquess of Wharton . . . to which is added his Lordship's character by Sir Richard Steele* (1715), 55.

10. *Wharton Memoirs,* 44.

11. Cornwall RO, BO/23/72/2–69: 'The case of the borough of Liskeard'.

12. BL, Add. MS 34125, fos 138–52: 'Case book of Chief Justice Holt'.

13. Howell, *State Trials,* XIV, 843–61.

14. Wharton had won possession of lead mines in the honour of Richmond in Yorkshire by having the case called up to the House of Lords and depriving the other claimants (Robert Squire, M.P. Scarborough 1705–7, and Charles Bathurst of Clints in Richmond) of the use of a vital piece of evidence; the survey of the honour of Richmond, a public record. This was condemned by the Commons as 'unwarrantable' and tending to subject 'the rights and property of the Commons of England to an illegal and arbitrary power'; see Howell, *State Trials,* XIV, 890–5; *CJ, xiv,* 560.

15. *CSP Dom., 1703–4,* 395–6.

16. Howell, *State Trials,* XIV, 778–99; PRO, C104/116, pt 1: Lord Ossulton's diary, 14 [January 1704] ; BL, Loan 29/359. The 13 were: Scarsdale; Rochester; Compton, Bishop of London; Sprat, Bishop of Rochester; Guernsey; Hooper, Bishop of St Asaph; Guilford; Weymouth; Northampton; Abingdon; Granville; Strafford, Bishop of Chester; and Gower (*LJ, xvii,* 369).

17. BL, Add. MS 17677 WWW, f. 458: L'Hermitage to the States General 'très secret, Londres 25 janvier 1704'.

18. See Mary Frear Keeler, 'The emergence of standing committees for privileges and returns', *Parliamentary History, i* (1982), 25–46.

19. Howell, *State Trials,* XIV, 696. Sir Samuel Barnardiston, 1st Bt, stood at a by-election for Suffolk in February 1673 and was seated on petition by the Commons a year later. He then sued Sir William Soames in King's Bench for making a double return to keep him out of the House and was awarded £800 damages. (Barnardiston was backed by the 1st Earl of Shaftesbury and Philip, 4th Baron Wharton, Thomas's father, over this action.) The judgment, however, was reversed in the Court of Exchequer. In 1689 Barnardiston attempted to get the House of Lords to reverse the Exchequer judgment, but the Lords ruled

that the Commons had an exclusive right to determine the legality both of the returns and of the conduct of returning officers in making them (Howell, *State Trials*, VI, 1063–1120).

20. *Ibid.*, XIV, 705–12.
21. *Ibid.*, 712–42.
22. *Ibid.*, 743–52; for the suit see *ibid.*, 546–58. Bishop Lloyd who was mentally unstable (see *DNB*, XII, 1315–18) had not only directly intervened against Pakington in the Worcestershire election of December 1701, but had accused Pakington of 'whoredom, drunkenness' and seeking to bring in the Pretender.
23. Howell, *State Trials*, XIV, 752–5.
24. *Ibid.*, 761–5.
25. *Ibid.*, 769–75; Beinecke Library, Yale, Osborn Coll., Southwell MSS, Box 1: John Ellis to Edward Southwell, 22 Jan. 1704.
26. Howell, *State Trials*, XIV, 776.
27. Beinecke Library, Osborn Coll., Southwell MSS, Box 1: John Ellis to Edward Southwell, 22 Jan. 1704.
28. Howell, *State Trials*, XIV, 776–8.
29. *Letters Illustrative of the Reign of William III from 1696 to 1708 Addressed to the Duke of Shrewsbury by James Vernon*, ed. G. P. R. James (3 vols, 1831), III, 250–1; BL, Add. MS 17677 WWW, f. 475.
30. BL, Add. MS 17677 WWW, fos 553–4.
31. Howell, *State Trials*, XIV, 799–800; *LJ*, xvii, 554–5.
32. James, *Letters Illustrative . . .*, III, 257–8.
33. Beinecke Library, Osborn Coll., Richard Hill papers: J. Tucker to Richard Hill, Whitehall, 4 April 1704.
34. BL, Add. MS 17677 WWW, fos 562–3.
35. *The Report of the Lords Committees Appointed to Draw up the State of the Case upon the Said Writ of Error, Lately Depending in the House of Peers; Wherein Matthew Ashby was Plaintiff and William White and Others Defendants with the Resolutions of the House of Peers Relating Thereunto* (1704).
36. *Free Parliaments or a Vindication of the Fundamental Right of the Commons of England in Parliament Assembled, to be Sole Judge of all those Privileges of the Electors, and of the Elected, which are Absolutely Necessary to Preserve Free Parliaments and a Free People. Being a Justification of the Proceedings of the Honourable House of Commons in the Case of Ashby against White. Nolumus Leges Angliae Mutari!* (1704). It is attributed to Harley in Horace Walpole, *A Catalogue of the Royal and Noble Authors of England* (2 vols, Dublin, 1759), II, 213–14.
37. *The Ancient and Fundamental Right of English Parliaments in General Asserted and the Particular Right of the Commons of England Justified Both from Reason and Antiquity, and the Constitution of the English Laws; with Some Necessary Reflections and Observations in Answer to Sir Humphrey Mackworth's Late Pamphlet Called Free Parliaments etc. wherein He Asserts that the Commons of England are the Sole Judges of all those Privileges of the Electors and of the Elected, are Absolutely Necessary to Preserve Free Parliaments and a Free People. Tempora Mutantur & nos Mutari!* By J. B. L.L.M.D. [John Bateman] (1705) in the Huntington Library, San Marino, Calif.
38. Those said to have opposed the preparations for war against France in the spring of 1701: *A List of one Unanimous Club of Members* (1701). See *A Register of Parliamentary Lists 1660–1761*, ed. David Hayton and Clyve Jones (University of Leicester Department of History Occasional Publication no. 1, 1979), 94.
39. See Snyder, 'Defeat of the Occasional Conformity Bill', 181–6.
40. Howell, *State Trials*, XIV, 800–4; Nottingham UL, PW 2 Hy 871: 'Robert Mead's proceedings in the case of Ashby and White'.
41. Bodl., Tanner MS 301, f. 231.

42. Howell, *State Trials*, XIV, 801-5.
43. *Wharton Memoirs*, 51; G. M. Trevelyan, *England under Queen Anne* (3 vols, 1930-4), II, 24.
44. Keith Feiling, *History of the Tory Party 1640-1714* (1924), 377 n. 3.
45. Howell, *State Trials*, XIV, 805-6; Beinecke Library, Osborn Coll., Biscoe-Maunsell newsletters: London, 3 Feb. 1704/5.
46. *Wharton Memoirs*, 51.
47. Abel Boyer, *The History of the Reign of Queen Anne Digested into Annals* (11 vols, 1708-13), III, 194-208.
48. *Ibid.*, 209-10; *The Judgments Delivered by the Lord Chief Justice Holt in the Case of Ashby v. White and Others and in the Case of John Paty and Others* (1837), 41-2.
49. BL, Add. MS 17677 AAA, fos 161-2; Howell, *State Trials*, XIV, 807-10.
50. Kenneth A. Spencer Research Library, University of Kansas, MS C163: Simpson to Methuen, 27 Feb. 1705.
51. *Ibid.*
52. Boyer, *Annals*, III, 210.
53. *LJ, xvii*, 676.
54. Howell, *State Trials*, XIV, 809-10.
55. Spencer Research Library MS C163: Simpson to Methuen, 27 Feb. 1705.
56. *LJ, xvii*, 677-8.
57. *CJ, xiv*, 555.
58. *Ibid., xiv*, 559-63.
59. Boyer, *Annals*, III, 212.
60. Howell, *State Trials*, XIV, 831: for Ferrers see Snyder, 'Defeat of the Occasional Conformity Bill', 172-92.
61. *CJ, xiv*, 569-75; *LJ, xvii*, 694-715; BL, Add. MS 17677 AAA, f. 183.
62. Boyer, *Annals*, III, 239.
63. *Ibid.*, 212-24.
64. *A Defence of Liberty and Property, giving an Account of the Conflict between the Lords and Commons of Athens* (1705).
65. *Pro Aris & Focis: or a Vindication of the Proceedings of the Commons on the Writs of Habeas Corpus and Writ of Error in the Case of the Aylesbury Men. In a Letter from a Member of Parliament to a Friend in the Country* (1705).
66. Beinecke Library, Osborn Coll., Biscoe-Maunsell newsletters: London, 17 March 1705.
67. *Wharton Memoirs*, 55; Northamptonshire RO, Isham MS 3759.

4 'The Most Corrupt Council in Christendom': decisions on controverted elections, 1702-42

W.A. Speck

'This night was the Norwich petition examined by the Committee, which is certainly the most corrupt Councill in Xtendom, nay in the world.'

Diary of Sir Richard Cocks, 25 February 1702[1]

Between 1604, when the Commons finally wrested adjudication of elections from the Crown, until 1868, when they handed it over to the courts, defeated candidates who wished to protest against the return of sitting Members on the grounds of electoral irregularities did so by petitioning Parliament. After 1672, when Parliament met the House would decide to hear such petitions either by setting up a Committee of Privileges and Elections for the purpose or else by simply having them heard at the bar.[2]

In theory the committee was a judicial body impartially judging the merits of a case. There were various grounds on which a candidate might appeal for jurisdiction in a disputed election, though by and large they can be divided into two categories: disputes arising from the franchise, and those concerning the conduct of an election. Although the right to vote in the counties had been established in the fifteenth century as residing in those possessing freeholds to the value of forty shillings a year, the heterogeneous nature of the borough franchise was a fruitful source of contention. Above all, perhaps, the inhabitant boroughs, where some sort of residential qualification was requisite, afforded most opportunities for the House to determine the right to vote. Rival candidates would dispute the precise qualification in such boroughs — for example, one side insisting that it lay in the inhabitants at large while the other contended that it was confined to householders paying Church and Poor rates. Disputes about the conduct of elections were more frequent, and could involve counties. Thus defeated candidates could petition on the grounds that the returning officer had acted partially in favour of those he had returned, or they could complain that the sitting Members had been in breach of the laws against bribery and treating at elections.

In practice the Commons decided these petitions on political rather than judicial grounds, and throughout the seventeenth century the prevailing majority blatantly used petitions from unsuccessful candidates who would vote with them, to unseat sitting Members who sided with the minority. The polarization of the House into parties under the later Stuarts ensured that a Tory majority would unseat Whig Members, and vice versa. By Anne's reign this had developed to a fine art.

Because the procedure for hearing election petitions was in practice a machinery for increasing the majority of the party which had been victorious at the polls, some pains were taken to ensure that that party controlled it. The political rather than the judicial nature of the trials of petitions was most blatant if they were heard at the bar of the House rather than in committee, and, as we shall see, decisions on where to hear them were usually taken by the majority of the Commons on the sole grounds of party advantage. A hearing at the bar decided the issue immediately, whereas decisions taken in committee had to be endorsed by the House, giving the opposition a second chance to rally its forces to reverse a close vote. By and large the prevalent party would order hearings at the bar of petitions from leading Members of their own side or against leading Members of the other side, and refer to the committee less crucial petitions from their own side and almost all those from the other side. It is therefore politically significant that the majority of petitions to be tried at the bar were heard, while most of those referred to the committee were either withdrawn or not heard.[3] The session of 1708–9 was notorious in this respect. Here the Whigs demonstrated their partiality in the hearing of petitions by ordering them all to be tried at the bar and by not even bothering to appoint a Committee of Elections.[4]

In every other session during the period such a committee was appointed when the House met. This was virtually a Committee of the Whole House in practice, though ostensibly its membership was restricted to a number named in orders of the House.[5] These names were pointers to the prevalent majority. In 1702, 1710 and 1714 the lists were overwhelmingly Tory, while in 1715 Whigs predominated. The chairmen were also extremely partisan, being William Bromley, the sponsor of the Occasional Conformity Bill, from 1702 to 1705; Ralph Freman, a leading October Club member, from 1710 to 1713; and Sir Gilbert Dolben, another prominent Octobrist, in 1714. Richard Hampden, the chairman of the committee in 1715, though previously a staunch Junto Whig, had, it is true, trimmed his sails during the previous four years and had earned the enmity of Lord Wharton as a result. But though the animosity between them had reached a peak in the general election of 1715, their differences had been resolved during that contest, and it appears that Hampden's nomination to the chair of this committee signalled his return to the true Whig fold.

The situation was rather different in 1705, which witnessed the only contest for the chair of the Committee of Privileges and Elections during Anne's reign. The general election of that year had not produced a clear party majority, and the stalemate at the polls was to some extent reflected in the list of those named in the orders of the House to form the committee, which, though containing a sizeable proportion of Members from both parties, gave the Whigs the edge. In this situation it was essential for the Whigs to get control of the committee, or the Tories might use it to swing the balance in their favour. The Court, which had decided to use its influence to throw the balance the other way and had already signalled this by supporting a Whig in a hotly contested division over the Speakership on 25 October, made efforts to ensure that the Whig candidate was also successful in the contest for the chair of this committee. In November the Whigs put up Spencer Compton, and Sir Gilbert Dolben 'was set up by those who opposed the present Speaker' — that is, the Tories.[6] Lord Treasurer Godolphin rallied government supporters to Compton's side, writing to Secretary of State Robert Harley on 6 November, 'it will be very necessary to take a little pains with our friends not to mistake their interest tomorrow about the chairman of the Committee of Elections'.[7] Next evening 'the Committee of Privileges and Elections met, and Spencer Compton Esq., was chosen chairman by 16 more than Sir Gilbert Dolben, the former having 188 voices and Sir Gilbert 172'.[8] With voting strength so evenly balanced, the Whigs could not afford to lose control of a committee which was to be used flagrantly to build them a stable majority in the ensuing months.

On 2 November 1705 petitions relating to 31 controverted elections were read out to the House, presumably in the order in which they had been received by the clerk. The first three to be heard by order of the House, however, were the first, third and tenth of those read out. These concerned disputed returns in St Albans, Amersham and Hertford. All three were elections in which the Whigs were very concerned to see that the Whig petitioners succeeded against Tory sitting Members. St Albans took precedence not, one suspects, because it had been read first, but because the tempestuous Duchess of Marlborough had been involved in it. Her Grace had made interest for Henry Killigrew, a retired admiral but an active Whig, while the mayor had returned John Gape, a Tacker. Judging by the evidence reported to the House, both sides had overstepped the legal mark in canvassing at this election, and in all probability it would have been declared void by an impartial court of justice. However, after four divisions along party lines Gape was ousted and Killigrew installed. The Whigs did not fare so well in the trial of the Amersham election, at which the Whig Sir Thomas Webster had unsuccessfully stood against Sir Samuel Garrard, a Tacker. The committee found Garrard duly elected, largely because some of Harley's Tory supporters deserted the government and went over to the opposition, despite Godolphin's attempt to forestall this by informing Harley that there was not 'a more powerful man against us in the whole House' than Sir Samuel.[9] An attempt in the House to reverse the committee's decisions was equally unsuccessful. Lord Keeper Cowper was closely involved in the Hertford election, at which the Whig

Thomas Clarke filed a petition against the return of Richard Goulston, yet another Tacker. Cowper drew up the resolution on the prevailing franchise in Hertford, which the committee eventually adopted and which the House accepted by four votes. They also rejected Goulston and seated Clarke by similar narrow majorities, despite Cowper's impression that Harley was doing 'all he could underhand to spoil the Hertford business'.[10]

It was no accident that the first petitions to be heard in the session of 1705–6 were all filed by Whigs against Tackers. During the general election the government had done all in its power to prevent the returns of Tackers at the polls, yet despite its efforts some 90 of the notorious 134 had got back into the House.[11] The machinery for trying election petitions was therefore deliberately used by the Court and the Whigs to effect in the House what they had been unable to achieve at the hustings, and to remove Tackers from the Commons systematically.

So partisan was the trial of election petitions that some back-bench M.P.s revolted against the ruthlessness of their leaders and attempted in the session of 1707–8 to reform the procedure. On 27 January 1708 a committee was set up 'to consider of methods for the more speedy and easy trying the determining of controverted elections'.[12] This committee represented all parties in the House, but had a distinctly 'Country' flavour, its chairman being Peter King, at the time of his appointment one of the leading Country Whigs. The committee's brief was ironic in view of its recommendations, one of which was guaranteed to make the judging of returns anything but speedy and easy: this was 'that all questions at the trial of elections shall, if any member insist upon it, be determined by ballot'. The recommendation was adopted only once, at the trial of a disputed election in Ashburton on 26 February 1708. On that occasion

> the balloting was prepared, according to the Orders of the House for that purpose; and Sir Godfrey Copley and Mr. Henley were appointed by Mr. Speaker to attend the Box: And the Clerk, and Clerk-assistant, went with the Box, and Balls, and the said Two Members with them, round the several Benches of the House; and the Members sitting in their Places, took the Balls, and put them into the Box: After which the Box was carried to the Clerk's Table; and after counting the Balls at the Table by the Clerks, in the Presence of the said two Members (who stood one at each End of the Table) the two Members went to the Bar, and came up to the Table (as usual, on other Occasions of reporting) and reported to Mr. Speaker;
> That the Yeas were 189, and the Noes 148.[13]

Thereafter the method was abandoned, partly because it was so unwieldy but mainly because the government disliked this move towards impartiality in the hearing of election petitions. As Addison put it, 'The House of Commons are upon a project of deciding all elections by balloting, which some think may be as prejudicial to the Court as a place-bill; besides that, it is apprehended the election of a Speaker may hereafter be brought to the same decision, unless some method be still found for preventing it'.[14] Fortunately for the Court they were able to stifle the scheme in this session, though an attempt to revive it in the next was only just defeated by nine votes.[15]

Indeed the session of 1708–9 was notorious for the partiality shown by the Whigs in deciding election petitions. By ordering them all to be heard at the bar, and by neglecting to appoint a Committee of Elections, they ostentatiously drew attention to the fact that petitions were to be decided by party voting. As in the previous Parliament, petitions from supporters against Tory sitting Members were dealt with first, while those lodged by opponents were ignored.

Yet the very first petition to be heard in fact went in favour of the Tories. This came from the Whig Sir William Rich and complained about the return of Anthony Blagrave, a Tory sitting Member for Reading. At first all went smoothly for the Whigs. A resolution on the franchise obtaining in Reading, which favoured Rich's case, was passed on 2 December by a majority of 20. Nine days later, however, 'the Court lost the Reading election contrary to all expectation' when Blagrave was found duly elected by 129 votes to 82.[16]

Judging by the fate of a petition concerning the Westminster election, the outcome of the election was due to mismanagement rather than defections from the Whig side. Thomas Medlycott, a Member returned from Westminster by the Tory interest, was petitioned against by Sir Henry Dutton Colt, a Whig candidate who had had the support of the lord treasurer and three Whig dukes in the general election.[17] As in the case of Reading, preliminary resolutions were passed in favour of the petitioner, albeit by very narrow majorities. On 14 December, however, Medlycott was declared duly elected by 154 votes to 142. This surprising outcome was attributed to the negligence of the government. About 34 or 35 Whigs, thinking that the debate would be adjourned, left the House to hear Signor Nicolini sing. Scenting their opportunity the Tories pressed for a division, and carried it with the help of several Scots who disliked Sir Henry because he had been opposed to the Darien scheme. The news of his defeat caused consternation at the opera.[18]

The Whigs were much more on their guard after the Christmas recess. In January and February 1709 they carried two disputed election cases which became *causes célèbres* of party animosity: Abingdon and Bewdley.

In the Abingdon case William Hucks petitioned against Sir Simon Harcourt, claiming

that Sir Simon, by menaces and other illegal practices of himself and agents, procured several votes for him, and several were admitted to vote for him, that had no right, and that Sir Simon hath prevailed with John Sellwood, mayor of the said borough, to return him, though the petitioner was duly elected by a majority of qualified and uncorrupt voters, and ought to have been returned instead of the said Sir Simon Harcourt.

Of these claims the most crucial was that relating to the qualifications of voters, and on 18 January a resolution disqualifying many of Sir Simon's supporters was carried by 187 to 172. The partiality of this decision caused a great stir. Harcourt himself made a speech to the House upon it, which was subsequently published. In it he lashed the Whigs, asserting that 'any opposition may give a handle to a petition. No matter for the justice of it, power will maintain it.'[19] Two days later he was ousted from the House, after a heated debate. On 21 January Robert Walpole informed the Duke of Marlborough of the struggle:

> I had yesterday the hardest service I ever [had] in Parliament, the House sitting till past two of the clock in the morning upon Sir Simon Harcourt's election for Abingdon, which was at last carried against him by a majority of 47, and the petitioner voted in. It was much the fullest House that has been this Parliament, and the whole affair carried on with greater heat and warmth on both sides than usual.[20]

The manner in which party passions had made a travesty of justice in this determination 'made a great noise in town'.[21]

If anything, the Bewdley affair created an even greater noise. As with Abingdon the crux of the case concerned the franchise. Both sides agreed that this was restricted to the 13 members of the corporation. The issue at stake was whether a new charter granted to the borough in 1708 had superseded a charter conferred earlier. If so, then the Whig candidate Henry Herbert had been duly elected by the corporation set up under the terms of this new charter. If not, then Salwey Winnington, a Tory friend of Robert Harley, could carry his petition on the grounds that he had been rightfully returned by the corporation based on the old charter.[22] The granting of a new charter had already been a source of bitter debate between the Tories and the Whigs before ever its merits came to be decided in the hearing of this election petition. During the general election Harley had asked the pointed question, 'whether the taking away of charters and forcing new ones upon parliament boroughs was one cause of the Revolution?'[23] On 8 February 1709 the matter came before the House of Commons, and after two divisions both the new charter and Herbert's return were upheld. As Walpole reported the result to Marlborough,

> the House sat till almost 12 at night upon the Bewdley election, the last effort that the adverse party will attempt this session in my poor opinion. The spirit that has been shown in this election

where Mr. Harley was so nearly concerned and in that of Abingdon of Sir S. Harcourt has chiefly contributed to make this the easiest sessions of parliament I ever saw, wherein I think we may depend upon meeting no more trouble in public affairs.[24]

During this session the Whigs were motivated by a spirit of revenge. As one observer put it, 'more of that corner will follow the same fate [as Harcourt] till they have made up the number that the Tories in the days of peace turned out in one session, I think 13 in which Sir Simon was particularly eminent'.[25] In fact the Whigs did not rest until they had turned out 16 Tories and brought in 16 of their own number. This was to turn a majority of 69 after the general election into one of 101, not counting Scottish Members or by-election results.

The Tories were not quite so vindictive after their victory of 1710. In June 1711 Henry St John claimed that 'no man has been forced from his seat purely because we did not like him'.[26] There was some substance in this claim. Thus when a Tory, John Orfeur, petitioned against the Whig James Stanhope, asserting that the latter had been illegally returned at Cockermouth, and hoping to replace him as the sitting Member, the House declared it a void election and Stanhope was returned in the subsequent by-election. As one of his supporters commented, referring to the Tories in Cockermouth, 'their greatest dependence was that the House would take it for a party cause between High and Low, but I'm glad that that House has a greater regard for justice than for persons'.[27] As we have noticed also in the affair of balloting in 1708, although the hearing of petitions was on the whole a machinery for increasing the prevalent majority, the Commons was not utterly partial to the exclusion of all thoughts of justice. By and large the Tories appear to have been rather more scrupulous than the Whigs. Nevertheless the Parliament of 1710–13 witnessed the greatest number of changes due to the replacements of sitting Members by petitioners of any Parliament in Anne's reign, a Tory majority of 151 at the polls being boosted to one of 199 thanks to the dislodging of 24 Whigs by Tory petitioners.

When the Whigs came into their own in 1715, however, the greatest purge of the period took place. Edward Wortley Montagu, a leading Country Whig, admitted that 'the injustice shown in trying of elections has perhaps this session been greater than ever'.[28] Following the general election held in that year, no fewer than 82 petitions were presented, a record for these years and indeed the highest number of the eighteenth century apart from 1722. Of the 82, 21 were determined. Eighteen of these determinations upheld the petitioners' claims, and as a result 25 Tory sitting Members were ousted and the same number of Whigs were seated. Of the rest, 32 were withdrawn and 27 were never determined. Those withdrawn were from 35 Tories and 11 Whigs. Those never heard were from 25 Tories and only 9 Whigs. The hearing of election petitions

confirmed the Whig triumph of 1715, and within one session a Whig
majority of 65 at the polls was turned into a majority of 115.

The Tories alone could never again challenge the Whigs for control of
the Committee of Privileges and Elections. Unrestrained by the consideration that their rivals might mete out revenge after the next general
election, the Whigs under Walpole became even more outrageously partisan
than they had been in Anne's reign. The prime minister's own supporters
admitted as much. Lord Hervey thought that after the 1727 elections
'the manifest injustice and glaring violation of all truth in the decisions of
this Parliament surpass even the most flagrant and infamous instances of
any of their predecessors.'[29]

> What can I say for the judgments of the house of commons in their
> election causes? [confessed Speaker Onslow] It is really come to be
> deemed by many a piece of virtue and honour to do injustice in
> these cases. 'The right is in the friend and not in the cause' is almost
> avowed, and he is laughed at by the leaders of parties who has
> scruples upon it; and yet we should not bear this a month in any
> other judicature in the kingdom.[30]

Realizing the hopelessness of their cause, Tories virtually ceased to
petition against Whig candidates during Walpole's ministry. This partly
accounts for the decline in the number of petitions from a peak of 99 after
the 1722 election to 61 in 1727, 69 in 1734 and 43 in 1741.[31] Indeed the
numbers were to some extent maintained by ministerial supporters, who
were now able to intervene in constituencies and petition against the
return of their opponents — sometimes on the most specious grounds — on
the assumption that their complaints would be automatically upheld by
the House of Commons. Newtown, Isle of Wight, for instance, was a
borough which returned Tories without a contest throughout the reigns of
Anne and George I. In 1727, however, the Whig governor of the island, the
Duke of Bolton, put up his cousin, Charles Armand Powlett, and Sir John
Barrington of Swainton, near Newtown. Although the two Tory sitting
Members obtained a clear majority of the votes polled, Bolton's candidates
petitioned on the grounds that the returning officer had refused to poll
qualified voters on their side. The dispute turned on the franchise in Newtown, the Tories insisting that it was in the freemen elected by the
corporation while the Whigs claimed that it was in freemen holding bur-
gages in the borough. Significantly it was decided at the bar of the House
of Commons, and not in the Committee of Privileges and Elections, on
22 April 1729 'that the right of election of burgesses to serve in parliament for the borough of Newtown in the Isle of Wight . . . is in the mayor
and burgesses of the said borough lands within the said borough.' Powlett
and Barrington were therefore declared to have been duly elected.[32]

The chances of challenging this ruling, if ever political circumstances
presented the opportunity, had technically been curtailed in the very same

session by the passage of the so-called Last Determinations Act. This takes
its name from a clause in a statute 'for the more effectual preventing
bribery and corruption in the election of members to serve in parliament.'
The clause stated 'that such votes shall be deemed to be legal, which have
been so declared by the last determination in the House of Commons;
which last determination concerning any county, shire, city, borough,
cinque port or place shall be final to all intents and purposes whatsoever,
any usage to the contrary notwithstanding.'[33] This did not prevent petitioners from disputing the validity of the last determination of the Commons, necessitating a standing order in 1736 disallowing evidence concerning the legality of votes other than those so determined.[34] Even
thereafter some petitioners were prepared to call previous determinations
in question. In 1737, for example, upon hearing a petition from Windsor
the House overlooked rulings of 1690 and 1697 in favour of one from
1680.[35]

Nevertheless, the passage of the Last Determinations Act in 1729 shows
that, even during Walpole's administration, the House of Commons did not
totally lose sight of the principle that objective rather than subjective
criteria ought to affect decisions upon controverted elections. There was a
limit to the extent to which the great man himself could persuade the
House that black was white. He overstepped it after the 1734 election, in
the case of Marlborough. Two Tories had topped the poll in the borough
with the backing of Lord Bruce, defeating two Whig carpet-baggers from
London put up by Lord Hertford with Walpole's blessing.[36] When the
defeated candidates petitioned against the return of the Tories, Lord
Hertford wrote to the prime minister:[37]

> I don't doubt but by your help to carry my petition for my two
> Members, and then to secure the corporation for ever, so therefore
> to shew the town that my interest is not so despicable I must desire
> that the two companies [of troops] now at Hungerford may be sent
> hither, which will be no burthern for we have above forty public
> houses and it will be of great use to my interest, the keeping up
> which is a great expense to me but I will keep it as long as I have
> any money, but this trifle I now ask must be granted me, for if I am
> not supported I must give it up, and also the few honest men we
> have amongst us and this I am sure you will not let me do.

The petitioners sought to disqualify 11 electors who had polled for their
rivals by challenging the election of one Edward Bell as common-council-
man in Marlborough. Bell's right to sit on the council had actually been
upheld by the Court of King's Bench, a fact exploited by those who supported the sitting Members to discredit the petition. They tried to prevent
the admission of evidence controverting Bell's election on the grounds
that there was a verdict and judgment in his favour, but the House agreed
to hear it, albeit by only four votes. However, when it was heard, the small

majority melted away. Although Sir Robert personally tried to persuade the Commons to accept the evidence, staying throughout the debate and speaking at length to the proposition, the invidiousness of reversing by a vote a judicial verdict proved too much for his supporters. Dudley Ryder, the attorney general, actually refused when the prime minister asked him to reply to the argument that this was setting a vote of the House of Commons above the law. Henry Pelham and even Sir William Yonge left before the vote, so that 'Sir Robert, finding he could not spirit up his tools, gave up the question.'[38]

While Walpole's majority after the 1734 election was large enough for him to overlook the occasional defeat on a disputed election, it was so narrow following the general election of 1741 that he could not afford to lose control of the machinery for judging controverted returns. In this respect the voting on a petition from Bossiney on 9 and 11 December, in the first divisions of the new Parliament, seemed to augur well for Walpole. On the crucial questions he obtained majorities of six and seven. These were so narrow, however, that the opposition took comfort from them, while the government's supporters were filled with apprehension. As Horace Walpole gloomily observed, 'one or two such victories, as Pyrrhus, the member for Macedon said, will be the ruin of us. I look upon it now, that the question is, Downing Street or the Tower.'[39] The vote for the chairmanship of the Committee of Privileges and Elections on 16 December was therefore crucial to the survival of his ministry. On that day William Hay, Member for Seaford, recorded in his diary:[40]

> The committee of privileges and elections now met for the first time and both parties had determined long before to exert their whole strength in the choice of a chairman and the candidates were known. [Giles] Earle chairman in the two last parliaments was proposed by the ministry, and Doctor Lee a civilian of good capacity and character . . . by the opposers. Lee was chosen by 242 against 238.

This was the beginning of the end for Walpole. As Archdeacon Coxe observed, 'the fatal consequences were immediately visible; several unsuccessful candidates, who had depended on his support, withdrew their petitions.'[41]

The next challenge to the government over a controverted election was in fact heard not in the committee but at the bar of the House. On 22 December the hearing of a petition concerning the conduct of the returning officer at the Westminster election provoked as many as four divisions.[42] At the general election two government supporters had stood against Admiral Vernon, an opposition hero after his capture of Porto Bello in the war with Spain, and Charles Edwin, a Welshman who had been somewhat casually nominated at the meeting which had adopted Vernon as a candidate.[43] When John Lever, the high bailiff and returning officer for Westminster, returned Lord Sundon and Sir Charles Wager (the

ministerial candidates), supporters of Vernon and Edwin petitioned
protesting

> that the said John Lever was determined at all events to return
> the said Lord Sundon and Sir Charles Wager; that during the first
> three days of taking the poll, the said John Lever contented himself
> barely with doing injustice, under colour of exercising his judgment,
> and under that disguise refused the votes of several persons duly
> qualified and desirous to vote for the said Edward Vernon and
> Charles Edwin; and at the same time admitted others to poll for the
> said Lord Sundon and Sir Charles Wager who had no right of voting
> ... That the said John Lever, not satisfied with injustice and impar-
> tiality only, had recourse to violence; and, in conjunction with
> Arthur Rawlinson, the High Constable of the said City and Liberty,
> and others, did hire and pay a great number of loose, and dissolute
> persons, and furnish them with clubs, bludgeons, and other offensive
> weapons; and did direct the persons, so armed, to attend the place
> of poll, and insult the friends and voters of the said Edward Vernon
> and Charles Edwin.

The most serious charge against the high bailiff was that he had arbitrarily
closed the poll on 8 May against the protests of Edwin and his supporters,
and had announced the return of Sundon and Wager, attended by a guard
of over fifty soldiers 'drawn up in a military manner' at St Paul's Covent
Garden, 'the place of polling.'[44]

Although it seems clear that Lever had been guilty of gross partiality —
and indeed received £1500 from the secret service fund for his pains — the
decisions of the House rested on political rather than judicial considerations.[45] On the first question, that Lord Sundon had been duly elected,
Members voted 216 for and 220 against. Sir Charles Wager was similarly
declared not duly elected by 220 to 215. The election was consequently
declared void. The ministerial side then tried to adjourn the House, but
were defeated by 217 to 215, whereupon Lever was ruled to have acted
illegally, and ordered into custody. The Court again failed to adjourn the
House by 206 votes to 200, even though it was by that time about three
o'clock in the morning. The Commons went on to pass resolutions deplor-
ing the presence of troops at the election, and finally broke up at five
o'clock.[46]

Despite these reverses the prime minister still hoped that, after the
respite of the Christmas recess, he would be able to command a majority
in the lower House. He told the attorney general on 8 January that 'he had
made a very exact computation of the numbers on each side in the House
of Commons and was satisfied that setting aside all doubtful votes he had
now a clear majority of 19, expecting one who would at most only keep
out of the way.'[47] Certainly on 21 January he managed to avert the setting
up of a secret committee to inquire into his administration, albeit by only

three rather than by 19 votes. Nevertheless, decisions upon controverted elections continued to go against him, so strongly supported by the opposition and so weakly resisted by his own side that he did not even risk dividing the House.[48]

On 28 January 1742, however, he decided to make a last stand over a petition from Chippenham. At the general election this Wiltshire borough had returned two opposition candidates, Edward Bayntun Rolt and Sir Edmund Thomas, who defeated two government supporters, Alexander Hume and John Frederick. Hume took the initiative in petitioning against the result on behalf of himself and his brother-in-law Frederick, spending some £4,057 on the election and the petition.[49] They complained that on the day of the election 'a considerable number of armed men were brought into the said borough by the agents of the said Sir Edmund Thomas and Edward Bayntun Rolt in order to terrify and intimidate the voters in the interest of the petitioners.' They also claimed that one of their supporters, Anthony Guy, sheriff of the county, had been taken into custody on a trumped-up charge and not allowed his liberty until after the poll had closed, despite the fact that 'unexceptionable bail of ten thousand pounds was tendered'. They finally asserted that the returning officer had acted partially, refusing qualified votes for them and accepting illegal votes for their rivals. This last claim brought up the question of the right to vote in Chippenham, which became a crucial consideration notwithstanding the Last Determinations Act. The franchise had in fact been determined as long ago as 1624, when it was resolved that the burgesses and freemen had the right to vote. The petitioners 'insisted that the words "burgesses and freemen" mentioned in the last said determination of this House, mean only such burgesses and freemen as are inhabitants, householders of the ancient houses called free or burgage houses within the said borough.' Counsel for the sitting Members, on the other hand, interpreted the phrase to mean 'persons possessed of ancient burgage houses within the said borough.'[50] It would appear from this that they had polled burgage-owners who did not reside in Chippenham, whereas the defeated candidates wished to confine the franchise to those who were resident there.

The House decided between these rival interpretations by the narrowest possible margin. Although the government side 'came in with full assurance of victory', they 'lost the question upon which the right of election at Chippenham depended by a majority of one.'[51] The sitting Members' version of the franchise was upheld by 236 votes to 235. This was the crucial vote which persuaded Walpole to resign. It was followed on 2 February by another vote to admit counsel for and against the petition to proceed on the basis of the resolution on the franchise. This time the opposition carried it by 241 to 225. Their victory persuaded a ministerial supporter that 'the other party in three weeks' time must get a majority by the alterations in elections, for we have a great many people that have declared they will not attend 'em any more.'[52] Walpole himself is said to have declared that he should never again sit in that house.[53] Certainly he never did, for Parliament was adjourned the following day until 18 February, while on the 9th he was ennobled and on the 11th he resigned.

The machinery for deciding controverted elections thus played a central role in parliamentary politics from the accession of Queen Anne until the fall of Walpole. During those forty years, however, the operators of the machinery changed considerably. Under Anne it was employed as a weapon in the party battle between the Tories and the Whigs in the House of Commons. Gradually under her successors it was used by the Whig government not only against Tory opponents but also against dissident Whigs. Rolt and Thomas, the two sitting Members for Chippenham against whom Frederick and Hume petitioned, were both Whigs. How far alignments had changed since Anne's reign is indicated by the fact that their tellers in the crucial vote of 18 January were Sir John Hynde Cotton, a Tory, and George Lyttelton, an opposition Whig. This creates difficulties in describing the politics of Walpole's last years in the terminology that had been appropriate to those of Godolphin. Contemporaries recognized this when they revived the terms 'Court' and 'Country' to account for political partisanship. Lord Egmont described the crucial divisions in the session of 1741-2, writing on 2 February after hearing the result of the vote on the Chippenham petition, thus: 'On the choice of a chairman of committees of election the Country party were 242 to 238, 6 majority; on the Westminster election they were 220 to 216, 4 majority; afterwards with strong endeavours the Court warded off the appointment of a secret committee by 3 majority; but this day we see the Country party carried the election by 16.'[54]

After the fall of Walpole the trial of election petitions never again played a central part in the political battle, whether between Tories and Whigs or Court and Country. For one thing, the number of petitions dropped sharply along with that of contests at general elections. In 1747, for example, there were only 17.[55] For another they ceased to be as partisan. 'In the majority of elections cases between 1754 and 1770,' according to Philip Lawson, 'there was no party interest involved in the original dispute and if anything this emphasised the shortcomings of the procedure. The absence of a struggle between government and opposition reduced proceedings to a boring ritual.' This prepared the ground for Grenville's Election Act in 1770, which produced 'a method of trying election petitions in which justice could not only be done but be seen to be done.'[56] When disputed elections once more began to rouse violent partisanship, therefore, they were decided by a select committee randomly chosen, and not by 'the most corrupt Council in Christendom'.

NOTES

1. Bodl. MS Eng. hist. b. 210, f. 5. I am indebted to Dr David Hayton for this reference.
2. Petitions and the reports upon them are scattered throughout the *Commons Journals*. The information relating to them was extracted and arranged alphabetically by constituency in T. Carew, *An Historical Account of Elections* (1755).
3. O. C. Williams, *The Clerical Organisation of the House of Commons 1661-1850* (1954), 218.
4. See below, p. 111. They could claim to be following a recommendation of the committee set up in the previous session to consider methods for greater dispatch in the hearing of petitions — that they should all be heard at the bar. *CJ, xv*, 551. Certainly it speeded up proceedings, but the other concern of the committee, that they should be made less partial, was very far from being realized.
5. Williams, *Clerical Organisation*, 214. After the lists of names was added: 'all that are to come are to have voices'.
6. BL, Blenheim MS A1-25: Harley to Marlborough, 9 Nov. 1705.
7. BL, Loan 29/64/8: 'Tuesday at 2'.
8. Narcissus Luttrell, *A Brief Historical Relation of State Affairs* (6 vols, 1857), V, 609.
9. BL, Loan 29/64/4: 'Monday morning'.
10. *The Private Diary of William Lord Cowper*, ed. E. C. Hawtrey (1833), 18.
11. W. A. Speck, *Tory and Whig: The Struggle in the Constituencies* (1970), 107-8.
12. *CJ, xv*, 616-17, 551.
13. *Ibid.*, 577.
14. *The Letters of Joseph Addison*, ed. W. Graham (1941), 93.
15. Luttrell, *Brief Relation*, VI, 375.
16. HMC, *Portland MSS*, IV, 514.
17. BL, Add. MS 17677 CCC, f. 455.
18. BL, Add. MS 22202, fos 2-3: newsletter, 21 Dec. 1708.
19. BL, Egerton MS 3354 (3): 'Sir Simon Harcourt's speech immediately before he left the House'. Cf. Lord Campbell, *Lives of the Lord Chancellors* (8 vols, 1845-69), IV, 449.
20. BL, Blenheim MS B1-23.
21. HMC, *Portland MSS*, IV, 517.
22. For a detailed narrative of the whole episode see P. Styles, 'The corporation of Bewdley under the later Stuarts', *University of Birmingham H. J., i* (1947-8), 92-133.
23. BL, Loan 29/10/22.
24. BL, Blenheim MS B1-23.
25. BL, Add. MS 33225, f. 17: F. Hare to H. Watkins, 28 Jan. 1709.
26. *Letters and correspondence . . . of Henry St. John*, ed. G. Parke (4 vols, 1798), I, 152.
27. Cockermouth Castle MSS, box 110: Christian to J. Relfe.
28. *The Letters and Works of Lady Mary Wortley Montagu*, ed. Lord Wharncliffe (3rd edn, 2 vols, 1861), I, 18.
29. Lord Hervey, *Memoirs of the Reign of George the Second*, ed. J. Wilson Croker (3 vols, 1884), I, 102.
30. G. Burnet, *History of His Own Time* (6 vols, 1823), V, 192: Onslow's note.
31. *The House of Commons 1715-54*, ed. R. Sedgwick (2 vols, 1970), I, 14.
32. *CJ, xxi*, 48, 337-8. Sir Edward Knatchbull noted that the motion for hearing the Newtown petition at the bar was made 'although but 2 days before the Committee of Elections had been closed with intention to hear no more, upon

which Worsley, the sitting Member, had sent his witnesses out of town and they might be gone into other parts'; however, on a division, it was carried by 166 against 147. *The Parliamentary Diary of Sir Edward Knatchbull, 1722-1730*, ed. A. N. Newman (Camden Soc., 3rd ser., XCIV, 1963), 93.

33. 2 George II c. 24.
34. *CJ, xx*, 498: 16 Jan. 1735/6.
35. T. H. B. Oldfield, *An Entire and Complete History . . . of the Boroughs of Great Britain* (3 vols, 1792), II, 20-2.
36. Sedgwick, *House of Commons*, I, 349-50.
37. Quoted *ibid.*, citing Cholmondley (Houghton) MSS in Cambridge UL.
38. *Ibid.*, citing Edward Harley's diary in Cambridge UL; HMC, *Egmont Diary*, II, 167.
39. J. B. Owen, *The Rise of the Pelhams* (1956), 20.
40. Northamptonshire RO, MS (4 vols) L(c) 1732-5: William Hay's Journal, 16 Dec. 1734. I owe this reference to Dr Linda Colley.
41. W. Coxe, *Memoirs of the Life and Administration of Sir Robert Walpole* (4 vols, 1816), IV, 248.
42. *CJ, xxiv*, 37.
43. Sedgwick, *House of Commons*, I, 286. Vernon was actually still at sea when he was nominated for Westminster and five other constituencies.
44. *CJ, xxiv*, 13.
45. N. Rogers, 'Aristocratic clientage, trade and independency: popular politics in pre-radical Westminster', *Past and Present, lxi* (1973), 74.
46. Harrowby MSS (Earl of Harrowby, Sandon Hall, Staffordshire: transcript at the History of Parliament Trust), diary of Sir Dudley Ryder, 22 Dec. 1741. I owe this reference to Dr Eveline Cruickshanks.
47. *Ibid.*, 8 Jan. 1742, quoted in Sedgwick, *House of Commons*, I, 48.
48. *Ibid.*, 49.
49. *Ibid.*, 343-4; II, 158.
50. *CJ, xxiv*, 15-16, 65-6.
51. Devonshire MSS 257/18 (Duke of Devonshire, Chatsworth, Derbyshire: transcript at the History of Parliament Trust): H. B. Legge to the Duke of Devonshire, 30 Jan. 1742. I owe this reference to Dr Eveline Cruickshanks.
52. Devonshire MSS (transcript at the History of Parliament Trust): Lord Hartington to Devonshire, 2 Feb. 1742.
53. Coxe, *Walpole*, IV, 254.
54. HMC, *Egmont Diary*, III, 247.
55. Sedgwick, *House of Commons*, I, 14.
56. P. Lawson, 'Grenville's Election Act, 1770', *BIHR, liii* (1980), 218, 228.

5 'The Scheme Lords, the Neccessitous Lords, and the Scots Lords': the Earl of Oxford's management and the 'Party of the Crown' in the House of Lords, 1711-14

Clyve Jones

'The Scheme Lords, the Neccessitous Lords, and the Scots Lords
Vote according to the Ministry, but the wise and Independent Vote
according to Judgement.'

Lord Cowper, 20 January 1711[1]

The ex-Lord Chancellor Cowper's assessment of the composition of
Robert Harley's[2] ministerial support in the House of Lords was an early
analysis of the future lord treasurer's system of management. The three
groups named by Cowper match closely two of those three elements that
formed 'the party of the Crown' in the late eighteenth-century Lords: 'the
thanes, high priests and household cavalry'.[3] Only the high priests are
missing from Cowper's analysis, and Oxford clearly lacked the asset of a
pliant bench of bishops. By 1711 the bench was dominated by a strongly
coherent group of Whig Low Church bishops ably directed by the often
absent Thomas Tenison, Archbishop of Canterbury. They were so well
disciplined that Henry St John (later Lord Bolingbroke) complained that
if the Whig leaders proposed to vote 'to un-Bishop them, he believed they
would concurr in it'.[4] Oxford during his four-year ministry had little
chance of changing the balance of the bench in his favour; thus his
management of the Lords was largely dependent upon his control of the
three elements of a party of the Crown named by Cowper.

A month before the new Parliament met on 25 November 1710, the
Duke of Shrewsbury wrote to Harley that 'the state of the House of Lords
is bad'. Peter Wentworth, brother of Lord Raby, then British minister in

Berlin, agreed: 'the Torys will be so strong in the house of Commons that they may call some of them to the house of Lords, where they won't be altogether so strong without some help'.[5]

Nearly three weeks previously, with typical thoroughness, Harley had bent his parliamentary skills to analysing the membership of the Lords into supporters, opponents and doubtfuls.[6] The results on paper were not encouraging: of the 133 lords included in his tabulation, there were 63 supporters, 51 opponents and 19 doubtfuls. Harley had omitted from his calculations the 16 representative peers of Scotland who had yet to be elected to the House.[7] He was not to know that all the ministry's list would be elected on 10 November 1710, the first time this had happened since the Union in 1707. The previous record of the factionalism of the Scots[8] was not an encouraging one. Clearly their votes and the votes of the 19 doubtfuls in his calculations would be important to the ministry's position in the Lords. The doubtfuls — largely Court Whigs whose natural inclination was to support the ministry in day-to-day affairs — were liable, in a crisis, to turn to the Whigs and abandon the ministry. The management and voting lists tabulated below in Appendix 1 show that in the crises over 'No Peace without Spain', the Hamilton peerage, the French Commerce Bill and the Schism Bill, 14 opposed the ministry while only four supported it.[9] Thus it would appear that the House was finely balanced at 66 for the ministry and 65 against (excluding the Scots).[10]

Swift's comment, therefore, at the opening of the new parliamentary session in November 1710, that 'even after some Management, there was but a weak and crazy Majority',[11] might seem correct. Certainly during the first parliamentary session of the ministry there were some defeats. But there were numerous victories, largely led in this first session by Harley's lord president of the Council, Lord Rochester (who died 2 May 1711). On the first division of the session of 9 January 1711, on the contentious issue of the state of the war in Spain, the Court's victory was so decisive that Peter Wentworth wrote, 'the Torys has such a majority even in the house of Lords that they carry what they please, much to the surprise of the late Ministry and their friends, who thought themselves sure of a majority of 14 at least which was the number the Tories carry'd their first question'.[12] Clearly, the difference between Wentworth's optimistic view and Swift's 'weak and crazy majority' lay in the ministry's ability to retain the allegiance of the Scots (fairly easy to do in the first session) and the Court peers. By the beginning of the second session on 7 December 1711, Oxford had lost the allegiance of both. A majority of Scots had remained in Scotland frustrated by the ministry's lack of progress over the Duke of Hamilton's British peerage, while the Court Whigs were unhappy about the ministry's peace negotiations. As Lord Halifax, Oxford's regular informant on Junto feelings, wrote the day before the ministry's defeat by one vote on the 'No Peace without Spain' motion on 7 December 1711: 'You know best your own calculations but according to mine there will be

a majority in our House against the terms of peace offered by France.'[13]
After the débâcle of that defeat, Oxford calculated that between 14 and
19 Court peers and office-holders had voted against the ministry.[14] Swift's
comment of a year earlier had come true.

Besides a change in political circumstances between November 1710
and December 1711, Oxford was faced with an altered membership in the
House of Lords which narrowed the paper majority he had calculated in
October 1710. Indeed a correspondent of his son had noted with some
concern in December 1710 that 'Tory Lords drop apace'.[15] Death ought
to have been indiscriminate, taking no account of party, but in the first
session of Oxford's ministry the 'grim reaper' seems to have been a close
associate of the Whig Junto. An examination of those lords in Oxford's
initial calculation of October 1710, who do not reappear on his later
management lists, reveals that eleven had died by December 1711, and of
these ten were supporters and only one an opponent.[16] The laws of peerage succession, however, softened the harsh impact of death's pro-Whig
bias: of the ten supporters who died, four were succeeded by heirs who
supported the ministry.[17] Even so, Oxford's theoretical majority had been
reduced and little had been done, by new creations, to restore the balance.
Besides Oxford himself, only two other new peers had been made.[18] But the
creation of the twelve new peers during the Christmas recess of 1711/12
did something to restore the ministry's theoretical majority. Death continued to take its toll during the second and third sessions of Parliament,
so much so that at the end of the third session Oxford compiled a
memorandum of 27 peers and three bishops 'Dead in this Parliament'.[19]
Again, death wore a Whig mantle: of the 27, the political persuasion of
23 is known, and of these 16 were supporters and seven opponents of the
ministry. By mid-1713, however, this seems to have only marginally
changed the composition of the Lords in favour of the Whigs.[20] This may
be why Oxford made little attempt to boost his majority further with
many more creations: only three peers were added by mid-1714. His
creation of bishops was, of course, limited to replacing those who died.
During his ministry he introduced six new Tory bishops,[21] but as the six
who had died were Tories, this did not bring about any change in the
political balance. In fact, as we shall see, two of these new bishops voted
against the ministry in 1714 over the Protestant Succession.

An analysis of the membership of the House in 1710 and of the changes
which took place by mid-1714 shows that the narrow paper majority of
1710 was much the same at the end as at the beginning of the ministry,
despite the mass creation of 12 peers. The final collapse of Oxford's more
substantial working majority in the Lords was due to changed political
circumstances which altered the political allegiances of some of his early
supporters, rather than to a radical alteration in the composition of the
House.

A definition of the 'scheme lords' is not as easy to arrive at as might at first seem to be the case. The office-holders or the 'queen's servants' form the broadest definition. They either held offices of profit at a national or a local level — in government, the royal household or in the armed forces — or they held offices of trust or honour — largely privy councillorships or lord lieutenancies of counties. In November 1710 there were 63 such peers or bishops (41 holding offices of profit and 22 offices of honour).[22] By February 1714 the total number had risen to 69,[23] but though the number had only increased by six, the composition of the queen's servants had undergone significant changes. In February 1714 the number of holders of profitable office had increased to 50. More marked, however, was the shift in political balance in this group: in 1710, 18 of the 41 offices of profit had been held by Whigs, while in 1714 they held only eight out of 50.[24] With the honorific offices, the change had been from 15 Whigs out of 22 in 1710 to five out of 19 in 1714. Thus there had been a dramatic shift towards the Tories. This had taken place in stages, sometimes resisted by Oxford who wished to retain some of the more moderate Whigs in office.[25] September 1711 had seen the appointment of Bishop Robinson as lord privy seal in place of the late Duke of Newcastle, who had been the last genuine Whig to remain in the Cabinet. December 1711 and January 1712 saw the dismissal of the Dukes of Marlborough and Somerset as captain general and master of the horse respectively. And during 1712 and 1713 Tories were brought into minor offices so that by 1714 they predominated in the ranks of the queen's servants in the House of Lords.

Within this broad definition there is to be found a smaller group who were the important controlling element in the ministry, and who can be considered to form the core of the scheme lords. These were the members of Oxford's Cabinet. In 1710 eight members of the Cabinet sat in the Lords and by 1714 the number had risen to 12. This increase had largely been the result of the removal of important politicians such as Harley himself and Henry St John to the Lords, rather than a deliberate policy of increasing the strength of government supporters in the House. None the less, the large number of Cabinet members in the Lords ought, in theory, to have formed the nucleus of the party of the Crown, giving management and direction to the Court party in the upper House.[26] By 1714, however, the Cabinet had been riven into factions by the rivalry between Oxford and Bolingbroke.

The lord treasurer was placed in a position of not being able to trust certain members of his Cabinet, most notably Harcourt, Buckingham and later Shrewsbury, whom he suspected of conspiring with Bolingbroke.[27] These factors, based on personal rivalry, were compounded by the issues of the peace with France and the Protestant Succession. The latter became so crucial that on at least one vote on 13 April 1714 Bishop Robinson of London, Cabinet member, ex-lord privy seal and Oxford supporter, voted

against the ministry.[28] Thus towards the end of his ministry Oxford found
he could not always rely on Cabinet members, who ought to have formed
the nucleus of the Court party in the House of Lords.

Two further groups can be considered as part of Oxford's scheme lords.
The most important were those Court Whigs whom Oxford persuaded to
support his ministerial revolution of 1710, but who were mostly not
appointed to the Cabinet. These were in all likelihood the lords whom
Cowper regarded in the worst light: men of supposed right principle whose
better judgment had been suborned by the treasurer. They included
important political figures such as Somerset and Argyll (and, of course,
Newcastle, who had been retained in the Cabinet), and lesser men like
Peterborough, Rivers, Kent and Cholmondeley who retained or acquired
offices of profit under the Crown.[29] These men, of whom there were
perhaps more than a dozen in the Lords in 1710, were central, as we shall
see, to Oxford's scheme of management in the upper House. It was unfor-
tunate that over the four years of his ministry Oxford was to lose the
support of all of them.[30] Death claimed some: Newcastle in July 1711 and
Rivers in August 1712. Some proud and independent magnates eventually
found Oxford's ministry uncongenial and returned to the Whigs. Somerset,
always an unreliable ally (as the Whigs had found) parted company with
Oxford shortly after the formation of the ministry, though he was not to
lose his post of master of the Horse until January 1712.[31] Argyll remained
within the scheme until the early summer of 1712 (his first recorded vote
against the ministry being on 19 May 1712),[32] though he had been assailed
by doubts earlier.[33] There is some evidence to suggest that the final break
in the summer of 1713 was partly caused by a disagreement with the lord
treasurer over money due to a member of his family.[34]

Even the normally reliable Court Whigs, Cholmondeley and Kent, broke
with the ministry over the 'No Peace without Spain' motion debated on
7 and 8 December 1711, though they returned to the fold once the crisis
was over, supporting Oxford on the Hamilton peerage case on 20 December.[35] On the crucial vote of 2 January 1712 which tested Oxford's
strength in the Lords after the introduction of the 12 new peers, Cholmondeley along with many of the Court Whigs supported the ministry. His
stated reason was 'that he was let into noe secret of either, noding his
head to this side and that side, saying neither of this side nor that side,
so he was an impartial man, and in pure respect to her majesty shou'd be
for complying with her majesties' desire'.[36] Oxford, however, must have
retained suspicions of the loyalty of the Court Whigs in a crisis, suspicions
no doubt confirmed by a meeting in late February 1712 at Lord Halifax's
where the Whigs Portland and Somerset, along with the Tory Nottingham
(who had deserted the ministry over Spain in December 1711), met Kent,
Cholmondeley and Longueville.[37] Cholmondeley's support wavered during
the debates over the Grants Bill in May 1712,[38] but he finally went too
far when he condemned the peace negotiations at a Privy Council meeting

in April 1713, and he was sacked from his post of treasurer of the Household. The peace and particularly the Protestant Succession were by 1714
to drive all the Court Whigs, even the pliant Duke of Kent, out of the
ministry.[39]

The last group in the scheme lords were the newly created peers raised
to the House of Lords during the life of the ministry. Besides the famous
dozen created to ensure the passing of the peace negotiations,[40] there were
only six other peerages created during Oxford's ministry:[41] Oxford himself, Harcourt and Boyle of Marston (the Irish Earl of Orrery) in 1711,
Bolingbroke in 1712, and Lords Osborne and Bingley in 1713. All, with
the exception of Boyle (a Court Whig who supported Oxford from 1711
to 1713),[42] were Tories. The support of Bolingbroke and Harcourt was in
doubt in 1714, Cabinet in-fighting spilling over into the Lords, but even
some of Oxford's dozen voted against the ministry (or were forecast as
opponents) over the French Commercial Treaty in 1713, and over the
Protestant Succession and the Schism Bill in 1714.[43] This was despite
many of the twelve being closely related politically to Oxford, some since
his early days in the Commons.

At the same time as the composition of the 'scheme lords' became
increasingly Tory, as Court Whigs were weeded out over their opposition
to the peace and to the ministry's ambivalent stand on the Protestant
Succession, these very same issues were driving the ministry apart. The
developing Cabinet factions in 1714 called into question Oxford's paper
majority in the Lords, for doubts over the ministry's commitment to the
Protestant Succession led to the formation of a new group, the Hanoverian
Tories — former ministerial supporters, who harboured the gravest suspicion of Bolingbroke and did not trust Oxford.[44] But the lord treasurer,
with consummate parliamentary skill, as we shall see, contrived to hold
together sufficient of his battered groupings in the Lords, despite the
many defections, until almost the end of his ministry in July 1714.

By 'the neccessitous lords' Cowper did not necessarily mean those in
receipt of financial benefit from Oxford, who numbered over 50 between
1710 and 1714.[45] Many among them were not in serious financial need
and often they received pensions and bounties in addition to holding office.
The necessitous lords — or as they were more commonly termed the 'poor
lords' — are rather to be defined as those whose needs were so great that
they required financial assistance in order to perform their political
functions. Some, however, were poorer than others. They ranged from the
Duke of St Albans, bastard son of Charles II, with a pension (fitfully paid)
of £1000 a year and three offices (one of which he lost in 1712), to the
Lords Willoughby of Parham with meagre estates in Lancashire worth about
£150 a year.[46] St Albans' income was not enough to maintain his status
as a duke and a member of the royal family.[47] He was considered doubtful
by Oxford in 1710 but consistently opposed the ministry. Consequently

he lost his place as captain of the Band of Gentlemen Pensioners in January 1712, and his pension fell into arrears until its settlement in 1713. His parlous financial position was the reason for his inclusion (along with the truly poor lords) in a list of poor lords sent to the Elector of Hanover in late 1713, with the object of identifying those who through financial need had voted against the ministry, as well as those poor lords who supported Oxford but who might be tempted away.

This extremely useful contemporary list (along with one sent to Hanover in January 1712), together with other sources, enables a total of 28 peers to be classified as necessitous.[48] Of these 19 received pensions or office from the ministry,[49] while nine did not.[50] It is not surprising that of the 19 helped by Oxford we should find that 11 were Tories of various hues, while of the remaining eight, six were Court Whigs whom Oxford may have hoped to win over to the ministry.[51] As things turned out, all six seem usually to have opposed the ministry despite any aid they received, though there is evidence to show that on occasions some of the six voted with Oxford: Grantham over the Hamilton peerage case on 20 December 1711, and Howard of Effingham and Radnor on the peace address on 7 June 1712.[52] Oxford had more success with the two remaining Junto Whigs, both of whom supported the Court for the best part of one or more sessions: Cornwallis in 1712 and Herbert in 1713 to 1714.[53]

There is some evidence to show that, while generally supporting the ministry, at least two of the 11 Tory poor lords who received aid from Oxford were not above voting against the ministry: Sussex over the questionable constitutional point of trying to reverse the previous day's vote on 8 December 1711, and Stawell over the Hamilton peerage case on 20 December 1711.[54] Both these divisions were, however, occasions which saw many Tory defections.[55] On the whole the Tory poor lords in receipt of pensions supported the ministry, while the Whigs did not. There were exceptions on both sides, but generally pensions did not alter the voting pattern of any poor lord.

When we look at those necessitous peers who did not receive money from the ministry, we see a similar voting pattern. Only three of the nine (Chandos, Howard of Escrick and Plymouth) generally supported Oxford, and not surprisingly they were Tories. But Howard of Escrick and Plymouth did vote against the ministry on at least one occasion, 8 and 20 December 1711 respectively. Of the remaining six Whigs, four (Colepeper, Fitzwalter, Mohun and Stamford) were regarded by Oxford in October 1710 as possibly open to pressure.[56] In the event all, except Fitzwalter, seem to have consistently opposed the ministry. He was listed by Oxford as a supporter in December 1711 over the Hamilton case, but abstained in the vote. He did, though, support the government on the adjournment motion on 2 January 1712, despite strenuous efforts by the Whigs to defeat the ministry.[57] His performance failed to gain him assistance from

Oxford. Fitzwalter was, however, the only peer between 1710 and 1714 to receive money from Hanover.[58]

There was one occasion during the Oxford ministry when the bribery of a peer in need of money did secure a crucial division. The incident was probably the most audacious piece of brinkmanship practised by Oxford in his management of the Lords. On the morning of 5 June 1713, calculating that his majority was in question, Oxford offered Lord Warrington the full arrears outstanding on his father's pension (amounting to £6500) if he would vote for the ministry. Warrington, despite his independent Whig background, agreed and his one vote saved the day. Characteristically Oxford was slow in paying the arrears and eventually only £1000 was paid in December 1713.[59] This seems to indicate that though Oxford was prepared to bribe in emergencies it was a method that he was not willing to employ widely. There were many complaints from pensioners that payments were in arrears. Oxford often used the prospect of payments as a means to cajole a peer, but this sometimes did not work. Though Warrington offered his support upon completion of the payments of his father's arrears, he never voted for the ministry again.

Money distributed to poor lords may well have tipped the balance in favour of the Court on issues that were not contentious. More importantly it probably ensured a more regular attendance at Parliament of those poorer peers who would have supported the ministry in any case. Warrington reckoned that attending the Lords cost him about £200 a session, but this was more than many poor lords could afford.[60] Financial incentives in such cases were essential. The case of the 13th Lord Willoughby of Parham well illustrates the point. With only a small estate he none the less attended in the winter of 1713 and was rewarded with a pension of £400.[61] His younger brother, who succeeded him in April, was a confirmed Whig and had to rely on the generosity of the Junto to pay his expenses. In the game of pensions, however, Oxford, as lord treasurer, with access to government patronage, always held the trump card over the Junto with their dwindling resources. Even Hanover's bounty, had it become available to the Whigs, would have been no match for Oxford.

The necessitous lords did form a part of Oxford's party of the Crown, but their numbers were small and consisted mainly of natural supporters of the ministry who were enabled by their pensions to attend and, when necessary, vote for the government. Cowper's remark implied that those of 'independent judgement' could be bought if their financial circumstances were pressing enough. The case of the Earl of Lincoln disproves this. Perhaps the most consistently wooed of the poor lords — and in receipt of around £1500 between 1711 and 1713 — he steadfastly supported the Whigs.[62]

> From a Tr[easure]r that will drink lye swear and pray
> And bribe Scottish Lords with Civil List pay . . .
> Lebera nos[63]

The idea that the 16 Scottish representative peers were in the pay of
Oxford and therefore at his command was widespread. Their venality was
the popular explanation for their apparent political subservience. Typical
stories which had wide currency at the time were that the Duke of Beaufort (who ironically did receive a £1000 bounty in 1711)[64] sent £1000
back to Oxford, indignantly claiming he was not a Scottish lord to be
bought, while a Scottish peer had a paper pinned to his back proclaiming
that his carriage had been paid.[65]

We shall see that, while it was true that the Scottish peers on average
were more penurious than their English counterparts[66] and were thus more
vulnerable to pressure from the government, the idea that the Scots were
a tightly knit homogeneous pro-ministerial bloc of votes who meekly
followed Oxford's call was a myth. It is true that the 16 peers elected in
November 1710 had all been on the ministry's list and that all Oxford's
nominees were elected in 1713. The government's position was so strong
at the 1713 election that the opposition peers, though in Edinburgh, did
not bother to vote despite vigorous activity by Lord Ilay.[67] These two elections were in contrast to the first peerage election in 1708, when only ten
of the government's list had been elected, with the result that the six
opposition Squadrone/Hamilton peers sided with the Junto when it was in
their interest.[68] The 16 elected in 1710, however, were all nominal Tories
but by no means a homogeneous group. A list of November 1710 classifies
them into either Court or Episcopal Tory, with Loudoun described as a Presbyterian Court Tory.[69] Loudoun, significantly, was the first Scot to break
with the ministry in 1714 over the Protestant Successsion, and the only
Scot to become a Hanoverian Tory.[70] Even among the eight so-called
Court Tories, who could have been expected to be the closest to the
ministry, there were some fairly independent figures who were eventually
to leave the lord treasurer. The most important was Ilay, who was to
follow his brother Argyll into opposition in 1712,[71] losing his seat in 1713
for his pains. The Campbells' crony, Lord Blantyre, was probably saved
from a similar fate by his timely death in the summer of 1713.[72] By the
end of the 1713 session an observer believed that Argyll 'and 3 more of his
Party will oppose the Court', while the rest of the Scots had returned to
the ministry.[73]

Annandale and Balmerino, Episcopal Tories, were also of an independent mind, and during the crisis early in 1712 following the Hamilton
peerage case they were in the van of organizing a boycott of the House
by the Scots.[74] Annandale was dropped in 1713 by the ministry, but
Balmerino survived despite his prominent role in the Malt Tax crisis of
May–June 1713 when, though of high Tory principles, he was not above

working closely on certain occasions with the Whigs.[75] Perhaps the most uncooperative was the wayward and imperious Duke of Hamilton. His chagrin
in December 1711, when the Lords refused him a seat by right of his
British dukedom of Brandon, led to a personal boycott of the Lords which
lasted until he had made his peace with the ministry in the summer of 1712.[76]

Despite being government nominees, the 16 Scots elected in November
1710 were more liable to rebel than those elected in 1713. The 1713
election had been more tightly handled by the government, although
three strong Jacobite peers had been returned and even Oxford and Mar
could not prevent Breadalbane forcing his way on to the ministry's list
against their better judgment.[77] The presence of these Jacobites no doubt
confirmed Argyll's opposition to the ministry, which he had accused as
early as March 1713 of being pro-Jacobite.[78]

Could the Scottish representative peers, therefore, be regarded as a pro-
ministerial bloc whose vote Oxford could rely upon? Clearly at certain
times some peers were unreliable, and moreover there were two notable
crises in Oxford's ministry which were largely due to the defection of the
Scots: the Hamilton peerage case in 1711/12 and the Malt Tax crisis of
1713. These showed that only a great and widespread sense of national
grievance could completely unite the Scots, and the attempt to repeal the
union in June 1713 was the most dangerous moment for the ministry as
far as the representative peers were concerned. But even at this time the
unity was more apparent than actual: Balmerino, though strongly opposed
to the Union, thought that there was no chance of success over its repeal
and hoped to use the crisis to strengthen the Scots in the forthcoming
election; the Court Tory Mar, close to Oxford, would not oppose the
ministry over the French Commercial Treaty during the negotiations with
the Whigs over the repeal of the Union; while Findlater, unhappy at the possible outcome for Scotland, was pressurized against his wishes to introduce
the repeal. The defeat of the Junto's attack on the ministry over the Union
and the Malt Tax was also partly effected by the vote of the Scot, Lord
Dupplin, who supported the ministry, and by the absence of Lord Home.[79]

The boycott campaign instigated by the Scots in January and February
1712 has been shown to have been a failure which had little effect upon
the ministry's position in the Lords.[80] Again, innate differences within
the ranks of the Scots – what the Duke of Montrose described as their
lack of 'resolution'[81] – ensured that a united front could not be kept up
for long.[82] Furthermore, the bargaining position of the Scots in 1712 had
been weakened by the mass creation of 12 peers over the Christmas recess,
and more importantly by the return into the ministry's fold of the
majority of Court Whigs who had deserted over 'No Peace without Spain'
in December 1711. Numerically the Scots were now less important in the
ministry's calculations. This was demonstrated by the walkout of the Scots
on 31 January 1712 over the repeal of the 1709 Naturalization Act when
the government's majority without them was still 18.[83]

So long as the ministry held on to the Court peers, the position of the Scots as lobby-fodder was less important. This, of course, is not to say that the 16 Scottish votes were unimportant to the ministry. In a thin House they could be useful. When Oxford suffered his first major defeat in the Lords on 7 December 1711 over his peace policy, it was largely because 19 Court peers and office-holders had deserted the government, while at the same time there were only five Scots present and voting for the ministry.[84] Consequently Oxford worked hard to keep the Scots sweet. His attempt in the aftermath of the Hamilton case to devise a new system of representation which would do away with the despised elections showed how far he was prepared to go.[85] A more piecemeal but effective method was the bestowal of offices and pensions on the Scots. The extent of such largess was not as great as one would be led to believe by contemporary comment. Of the 23 different Scots elected between 1710 and 1714, ten held pensions at one time or another,[86] some of them holding office at the same time. In November 1710 six Scots held offices of profit under the Crown (two of whom held pensions), while in February 1714 that number had risen to only nine (of whom five had pensions). Thus at any one time about half of the Scots were tied financially to the ministry, and this goes some way to explaining the eventual failure of any Scottish revolt against the government.[87]

The ultimate weapon for bringing the Scots to heel, however, was the possibility of an intransigent peer being dropped from the government list at elections. After 1710 no peer not on such a list was elected to the Lords, and both Ilay and Annandale were discarded in 1713 for their opposition or non-cooperation.[88] Despite the strenuous efforts of Argyll and the Campbell clan, Ilay could not prevail against Oxford's revamped Scottish machine headed by Mar.[89] The ultimate threat of expulsion from the House at a general election was a clumsy weapon to wield for the daily management of the Scots. They had to be handled carefully, and Oxford had several Scottish 'lieutenants' in the House. The two Scottish secretaries of state — Queensberry until his death in July 1711 and Mar from September 1713 — were an obvious channel of management. Is it more than coincidence that the two great Scottish crises in Oxford's ministry occurred at a time of interregnum in the office of Scottish secretary? More informal channels were also used effectively and extensively. Mar himself, before his role was formalized in 1713, was an important link-man. His position became dominant after he became Scottish secretary.[90] At a more personal level Oxford used members of his 'family', particularly Lord Kinnoull and his heir the Viscount of Dupplin, Oxford's son-in-law.[91] There is also evidence of Oxford's son, Lord Harley, playing a part by entertaining Scottish peers at his country seat at Wimpole in Cambridgeshire.[92]

Oxford may at times have despaired of the wayward men from North Britain, who had had to adapt themselves since 1707 to a new parliamentary milieu in which they were, or often felt themselves to be, a despised minority. They brought south with them clan allegiances, religious divisions, different economic backgrounds, personal ambitions and competing dynastic loyalties which often separated them from their English counter-parts but which inevitably made concerted action against the ministry a short-lived affair. Oxford recognized that this important element of potential government supporters could be controlled (with the noticeable exception of Argyll, who sat in the Lords by virtue of his English peerage as Earl of Greenwich) by judicious use of the carrot (pensions and offices)[93] and the stick (deprivation of both their seats and their financial benefits). The Scots in the long run were important for the ministry's survival, and in the traumatic session of 1714 few of them broke with Oxford.[94]

The first session of the Lords that Oxford faced in person (December 1711 to July 1712) saw the first great crisis of the ministry.[95] For the four months beginning in October 1711 British politics was dominated by the making of the peace, and for virtually the only time in this Parliament (November 1710–August 1713) the Whigs united in their opposition were offered a real chance to recover power. For the three weeks of December the ministry's life hung in the balance. The cry of 'No Peace without Spain' was used to rally the Whigs, and they skilfully organized their attack for the opening day of the session. The House of Lords was chosen as the battleground, for only here could the Whigs hope for a majority. Their meticulous organization, their careful wooing of a dozen or so Court Whigs — who on the day were brought over by a ruse perpetrated by the Duke of Somerset, who misled them into believing that the queen sup-ported the Whig position — and the unexpected bonus of the apostasy of Lord Nottingham (whose personal rancour and jealousy of the lord treasurer left him open to Junto pressure),[96] enabled them to carry by one the vital vote on 7 December. Oxford had not been negligent in his pre-parations, but several factors — disaffection among the Scottish peers, less than half of whom responded to his appeal to hurry south; his own reluc-tance to use to the full the influence of the Crown, partly because of his personal objections to bribery and radical changes in the public service; commitment to an ideal of non-party government with the concomitant reluctance to lose any future manoeuvrability between the parties; and strained relations within the ministry over the peace proposals — all con-spired to defeat him. In the debate itself the ministry was on the defensive from the start, showing a reluctance to stand by its own case. Oxford, possibly through ignorance of procedure, tried to avoid the debate, which led to humiliation at the hands of Wharton, apparently aided by the Duke of Buckingham. The decisive reasons for the ministry's defeat were the success of the Junto in winning over 19 Court peers and office-holders, the firmness of the Whig bishops in the face of royal and ministerial pressure, and crucial absenteeism on the Tory side — particularly on the part of the Scots who were piqued over the ministry's sluggishness concerning the Duke of Hamilton's British title.[97] Significantly the five Scots present did vote with the government, and Nottingham singularly failed to carry any other Tories with him. These two elements — the ultimate reliance of the Scots on the ministerial patronage and the loyalty of the Tory rank and file — were to be the basis for Oxford's recovery.

Meanwhile, through a crass miscalculation on the part of the ministry (and Oxford must take the blame, though in the House on 8 December the lead was taken by the Tory hotheads, Abingdon and Anglesey), with some of Oxford's supporters dubious about the move, there was an attempt to reverse the vote of the previous day. This unparliamentary conduct so outraged the House that near-chaos broke out when a division was attempted and the ministry, finally realizing its error, tried to stave off a humiliating defeat: the vote was abandoned and the ministry declared to have lost the motion. There is strong evidence to show that, apart from the ministerial desertions of the previous day, several Tories were siding with the Whigs (even possibly Secretary of State Dartmouth).[98] This fiasco, no doubt partly due to Oxford's inexperience, must have been a cold douche for the lord treasurer, but worse was yet to come. Nottingham's price for supporting the Whigs — the Occasional Conformity Bill — passed the House within seven days. Though personally distasteful to Oxford, with his Puritan background — and he did indeed attempt discreetly to sabotage it — the bill, with massive Tory support, could receive nothing less than the ministry's public sanction.

The second disaster for the Court came on 20 December 1711, two days before the final passing of the Occasional Bill. On this occasion the issue was whether a Scottish peer given one of the new post-Union British titles could sit in the Lords by right of that peerage. The Junto, with visions of an influx of new peers firmly under the Court's influence, were determined to prevent Hamilton (already sitting as a representative peer) from sitting in the Lords as Duke of Brandon. The Whigs were taking a narrow party view of the issue, and were undoubtedly breaching the spirit of the Union. Unfortunately for Oxford, though he was naturally supported by the few Scottish peers present and by some of the more independent Whigs who backed Hamilton's undoubtedly strong legal position, many Tories shared the Whig prejudice against the possibility of being swamped by new Scottish peers. The Whigs won the vote by a majority of five. The result was acute dissatisfaction on the part of the Scots (which a month later led to a decision by them to boycott the House), a lowering of Tory morale, and a temporary seizure of the initiative by the Whigs, who were able to pass three surprise motions: leave was given to introduce a Hanover precedence bill, designed to underline Whig zeal for the Protestant Succession; an address was proposed requesting that the British negotiators at Utrecht should embark on no further negotiations without the allies; and a motion to adjourn the Lords only until 2 January 1712, two weeks before the Commons were to return after their Christmas recess, was an attempt by the Whigs to maintain the momentum of their recent victories.

Despite these severe setbacks, Oxford remained calm. He knew he had the full support of both the queen and the Commons, against which the Lords could not prevail. His three-pronged attack succeeded in regaining the initiative: the queen dismissed the Duke of Marlborough from his offices on 31 December 1711; an example was made of the most prominent Whig office-holders, particularly Somerset, who was dismissed in January 1712; and the boldest stroke of all — the creation by 2 January of 12 new Tory peers, many of whom were related or had strong personal connections with the lord treasurer. Distrusting the Scots, Oxford also attempted to solicit the errant Court Whigs back to the fold. His campaign was vindicated on 2 January, when in order to test and advertise his strength in the Lords, he manoeuvred the House into an uncontroversial adjournment debate. Oxford won by 13, but not solely by the votes of the newly created peers;[99] some Tories were absent, and many Whig placemen had succumbed to the blandishments of the ministry.[100]

The crisis was not over until the end of February 1712. The Whigs, resilient as ever, soon shook off their demoralization after the defeat of 2 January and put up a fight over the repeal of the Naturalization Act of 1709, but they lost by 18 votes, despite a walk-out by the Scots. The boycott by the Scottish peers, from 7 to 27 February,[101] over their disgust at the ministry's failure to come up with anything to sweeten the bitter pill of Hamilton's defeat, placed the Court in difficulties. These were compounded in early February when news of the French peace offer reached London. Made by a French government which had received an injection of confidence from the dissensions amongst the allies, the offer spelt the end to Tory hopes of a quick settlement. On 15 February Halifax's motion for an address against the French offer caught the ministry off balance. It attracted support from both parties, and the Court's efforts to get a postponement failed after Lord Guernsey, who till then had supported the peace negotiations, intervened on behalf of the Whigs. Pacification of the Scots became essential to the ministry's survival. Oxford believed, however, that when the representative peers realized that the Court would not redress their demands until the peace had been secured their resistance would crumble. Oxford underlined future promises with present *douceurs* to the neediest peers. In the final analysis, the Scots realized that the Court could outbid the Whigs in cash and promises. On 27 February all the Scots (except Hamilton and Annandale) returned to the Court. Two days later a place bill was decisively defeated by a combination of Scots, ministerial peers, the bulk of the independent Tories and a handful of Court Whigs. The 29th February saw the end of the crisis begun on 7 December, and the political pattern in the Lords stabilized for the rest of the session, which lasted until July 1712.

All was not plain sailing, however. The Grants Bill, which the ministry only lukewarmly supported, was defeated on 20 May by the narrowest of margins,[102] by a combination of Whigs and many Tories. The bill's defeat indicated no real shift in the balance of power in the House,[103] since the latter were largely voting out of self-interest.[104] A truer reflection of the ministry's position was given on 28 May when the Whigs launched an attack on the 'restraining orders' given to the Duke of Ormond, captain general of the land forces in Flanders. They failed to gain any Tory support, and even Argyll stood with the Court. By the time the official peace terms were announced in a speech from the throne on 6 June, the Tories were united and the Court Whigs who had deserted Oxford on 7 December were firmly back in the fold. Much of the Whig fervour over the restraining orders had cooled, and the ministry won the debate on the address of thanks on 7 June by a staggering 45 votes. It was a severe blow for Whig prestige, and Oxford ended the session at the high-water mark of his fortunes.

The summer and autumn of 1712 were spent by the ministry in frustrating bargaining at Utrecht. Eleven prorogations of Parliament resulted and the two Houses did not meet again until April 1713. In this long delay the ministry's supporters in the Lords grew fractious, while Whig spirits revived. In the New Year the Whigs mounted a strong anti-ministry campaign. Aimed at establishing in the public mind the association of the Court with the Pretender and the Whigs with Hanover, it was not completely successful as the Elector himself proved uncooperative. By the end of February, however, the campaign had produced some signs of wavering among the crucial 'centre' peers.

The Utrecht peace terms were ratified by the queen in Council on 7 April, and two days later Parliament met. Though the peace did not require parliamentary approval, the Commercial Treaty with France needed legislation to give it effect, for the crucial 8th and 9th articles could not come into force until the existing protectionist laws directed at France were repealed. These contentious clauses and the disaffection stirred up in Scotland over the Malt Tax enabled the Whigs to wrench back the initiative they had so spectacularly lost in February 1712.

The early days of the 1713 session saw the peace debated. The Whigs vigorously attacked on a request to have the treaties laid before the House, but they were routed on 9 April by 32 votes after some decisive debating from Oxford himself. The Junto, however, had managed to pick up the votes of a few Court Whigs, and the two Tory votes of Guernsey and Bishop Dawes of Chester.[105] These last two, the germ of the future Hanoverian Tory group in the Lords, were of considerable significance. The Commercial Treaty Bill, the government's keystone of the peace, aroused high feelings in the Commons in late May, and at the report

stage on 18 June it was rejected by 194 to 185. This was Oxford's first
major defeat in the Commons since November 1710.

It was in the Commons too that the seed of the Malt Tax crisis was
sown.[106] On 22 April the Committee of Ways and Means reduced the Land
Tax to 2s. in the pound (the government had wanted 3s.). This loss placed
a premium on the other sources of revenue. On 22 May the Commons
passed a Malt Tax bill which imposed 6d. per bushel on English and
Scottish malt alike — a technical breach of the Union, in which article
14 had granted the Scots exemption from a tax on malt for the duration
of the war. Ironically the controversial clause was not the work of the
ministry, but forced on the Court by the country back-bench elements in
the Commons.

The incensed Scottish M.P.s met on 23 May and decided to move for
a bill to dissolve the Union. Three days later a joint meeting of M.P.s and
representative peers agreed to proceed. Oxford was again faced with a
parliamentary revolt of the Members from North Britain, a revolt this time
which could have serious consequences for the security of the nation.
All his efforts to placate the Scots failed, and they chose the Lords as their
battleground. There Whig support, could the Scots secure it, would prove
more effective. The Whigs were placed in something of a dilemma: they
needed the Scots to defeat the ministry, but had themselves been the chief
architects of — and had claimed much of the credit for — the Union.
Under the leadership of Lord Somers, they decided to walk the tightrope
of securing the support of the Scots without doing any permanent damage
to the Union and without endangering the Hanoverian Succession. Their
basic tactic was to keep the question of the Union open for as long as
possible.

On 1 June the Earl of Findlater introduced the Scots' motion to repeal
the Union. Oxford, aware of the lack of close co-ordination between the
Whigs and the Scots, outmanoeuvred the opposition. They pressed for a
vote on the adjournment, while Oxford insisted on the motion on the
Union immediately to remove all uncertainties. The Court carried the
previous question by 71 to 67, the majority consisting of four proxy
votes. As the Scots perceived that the Whigs would not join them in a
vote on Findlater's motion, it was rejected without a division. Oxford
had weathered the first major crisis of 1713. The Malt Tax, however, faced
the combined opposition of the Scots and the Whigs. Oxford needed this
tax to make up the loss on the Land Tax, so he pressed hard for it, then
hoping to pressurize the amenable Scots by refraining from further anta-
gonizing them. Eventually, the Malt Tax was carried on 8 June by 64 to
56. It had, however, been a close-run thing. On 5 June at the second
reading, Oxford's calculations must have told him that he might well
lose the vote. His solution was daring in that it involved pressurizing one
of the amenable peers — the independent Whig Earl of Warrington. On the
morning of the 5th, as we have seen, Oxford visited Warrington and

offered to pay off the pension due to his father in 1694. Warrington accepted and the bill passed its second reading by 76 to 74. Oxford needed this victory to clear the decks for the French Commercial Treaty. He could now pacify the Scots and wean them away from the Whigs. He had to do this if the treaty was to be saved, for he saw that 13 or 14 Tories were likely to side with the opposition.[107] As we have seen, the Commons scuttled the treaty, but at least Oxford had removed the Scottish menace from the Lords. The Scots were growing in importance for Oxford, as the Court Whigs and the Hanoverian Tories moved away from the ministry.

The closing months of the Parliament were an anti-climax for the Whigs after their triumph in the Commons on 18 June when the Commercial Treaty was defeated. Apart from a private legal case, there were no more divisions in the House before the prorogation on 16 July. Oxford's prognostication over the behaviour of the Scots proved accurate: once the Malt Tax crisis was over, they were singularly unwilling to extend their temporary alliance with the Whigs. Yet Oxford was to suffer one more embarrassing display of Whig organization which would catch the ministry napping. On 29 June a motion for a full attendance on the following day was agreed to by the Court. This was a blind, which enabled the Whigs to lay the 'Lorraine motion' before the largest possible House. This proposal, calling upon the queen to press for the removal of the Pretender from Lorraine, not only put on the spot many a Tory with Jacobite sympathies, but brought into play the question of the Succession, the only card the Whigs could produce at this time which gave them hope of success. The tactic proved devastating, though even here Oxford's skills managed to stave off a vote on the motion, the Whigs accepting a Court amendment. But on 3 July, when the queen's answer to the motion was reported, Buckingham made a particularly wayward speech which rebounded upon the ministry. Both Oxford and Bolingbroke were absent, and thus unable to prevent the Whigs carrying a further address to the queen.[108] The dissolution shortly after, however, deprived the Whigs of any follow-up to their tactical victory.

During the 1713 session the conflict between Oxford and Bolingbroke, which had its origins several years previously when both men had served in the Marlborough/Godolphin ministry,[109] sharpened over Bolingbroke's criticism of Oxford's parliamentary tactics. By the end of the session there had been formed, under Bolingbroke's leadership, a definite 'confederation' against Oxford. This consisted of the Lord Chancellor Harcourt and the Duke of Shrewsbury (who was abroad at the time). Bolingbroke began to draw Atterbury, recently given the see of Rochester, and Lord Trevor (one of Oxford's 'dozen') into his designs. Oxford's answer was a Cabinet reshuffle in August, which made few concessions to his rivals: Sir William Wyndham was made chancellor of the Exchequer and the Duke of Shrewsbury lord lieutenant of Ireland. The government of Scotland was reorganized, Mar and Findlater, two Court placemen dependent upon

Oxford, being made third secretary of state and Scottish lord chancellor respectively. Oxford's supporters Dartmouth and Bishop Robinson were retained in the Cabinet, while Bromley, Hanmer, Lansdowne and Denbigh were brought into the government.[110]

Oxford had been ill during the last few weeks of the 1713 session. His recurrent bouts of illness and melancholia, brought on by the death of his favourite daughter in November, had serious effects on his relations with the queen for the rest of the reign. In Oxford's prolonged absence from Court in the summer of 1713 for his son's wedding to the daughter of the late Duke of Newcastle, Bolingbroke won over the queen's favourite Mrs Masham, who had been the instrument which kept Oxford in close contact with the queen. Oxford further alienated the queen by asking for the title of Duke of Newcastle for his son.

The general election in 1713 was a confirmation of the predominance of the Tory party in the country, except in Scotland where the Whigs triumphed due to Oxford's mishandling of the various Scottish problems culminating in the Malt Tax. None the less the Court list of 16 representative peers was carried.[111]

On Christmas Eve 1713 the queen became seriously ill. Bolingbroke took fright and suspended his campaign against Oxford, believing also that he had the treasurer in a corner. The cracks in the administration were papered over to face Parliament in February 1714. Oxford, Bolingbroke and Harcourt worked together over the management of the Lords, Bolingbroke trying to convert the Hanoverian Tories back to the ministry. The Succession was to dominate Oxford's last parliamentary session.

The margin against the Junto in the Lords was between 15 and 20 votes. There were two main sources from which the Whigs tried to obtain votes: the Court Whigs and poor lords, and the 'Whimsical' or Hanoverian Tories.[112] Hanover, however, failed to provide any money for the poor lords. Yet the Whigs had gained Argyll and Lord Cholmondeley, and both sides vied for the support of the Duke of Kent. He finally succumbed to the Whigs over the Succession question. Oxford assiduously courted the Hanoverian Tories, by assuring them of his loyalty. Some like Anglesey blew hot and cold (the question of the government of Ireland was paramount to him),[113] while the queen's illness (with the prospect of her sudden death) made some Court Whigs vulnerable to the Junto.

The opening of Parliament on 2 March 1714 had been delayed by Oxford until the treaty with Spain had been ratified and the negotiations between France and the Empire concluded. Oxford was hoping for a short session, and the queen's speech was confined to the immediate financial needs of the ministry. He felt that with a comfortable majority in the Commons he need not be unduly alarmed at the antics of the Whigs in the Lords. But he had badly miscalculated. The Whigs opened the offensive with a proposal to invite the Duke of Cambridge (son of the Elector) to England to take his seat in the Lords. Oxford had tried to stifle this initiative by making it clear in the queen's speech that she opposed it. It placed him in a cleft stick: he could not support it against the queen's opposition, while opposing it would harm his credit at Hanover, and more immediately with the Hanoverian Tories whose support he needed in the Lords. Fortunately in the early days of the session the Hanoverian Tories were prepared to grant the ministry a probationary period, as they distrusted the Junto's motives. Thus the Whigs toned down their campaign over the Succession, and were compelled to pursue an oblique course which consisted in attacking the government over their shameful neglect of the Catalans in the treaty with Spain, and over the commercial agreement with Spain.

Unfortunately for Oxford, the internecine quarrel within the ministry broke out again. After Easter, widespread rumours of Oxford's fall weakened the links of the Whimsical Tories with the ministry. The prospect of an administration led by Bolingbroke drove the Hanoverian Tories into the Whig camp. Argyll and Nottingham were the go-betweens in these negotiations, in which the Whimsicals undertook to 'live in friendship' with the Whigs to frustrate the Jacobites. Thus for nearly two weeks in early April the Court stood at bay in the Lords. Again, with his back to the wall, Oxford demonstrated his skills of management. On 5 April the Court forced a showdown on their own motion (introduced by Lord Ferrers) that the Protestant Succession in the House of Hanover was not in danger. It caught the Whigs on the hop. Oxford had ensured a full House with a maximum attendance of Court peers. Anglesey led the attack on the ministry and he was supported by other Hanoverian Tories. Yet the government won both votes by a majority of 14, despite the Whigs gaining the votes of three Court Whigs (Ashburnham, Herbert and Orrery), the six newly converted Hanoverian Tories (Abingdon, Anglesey, Archbishop Dawes, Jersey, Carteret and the proxy of Mountjoy), and all the bishops but three.[114] Oxford had the full support of the Scots, but the Whigs managed to carry two addresses unopposed. Thus the honours for the day were about even. It was clear that the ministry still held a majority in the Lords, though by no means a stable one.

Oxford now worked hard to improve this situation. On 8 April, when the Duke of Bolton reported to the House the address concerning the Pretender and the Court put two crucial amendments and carried them by 11 votes, four or five Hanoverian Tories temporarily returned to the ministry. On the following day Oxford scored a personal triumph over accusations of pensions to the Highland clans.

Outside pressure from Hanover (the demand by the Hanoverian envoy Schütz for the writ for the Duke of Cambridge) threw Oxford into a crisis which promised to bring a repetition of the dark days of December 1711. The news of the demand instantaneously galvanized the hitherto irresolute Hanoverian Tories. On 13 April the Whigs attacked the queen's answer to the address (voted on the 8th) on the Pretender remaining in Lorraine.

Wharton, leading the Junto, proposed an address on the Succession, which the ministry narrowly defeated by two proxy votes. At this vote there was the largest number of Tory desertions so far.[115] But this proved the zenith of the Whig attack. They took two months to recover their impetus lost on the 13th. Over the next four days the ministry defeated a place bill by narrow majorities ranging from one to six, but on two votes on an address on the peace on 16 April the ministry had majorities of 20 and 33. The veneer of unity presented by the ministry in Parliament, however, began to disintegrate in May, and the Whigs were given a fresh stimulus.

By May 1714 Oxford had lost his hold over the queen. The attitude of the Whigs to her severe illness in the winter of 1713/14 had completed her alienation from that party. She was now against a reconciliation of the parties, a position Oxford could not share. Oxford moved closer to the Hanoverian Tories, and by the end of April had begun to strike back at Bolingbroke's faction. He used his connections with the Junto, maintained through Halifax, to move towards a bargain with the Whigs. But so long as the intentions of Hanover were unclear, there could be no genuine under-standing between them. Both Oxford and the Whigs faced a new setback with the introduction by Bolingbroke of the Schism Bill into the Lords on 4 June. Having failed to emasculate or defeat the bill in the Commons, the Whigs worked hard to secure its expulsion by the Lords. The bill (and this had been one reason for its introduction) was supported by the Hanoverian Tories, who by no means favoured Oxford's general stance of moderation. Nottingham opposed it, and his forecast for the voting on the bill[116] showed little hope of its defeat. The Whigs, however, with the covert co-operation of Oxford and his friends, who obtained vital Tory votes, were able to secure amendments.[117]

Oxford then moved on to the offensive to maintain his pre-eminent parliamentary position. He had to prolong Parliament's sitting if he was successfully to damage Bolingbroke's position. With the help of his fol-lowers in the Commons, Oxford supported the Whig attack upon the finance bills. These delaying tactics succeeded, and Oxford offered con-crete proposals to the Whigs in the form of a proclamation of £100,000 on the Pretender's head. On 23 June the proclamation was issued, but the figure had been reduced to £5000 due to opposition within the Cabinet. The following day the Commons, carefully stage-managed, moved to in-crease the reward to the original £100,000. Bolingbroke had been out-manoeuvred by Oxford, and was roughly handled in the Lords by Notting-ham and the Junto over the address of thanks for the proclamation.

Bolingbroke now counter-attacked in the only areas left open to him — the assiento, the South Sea Company and Spanish trade. Oxford kept the Junto supplied with inside information through his brother during the examination of Spanish trade from 2 to 9 July. During this last crisis there was some realignment of support: Lord North and Grey abandoned Oxford, Shrewsbury again sided with Bolingbroke, some Hanoverian

Tories began to waver in their support for the Whigs — Anglesey in particular as he was offered high office (probably the Irish viceroyalty) by Bolingbroke upon Oxford's fall.[118] Oxford himself supported the Whigs as strongly as he could, but he could not afford to lose totally the queen's approval. She, however, refused to abandon Bolingbroke. The 8th July proved the decisive day. The Whigs in the Lords were in the middle of an attack upon Bolingbroke's crony, Arthur Moore, and his involvement in the assiento. The Whigs lost two motions by 12 and 18 votes, while a counter motion of Anglesey's was approved. Oxford had been cautious over the attack on Moore, maintaining a much more neutral position than hitherto.[119] Bolingbroke's triumph, however, was short-lived. On the following day the queen's answer to the Lords' address (secured by Anglesey the previous day), which had been drafted by Bolingbroke, was so provocative that uproar ensued in the House. The Whigs were furious, Anglesey offended, and many Tories supported them. Bolingbroke had lost all his recent hard-won ground. But the queen rode to his rescue and prorogued Parliament the same day. Thus ended Oxford's last session of Parliament as a minister, with the government riven asunder and Oxford himself, with the aid of the Whigs, trying to prevent the emergence of a Bolingbroke administration. On 9 July he did not know it, but he had succeeded. Though deprived of the lord treasurership on 27 July by an ailing queen, her death on 1 August 1714, after having given the treasurer's staff to Shrewsbury, denied Bolingbroke the final prize.

In his attempt to create a 'party of the Crown' in 1711 to 1714, Oxford had built upon the methods used by his predecessors: a hard core of personal or moderate party followers, aided by those who received employment or pensions from the ministry, plus the representative Scottish peers. He also extended and refined his techniques of management into what could be called, perhaps for the first time in the history of the Lords, a system of management. This system was later adopted and brought to such a peak of refinement by Robert Walpole, largely with the help of a pliant bench of bishops — an asset which Oxford conspicuously lacked — that the Lords for many of the middle years of the eighteenth century were regarded as the government's rubber stamp. Oxford's system served him well, and though it failed at times, as many prototypes do, it helped him on the whole to control the upper House at a time when it contained (with a few notable exceptions) most major politicians of his day, and when it may be considered as the more important of the two Houses of Parliament. That Oxford's system broke down in 1714 under the pressure of the Peace of Utrecht and the Protestant Succession, says more for the Tory party's inability to come to terms with a Hanoverian future, for the internal Cabinet dissensions which destroyed the ministry and the strength of the party system, than for the weakness of Oxford's management scheme. His ideal of a middle-of-the-road Court-led government could not survive the 'rage of party' generated in the final years of the reign of Queen Anne; 'Whig and Torie,' as Lord Mar put it, 'being alike afraid of the power of the Crown'.[120]

NOTES

1. *The Diary of Sir David Hamilton, 1709-1714*, ed. P. Roberts (1975), 29.
2. He was raised to the peerage as Earl of Oxford on 23 May 1711.
3. See D. Large, 'The decline of "the party of the Crown" and the rise of parties in the House of Lords, 1783-1837', *EHR, lxxviii* (1963), 676. Large's party of the Crown consists of members of the royal household, the bishops, the Scots, together with the new recruits and the newly honoured peers (*ibid.*, 669-73). This definition has been accepted by other historians, e.g. G. M. Ditchfield, 'The House of Lords and parliamentary reform in the seventeen-eighties', *BIHR, liv* (1981), 218.
4. See G. Holmes, *British Politics in the Age of Anne* (1967), 399.
5. HMC, *Bath MSS*, I, 199: 20 Oct. 1710; *The Wentworth Papers, 1705-1739*, ed. J. J. Cartwright (1883), 150: [Wentworth to Raby], 20 Oct. 1710.
6. BL, Loan 29/10/19: list of 3 Oct. 1710 (printed below, Appendix 1, col. 2).
7. An analysis of a complete list of the peers compiled in 1710, which included all the bishops except the four Welsh dioceses (printed in HMC, *Lords MSS*, n.s. IX, 365-7), shows that Harley had excluded 51 other lords from his calculations. In Oct. 1710, 40 of these lords (18 minors, seven Roman Catholics, seven abroad, three nonjurors, two outlawed, two 'elderly' and one who had 'retired at the Revolution') could, in effect, be ignored (though six of the minors and two of those abroad were to appear in Harley's future calculations). There is no obvious reason why the remaining eleven were excluded from Harley's initial calculation: eight (five pro and three con) subsequently appear.
8. See C. Jones, 'Godolphin, the Whig Junto and the Scots: a new Lords' division list from 1709', *Scottish Historical Rev., lviii* (1979), 172-4.
9. By their very nature management and voting lists tend to reflect moments of crisis, therefore the record of the Court Whigs as tabulated below is, for many, not typical of their daily political behaviour. Newcastle is omitted from these calculations as he died in July 1711.
10. If one adds the minors and those abroad in 1710 who subsequently appear in Oxford's calculations, the figures are 69 pro and 70 con.
11. Jonathan Swift, 'An Enquiry into the Behaviour of the Queen's Last Ministry', in *Political Tracts, 1713-19*, ed. H. Davis and I. Ehrenpreis (1973), 149.
12. *Wentworth Papers*, 173.
13. HMC, *Portland MSS*, V, 125.
14. *Letters and Correspondence of . . . Viscount Bolingbroke*, ed. G. Parke (4 vols, 1798), II, 49; BL, Loan 29/10/16 (see below, Appendix 1, col. 5).
15. HMC, *Portland MSS*, V, 127: R[obert] Friend to [Edward] Harley, 9 Dec. [1710], misdated by editor as 1711.
16. The supporters were Brooke (d. 22 Oct. 1710), Craven (9 Oct. 1711), Dover (6 July 1711), Haversham (1 Nov. 1710), Jersey (25 Aug. 1711), Leigh (12 Nov. 1710), Leominster (7 Dec. 1711), Rochester (2 May 1711), Willoughby de Broke (18 July 1711), and Lord Privy Seal Newcastle (15 July 1711). The opponent was Bedford (26 May 1711).
17. Jersey, Leigh, Rochester and Willoughby de Broke. Haversham was succeeded by a Whig son, and Brooke, Craven, Dover (Queensberry) and Leominster by minors. Newcastle had no male heir.
18. Lord Keeper Harcourt and the Irish Earl of Orrery, both given British baronies in Sept. 1711.

19. BL, Loan 29/10/3: undated, but from internal evidence c. mid-July 1713.
20. Some of these 23 peers never sat or sat so infrequently as to make little or no difference to Oxford's majority (e.g. Shaftesbury and Bishop Humphries of Hereford). Most of those who died were succeeded by heirs of similar politics, by minors or by heirs who were inactive, and two titles died out (Bolingbroke and Newcastle).
21. Robinson (Oct. 1710), Bisse (Nov. 1710), Ottley (March 1713), Atterbury (June 1713), Gastrell (March) and Smalridge (April 1714). There were also three promotions within the bench: Robinson from Bristol to London (1713), Bisse from St David's to Hereford (1712) and Dawes from Chester to York (1714). The queen's preferences in the making of bishops were strong and had to be balanced against any political advantages to be gained.
22. See Appendix 2. The three peers who only held pensions (Godolphin, Kinnoull and Leeds) have been excluded from these calculations.
23. See Holmes, *Politics in the Age of Anne*, 401, 436–9.
24. Some of these Whigs (e.g. Halifax, Lindsey and Montagu) held either hereditary offices or offices for life.
25. Only four Court Whigs survived in office by Feb. 1714.
26. Sometimes, however, direction in debate was sadly lacking from members of the Cabinet, and the ministry was caught napping more than once. One sidelight on this is that even as late as 1 June 1713 Bolingbroke, promoted to the peerage over twelve months before, had yet to make his maiden speech in the House: Niedersächsisches Staatsarchiv, Hannover, Cal. Br. 24 England, 113a: Kreienberg despatch, 2 June 1713 (hereafter cited as Kreienberg despatch).
27. The Duke of Buckingham had always been something of a rogue elephant in the Cabinet. For example, he had voted against the ministry early in its life on 24 Jan. 1711 (*Wentworth Papers*, 179), and he had embarrassed Oxford by siding with the Junto leader Lord Wharton over a crucial procedural point in the debate on 'No Peace without Spain' on 7 Dec. 1711. See A. Boyer, *The History of the Reign of Queen Anne Digested into Annals* (11 vols, 1703–13), X, 285.
28. He was followed into opposition on this vote not only by the Hanoverian Tory Archbishop Dawes of York, but by the two other Tory bishops, Hooper of Bath and Wells and Bishop Smalridge of Bristol. Robinson was back in the Court's fold by 16 April (*Wentworth Papers*, 368; Mellerstain Letters (Lord Binning, Mellerstain, Berwickshire), VI: [Baillie to his wife] 13, 15 April 1714).
29. Early in his ministry Oxford had doubts about some of these, e.g. Lord Privy Seal Newcastle was listed as doubtful in October 1710, Kent as an opponent, and Cholmondeley as a queried supporter (see below Appendix 1, col. 2).
30. Even the eccentric Lord Ashburnham, who supported the Court in 1712 to 1714 (Holmes, *Politics in the Age of Anne*, 227, 331–2, 425), voted against the Court on 5 April 1714 over the Protestant Succession (*Wentworth Papers*, 366; Mellerstain Letters, VI: [Baillie to his wife], 6 April 1714).
31. Though one of Harley's 'juntilla' in the summer of 1710 working for the fall of the Godolphin ministry, along with Shrewsbury, Rivers, Peterborough and St John (Holmes, *Politics in the Age of Anne*, 202), by Oct. Oxford regarded him as doubtful (Appendix 1, col. 2).
32. On the second reading of the Grants Bill, after deliberately abstaining on the first reading (Kreienberg despatch, 20 May 1712; Mellerstain Letters, V: [Baillie to Montrose and Roxburghe], 20, 22 May 1712). Argyll did, however, support the ministry on 28 May 1712 over the address on the 'restraining orders' (Mellerstain Letters, V: [Baillie to Roxburghe], dated 24 [? 28] May 1712).
33. Argyll, by abstaining, had helped the Whigs and the Court peers to throw out the Tory Naturalization Bill on 5 Feb. 1711. Shrewsbury and Queensberry were absent, and Ilay (Argyll's brother) and the other Scots, Mar and Loudoun, all voted against it (Kreienberg despatch, 6 Feb. 1711).

34. NLS, MS Acc. 7228/1 (Newhailes Papers), [George Lockhart to ? Sir David Dalrymple], 28 May [1713]; Atholl MSS (Duke of Atholl, Blair Atholl Castle, Perthshire), 45/11/29: John Douglas to Atholl, 13 June 1713. The family member was either Argyll's or Ilay's father-in-law.
35. See Appendix 1, col. 5–8.
36. *Wentworth Papers*, 240–1. The wishes of the queen in a particular case could, and did, have a crucial impact upon how the Court peers voted; see, for example, Somerset's ruse in Dec. 1711 (below, p. 134; Holmes, *Politics in the Age of Anne*, 390).
37. Nottingham's brother, Guernsey, who had remained loyal to Oxford on 7 Dec. 1711 (but voted against the ministry on 8 Dec.) was also present. He did not fully come out against the government until 1713: Staffordshire RO, D(W) 1778/v/151 (Dartmouth MSS): [Oxford to Dartmouth], n.d. [? 29 Feb. 1712]. Longueville's first recorded vote against the ministry was on 11 March 1714 over the 'Public Spirit of the Whigs' (*Wentworth Papers*, 360). Previously he appears to have supported the ministry (see Appendix 1, cols 4, 10 and 12).
38. Kreienberg despatch, 20 May 1712.
39. His first recorded vote against the Court, since December 1711, was on 11 March 1714, though he had been forecast as an opponent over the French Commercial Treaty in June 1713 (*Wentworth Papers*, 360; Appendix 1, col. 12).
40. Bathurst, Bruce, Burton (succeeded 1713 as 8th Lord Paget), Compton, Foley, Hay (Scottish Viscount of Dupplin), Lansdowne, Mansel, Masham, Middleton, Mountjoy (Irish Viscount Windsor) and Trevor. Twenty-one people had been considered for promotion to the Lords (BL, Loan 29/10/16: list dated 'Dec: 27: 1711').
41. Three barons were raised to earldoms in 1711: Dartmouth, Ferrers and Raby (Strafford); and the Scottish Duke of Hamilton was given the British dukedom of Brandon. There were rumours in early 1712 that Oxford intended to have six more peers created to secure his majority (Kreienberg despatch, 8 Jan. 1712).
42. He voted against the ministry on 11 March and 5 April 1714 (*Wentworth Papers*, 364; Kreienberg despatch, 12 March 1714).
43. They were Foley, Middleton, Mountjoy and the 8th Lord Paget. Mountjoy was the only one to vote against the ministry over the Protestant Succession on 5 April 1714, though only by his proxy which he had left with Orrery, by this time no longer a Court supporter. He was a follower of the Hanoverian Tory, Lord Anglesey, and as early as June 1713 it was noted that Mountjoy maintained a 'strict connection' with the Duke of Argyll. See Appendix 1, cols 12–14; *Wentworth Papers*, 364; G. Holmes and C. Jones, 'Trade, the Scots and the parliamentary crisis of 1713', *Parliamentary History, i* (1982), 76, n. 106.
44. They were led by the Earls of Anglesey and Abingdon and the Archbishop of York, Sir William Dawes. Other members were Carteret, Conway, Guernsey, Hatton (the latter two being closely connected to Nottingham), Loudoun, Mountjoy and Pembroke.
45. See Appendix 3.
46. For the lowly social status of the Willoughby family see P. J. W. Higson, 'A Dissenting northern family: the Lancashire branch of the Willoughbys of Parham, 1640–1765', *Northern History, vii* (1972), 31–53. The family had been granted a pension of £200 a year in 1680 to help them maintain the dignity of their peerage.
47. For the complaints of his duchess on this score see BL, Loan 29/307,308. Social status was probably as important a factor in determining the acceptance of financial benefits from the government as political principles. The Earl of Warrington, with an average annual income of around £4500, but encum-

bered with debts, regarded his father's acceptance of the dignity of an earl without a sufficient estate to maintain it as a mistake (J. V. Beckett and C. Jones, 'Financial improvidence and political independence in the early eighteenth century: George Booth, 2nd Earl of Warrington', *Bull. John Rylands University Library*, lxv, no. 1 (1982), 8–35.

48. See E. Gregg and C. Jones, 'Hanover, pensions and the "poor lords", 1712–13', *Parliamentary History*, i (1982), 173–80. For other sources see Holmes, *Politics in the Age of Anne*, under individual peers.

49. Byron (T), Clarendon (T), Cornwallis (W), Delawarr (T), Denbigh (T), Grantham (CW), Herbert (W), Howard of Effingham (CW), Hunsdon (T), Lincoln (CW), Radnor (CW), St Albans (CW), Saye and Sele (T), Stawell (T), Sussex (T), 13th Lord Willoughby of Parham (d. April 1713; T?), Westmorland (CW), Winchilsea (T), Yarmouth (T).

50. Chandos (T), Colepeper (W), Fitzwalter (W), Haversham (W), Howard of Escrick (T), Mohun (W), Plymouth (T), Stamford (W), 14th Lord Willoughby of Parham (W).

51. In Oct. 1710 all the six Court Whigs were considered by Oxford as 'doubtful' rather than as opponents: Grantham, Howard of Effingham, Lincoln, Radnor, St Albans and Westmorland. Four were also on a list of possible supporters in Dec. 1711 (see below Appendix 1, cols 2 and 3).

52. See Appendix 1; and Kreienberg despatch, 10 June 1712.

53. Holmes, *Politics in the Age of Anne*, 393. E.g. both Cornwallis and Herbert supported the ministry over the peace address on 7 June 1712, and Herbert over the Malt Tax on 8 June 1713. Cornwallis, however, opposed the ministry over the Grants Bill on 20 May 1712 (Kreienberg despatch, 20 May, 10 June 1712, 9 June 1713).

54. See Appendix 1, cols 6 and 8.

55. See C. Jones, 'The division that never was: new evidence on the aborted vote in the Lords on 8 December 1711 on "No Peace without Spain" ', *Parliamentary History*, ii (1983), 191–202; G. S. Holmes, 'The Hamilton affair of 1711–1712: a crisis in Anglo-Scottish relations', *EHR*, lxxvii (1962), 257–82.

56. See below Appendix 1, col. 2, where Mohun and Stamford are listed as 'con q', Colepeper as 'd' and Fitzwalter as 'pro'. Haversham and the 14th Lord Willoughby had not succeeded to their peerage at this time. Haversham was forecast as 'pro q' before the Hamilton case in Dec. 1711, but on the vote he was against the ministry (*ibid.*, cols 7 and 8). For Fitzwalter and Mohun see also BL, Stowe MS 248, f. 3.

57. Appendix 1, cols 7 and 8; Kreienberg despatch, 4 Jan. 1712.

58. He received £300 in the winter of 1713/14, and another £300 from the Whig Lord Sunderland (Gregg and Jones, 'Hanover, pensions and the "poor lords" ', 175).

59. Beckett and Jones, 'Financial improvidence', 26. In Dec. 1711 Lord Hunsdon had also sold his vote at a crucial moment for £1000 (Holmes, *Politics in the Age of Anne*, 385).

60. Beckett and Jones, 'Financial improvidence'. See Holmes, *Politics in the Age of Anne*, 391–2, for sample of peers requiring money to attend Parliament.

61. In the event only £100 was paid before his death in April 1713 (Appendix 3; Gregg and Jones, 'Hanover, pensions and the "poor lords" ', 179, n. 38; *LJ*, xix, 497–501).

62. See Appendices 1 and 3.

63. BL, Add. MS 40060, f. 88: 'A New Protestant Littany', dated Feb. 1711[/12].

64. See below, Appendix 3.

65. Mellerstain Letters, IV: [Baillie to Montrose], 4 Dec. 1711. These stories represent the attitude of many peers who despised the Scots; see, e.g. Scottish RO, GD 45/14/352/19 (Dalhousie MSS): [Balmerino to H. Maule], 2 June

1713; they also reflected the ignorance of many English politicians — Harley himself, in 1704, had the temerity to confess that 'he knew no more of the Scots business than of Japan' (Kenneth A. Spencer Research Library, University of Kansas, MS C163: Simpson to Methuen, 26 [Dec.] 1704). Even a Scot thought that the inability of the representative peers to 'resist money' had ruined their reputation: Mellerstain Letters, IV: [Montrose to Baillie], 31 Dec. 1711.

66. See Holmes, *Politics in the Age of Anne*, 393–4. Lord Home was undoubtedly the poorest representative peer (see *ibid.*, and HMC, *Portland MSS*, X, 213–14), but there were many poorer ones back home. The 5th Earl of Kellie succeeded to an estate in 1710 so disordered that he had 'not 15 p[oun]d st[erling] a year to mentaine him', while Lord Dunbarton, even with a bounty of £300 from Oxford in 1710, was 'really starving and has not wherewith to buy his dinner': Huntington Library, LO 8704 (Loudoun Papers): Balcarres to Loudoun, 10 April 1710: BL, Loan 29/222/1695; HMC, *Portland MSS*, X, 332: Mar to Oxford [dated ? 1710, but Nov. 1711].

67. P. W. J. Riley, *The English Ministers and Scotland, 1707–27* (1964), 250; Mellerstain Letters, V: [Baillie to his wife], Edinburgh, 'Thursday evening' [8 Oct. 1713].

68. See e.g. Jones, 'Godolphin, the Whig Junto and the Scots', 158–74.

69. D. Szechi, 'Some insights on the Scottish M.P.s and peers returned in the 1710 election', *Scottish Historical Rev.*, lx (1981), 62–3. There were eight Court and seven Episcopal Tories.

70. He voted against the ministry on 8 April 1714 (*Wentworth Papers*, 366–7) and may well have been influenced by the strongly Presbyterian and anti-Jacobite Duke of Argyll. Both were Campbells.

71. George Baillie recorded 'no good understanding between the Tr[easurer] and Argile' in Nov. 1711, but as early as July of that year the duke was described as in a state of 'uneasiness' (Mellerstain Letters, IV: [Baillie to Montrose], 4 Nov. 1711; Huntington Library, Stowe MSS 58, vol.. IX, p. 65: Anthony Hammond to [James Brydges], 28 July 1711). The Campbells were a powerful and independently minded clan, and clan rivalry between the various peers should not be underestimated. Argyll and Ilay appear to have first voted against the ministry over the Grants Bill on 19 and 20 May 1712, when they carried Blantyre and Orkney's proxy (cast by Loudoun, though he voted for the bill) with them. All the other Scots supported the ministry. Baillie believed the two brothers were working with the Whigs by this stage (Mellerstain Letters, V: [Baillie to Montrose and Roxburghe], 20, 22 May 1712).

72. Scottish RO, GD 45/14/352/26: [Balmerino to Maule], 23 June [1713]. Described as 'much a servant to two noble brothers' and strongly against the Union, yet he was forecast by Oxford in mid-June 1713 as supporting the ministry over the French Commercial Treaty, while Argyll and Ilay were opposed (see Appendix 1, col. 12). Blantyre had been expected to follow Argyll out of the ministry as early as 5 June 1712 (Kreienberg despatch, 5 June 1712).

73. Berkshire RO, Trumbull MSS Alphab. LV: Ralph Bridges to Sir William Trumbull, n.d., but c. 8 July 1713.

74. See Holmes, 'Hamilton affair', 275 n. 4.

75. Scottish RO, GD 45/14/352/23: [Balmerino] to Maule, 11 June [1713].

76. See Holmes, 'Hamilton affair', 279.

77. Riley, *English Ministers and Scotland*, 250; HMC, *Portland MSS*, X, 348–51. Breadalbane, Dundonald and Dunmore (the Jacobites) along with Portmore and Selkirk replaced Annandale, Ilay, Home, Linlithgow and Blantyre.

78. Riley, *English Ministers and Scotland*, 240. For a detailed analysis of the 1713 crisis see Holmes and Jones, 'Trade, the Scots and the parliamentary crisis of 1713', 47–99.

79. For details and the evidence see *ibid.*, 58, 60. Dupplin was not a representative peer but sat by right of his British barony conferred on him in the mass creation of 12 peers in 1711/12. He was Oxford's son-in-law. His father, Lord Kinnoull, however, appears to have supported the Scots over the attempted repeal of the Union and the Malt Tax.
80. See Holmes, 'Hamilton affair', 271–9.
81. Mellerstain Letters, IV: [Montrose to Baillie], 31 Dec. 1711. Montrose felt that if the Scots could act as a coherent group, they could 'break the neck either of Whig or Tory'.
82. For example, the summer of 1712 saw a struggle within the Scottish ranks between Argyll and Mar, which was focused on the choice of candidate to replace the dead Lord Marischal as a representative peer (Mellerstain Letters, V: [Baillie] to Montrose, Tweeddale and Roxburghe, 1, 3, 4 July 1712).
83. *Wentworth Papers*, 261. However, only seven (rather than 16 Scottish peers) are recorded as attending that day (*LJ*, *xix*, 367).
84. For details see Jones, 'The division that never was'. The Scots lost much credit with the ministry by loitering at home (Mellerstain Letters, IV: [Baillie] to Montrose, 4 Dec. 1711).
85. See Holmes, 'Hamilton affair', 273–4. The 16 elected peers were to be replaced by 25 or 30 hereditary peers, the others being allowed to be elected to the Commons (Scottish RO, GD 45/14/352/13–15: [Balmerino to Maule], 24, 26, 31 Jan. 1712; Mellerstain Letters, V: [Baillie to Montrose], 19 Jan. 1712). This idea could only have led to bitter wrangling amongst the Scots for the coveted 25 peerages, and to resentment amongst the English, many of whom had opposed the British peerage for Hamilton through fear of a swamping of their order both socially and politically.
86. See Appendix 3.
87. See Appendix 2 and Holmes, *Politics in the Age of Anne*, 436–9. Between 1710 and 1714 nineteen other Scottish peers who did not sit in the Lords were promised or received payments. The Earl of Selkirk (representative peer, 1713–15) also received a payment of £1733 in 1711. Some pensions or offices were granted as a result of financial necessity rather than outright expectation of political obedience, attendance at Parliament being too costly for many a slender estate (e.g. Northesk: HMC, *Portland MSS*, X, 265). Sometimes diligence in attendance was rewarded (e.g. Kilsyth: *ibid.*, 330). For information on pensions to non-representative Scottish peers see BL, Loan 29/45 I/22; 29/307; 29/222/1674, 1675, 1695, 1765; HMC, *Portland MSS*, IV, 638. The bounty dispersed was too small to have had any noticeable effect on the voting of peers in elections.
88. For Annandale's non-cooperation see Holmes, 'Hamilton affair', 262, 275, 279.
89. Riley, *English Ministers and Scotland*, 249–50; HMC, *Portland MSS*, X, 303.
90. HMC, *Portland MSS*, X, 264–72, 284–301, 309, 330–58.
91. For examples see HMC, *Portland MSS*, X, 267, 270–1, 286, 331, 348 (Dupplin); *Portland MSS*, IV, 558–9, 601 (Kinnoull).
92. BL, Loan 29/337: Edward Harley's commonplace book, 19 Sept. 1713; HMC, *Portland MSS*, X, 306.
93. In 1713 the Hanoverian envoy in London regarded several of the Scots peers as fair game, because of their poverty, for poaching from the ministry by means of pensions from Hanover. See Gregg and Jones, 'Hanover, pensions and the "poor lords" ', 177, 180, n. 43.
94. Loudoun was the only Scot to become a Hanoverian Tory, but Findlater, Orkney and Portmore also opposed the lord treasurer during the passage of the Schism Bill in June 1714 (Mellerstain Letters, VI: [Baillie to his wife], 10, 15 June 1714).
95. This section of the essay is based on five manuscript draft chapters of Geoffrey

Holmes's work on the Harley ministry. I am grateful to him for allowing me to use his unpublished material.

96. George Baillie of Jerviswood had forecast that if Nottingham opposed the peace there would be a 'frost in the house of Lords' (Mellerstain Letters, IV: [Baillie to Montrose], 29 Nov. 1711).

97. This concern had been voiced as early as June 1711 (HMC, *Mar and Kellie MSS*, 490: Mar to Oxford, 10 June 1711).

98. See Appendix 1, col. 6, and Jones, 'The division that never was'.

99. 'The Whigs say that Ld Pelham had gone out to lay the greater load upon the new creation'; Scottish RO, GD220/5/268/2 (Montrose Papers): Baillie to Monrose, 3 Jan. 1712.

100. The nine Scots present all voted with the ministry (*ibid., LJ, xix*, 352).

101. The Scottish boycott was temporarily suspended over the Scottish Treason Bill which passed the Lords in February.

102. The division was tied, 78 votes each side. By the rules of the House the negatives (Whigs) carried the question.

103. The Grants Bill had been sustained by majorities of between only one and three in seven divisions from 17 to 20 May. There were many deliberate abstentions among government supporters (Argyll, Ilay and Strafford on 17th; Arran, Northumberland and Ashburnham on 19th; Strafford, Mountjoy and Hunsdon on 20th), and also some outright opposition by voting against the bill (Arran, Northumberland and Rochester on 17th, Argyll, Ilay and Blantyre on 19th; Northumberland and Cornwallis on 20th). See Kreienberg despatch, 20 May 1712.

104. The Earl of Strafford (formerly Lord Raby) provided a fine example of Tory self-interest. He was due to be introduced into the Lords by his new peerage on 17 May, but put it off, 'not being willing to give the first vote against the Court and being unwilling to vote for resuming of Grants since I have one myself' (Bodl., MS Rawlinson A 286, fos 158–9: Strafford to Bishop Robinson, 16 May 1712; see also BL, Stowe MS 224, f. 286: same to [Electress Sophia], 26 May 1712).

105. BL, Add. MS 17677 GGG, fos 124–5: L'Hermitage despatch, 10 April 1713; Berkshire RO, Trumbull Add. MS 98: J. Bridges to Trumbull, 13 April; *ibid.*, Add. MS 136/3: R. Bridges to Trumbull, 10 April; *Wentworth Papers*, 328; BL, Loan 29/45/J: Newsletter, 10 April; A. Boyer, *The History of Queen Anne* (1735), 628.

106. For a full discussion of this crisis see Holmes and Jones, 'Trade, the Scots and the parliamentary crisis of 1713', 47–77.

107. See Appendix 1, col. 12. Among the fourteen were Nottingham's family connections, Pembroke, Bishop Dawes, Anglesey and Abingdon. The last two were important indicators of Oxford's loss of Tory support over the way the peace was developing.

108. BL, Add. MS 17677 GGG, fos 260, 265; Boyer, *Queen Anne*, 640.

109. For an analysis of this conflict see S. Biddle, *Bolingbroke and Harley* (1975).

110. For Shrewsbury being sent to Ireland see D. Hayton, 'The crisis in Ireland and the disintegration of Queen Anne's last ministry', *Irish Historical Studies, xxii* (1981), 199–202, and for the reorganization of the government of Scotland see Riley, *English Ministers and Scotland*, 246–9.

111. Of the 16, three were notorious Jacobites (see above, n. 77) while only four (Loudoun, Orkney, Selkirk and Portmore) could be said to support Hanover. Thus the Whigs could not count on the Scots again unless Anglo-Scottish relations deteriorated.

112. Anglesey, Abingdon, Carteret, Guernsey, Mountjoy, Weymouth and Archbishop Dawes of York.

113. See Hayton, 'The crisis in Ireland', 211–12.

114. Mellerstain Letters, VI: [Baillie to his wife], 6 April 1714; *Wentworth Papers*, 364–6.
115. Abingdon, Archbishop Dawes, Bishop Robinson (a Cabinet member), Bishop Smalridge, Loudoun, Anglesey and Carteret. Of the 19 bishops present, 15 opposed the Court (Mellerstain Letters, VI: [Baillie to his wife], 13 April 1714; *Wentworth Papers*, 368–9). The voting was 61 plus 11 proxies to 61 plus 9 proxies.
116. See Appendix 1, col. 14.
117. On 4 June, over the rejection of petitions from Dissenters against the bill, four Harleyites (Poulett, Dartmouth, Foley and Mansel) voted with the Whigs. Oxford left the House before the division (*Wentworth Papers*, 386; Boyer, *Queen Anne*, 705).
118. *Wentworth Papers*, 405; *The Correspondence of Jonathan Swift*, ed. H. Williams (5 vols, 1963–5), II, 51; Hayton, 'The crisis in Ireland', 213; J. Macpherson, *Original Papers* (2 vols, 1775), II, 634.
119. Oxford's motives for this curious backtracking were analysed at the time by Bothmar, the Hanoverian envoy (Macpherson, *Original Papers*, II, 634), as
    (1) his own character which would not allow him to support entirely one side;
    (2) the hardly realistic hope of maintaining some good graces with the Queen;
    (3) the hope of entering again into favour by degrees if he did not declare too openly against the Court party.
120. HMC, *Mar and Kellie MSS*, 495: 17 Jan. 1712.

Appendix 1 Oxford's management lists and division lists 1710–1714

Column numbers correspond to the numbering of the lists as given below. Peers' titles are indicated after their names, thus 5e = fifth earl; throughout, b = baron, d = duke, e = earl, m = marquess, v = viscount; the letter q = query throughout.

1. *12 Sept. 1710*, list of peers to be provided for: BL, Loan 29/10/19.
    + on list

2. *3 Oct. 1710*, analysis by Harley of the lords into those expected to support the ministry; Court Whigs and others doubtful; and those considered certain to oppose: BL, Loan 29/10/19.
    pro   expected supporters
    con   opposers
    d   doubtful

3. *c. Dec. 1711*, list, partly in the hand of Oxford, which is perhaps a calculation of support: BL, Loan 29/10/4.
    + on list

4. *2 Dec. 1711*, list of peers to be canvassed before the 'No Peace without Spain' motion: BL, Loan 29/10/16.
    + on list

5. *10 Dec. 1711*, list of office-holders and pensioners who had voted against the ministry on the 'No Peace without Spain' motion, 7/8 Dec., with some suggested replacements, and a separate list of loyal peers to be gratified: BL, Loan 29/10/16.
    con   voted against ministry
    pro   loyal peer

6. *8 Dec. 1711*, an assessment of those against presenting the address (vote confirming that of 7 Dec. on the 'No Peace without Spain' motion) in an abandoned division: Bute (Loudoun) MSS (Marquess of Bute, Mount Stuart, Bute), bundle A 249.
    x   con
    I   probable con

7. *19 Dec. 1711*, forecast for the division the next day on the Hamilton peerage case: BL, Loan 29/10/16 (two lists).
    pro   on list A
    con   on list B
    b   on both lists

8. *20 Dec. 1711*, those for and those against disabling Hamilton from sitting as an hereditary British peer, and those abstaining: BL, 29/163/10.
    pro   voted for
    con   voted against
    a   abstained (i.e. 'went out')

9. *29 Dec. 1711*, list of lords to be contacted during the Christmas recess: BL, Loan 29/10/16.
    +   on list.

10. *June/July 1712*, list of lords, possibly doubtful Court supporters: BL, Loan 29/10/5.
   + on list

11. *26 Feb. 1713*, list of lords Oxford intended to canvass or contact before forthcoming session: BL, Loan 29/10/14.
   + on list

12. c. *13 June 1713*, estimate of voting on the French Commerce Bill: BL, Loan 29/10/3.
   pro   expected to support bill
   con   expected to oppose
   d   doubtful

13. *13 June 1713*, list of Court supporters expected to desert over the French Commerce Bill: BL, Loan 29/10/13.
   + on list

14. *27 May–c. 4 June 1714*, Lord Nottingham's forecast for the Schism Bill: Leicestershire RO, Finch MSS, P.P. 161.
   pro   expected supporters
   con   expected opponents
   d   doubtful

For further descriptions of these lists see *A Register of Parliamentary Lists, 1660–1761*, and *Supplement*, ed. D. Hayton and C. Jones (University of Leicester History Department Occasional Publications nos. 1 and 3, 1979 and 1982). For a full discussion of list 6 see C. Jones, 'The division that never was: new evidence on the aborted vote in the Lords on 8 December 1711 on "No Peace without Spain" ', *Parliamentary History, ii* (1983), 191–202.

	1710		Dec. 1711							1712	1713		1714	
	1.	2.	3.	4.	5.	6.	7.	8.	9.	10.	11.	12.	13.	14.
Abergavenny, 13 b							con	con				con		con
Abingdon, 2 e	+	pro	+		pro		pro	pro				con[q]	+	pro
Anglesey, 5 e		pro				I	con	a	+			con	+	pro
Annandale, 1 m			+											
Ashburnham, 3 b		con				I	con[q]					pro		pro
Atholl, 1 d			+									pro		pro
Balmerino, 4 b			+				pro	pro				con	+	pro
Barnard, 1 b		pro	+	+			pro		+			pro		pro
Bathurst, 1 b												pro		pro
Beaufort, 2 d		pro	+		pro		pro	pro				pro		
Bedford, 2 d		con												
Berkeley, 3 e		con			con	x	con	con				con		con

	1710		Dec. 1711							1712	1713			171
	1.	2.	3.	4.	5.	6.	7.	8.	9.	10.	11.	12.	13.	14.
Berkeley of Stratton, 4 b	+	pro			pro		pro^q	a				pro		pro
Berkshire, 4 e		pro	+	+			pro	pro	+	+	+	d		pro
Bingley, 1 b														pro
Blantyre, 6 b			+				pro	pro			+	pro		
Bolingbroke, 1 v												pro		pro
Bolton, 2 d		con				x	con	con				con		con
Boyle of Marston 1 b					pro		pro	pro				pro		con
Bradford, 2 e		con										con		con
Breadalbane, 1 e														pro
Bridgwater, 4 e		con			con	x	con	con				con		con
Brooke, 6 b		pro												
Bruce, b					pro							pro		pro
Buckinghamshire, 1 d	+	pro					b	pro		+		pro		pro
Byron, 4 b		d					pro	pro			+	con		pro
Cardigan, 3 e		d	+		pro		pro	a				pro		pro
Carlisle, 3 e		con			con	I	con	con				con		con
Carteret, 2 b						I	con^q	con				con		pro
Chandos, 8 b		pro		+			pro	pro	+		+	pro		pro
Cholmondeley, 1 e		pro^q			con	x	con^q	pro				con		con
Clarendon, 3 e					pro		pro	pro			+	pro		pro
Cleveland, 2 d		d		+		I	con	a		+	+	con		con
Colepeper, 3 b		d				x	con					con		con
Compton, b									+			pro		pro
Conway, 1 b							pro	con			+	con^q	+	pro
Cornwallis, 4 b		con	+	+			con^q	con		+		con		con
Coventry, 4 e										+		pro		pro
Cowper, 1 b		con				I	pro	pro			+	con		con
Craven, 2 b		pro												
Dartmouth, 1 e		pro			pro	I	con	con				pro		pro

	1710		Dec. 1711							1712	1713			1714
	1.	2.	3.	4.	5.	6.	7.	8.	9.	10.	11.	12.	13.	14.
Delawarr, 6 b		pro					pro	pro				pro		pro
Denbigh, 4 e		pro	+		pro		pro	pro	+		+	pro		pro
Derby, 10 e		con				x	con	con				con		con
Devonshire, 2 d		con				x	con	con				con		con
Dorchester, 1 m		con				x	con	con				con		con
Dorset, 7 e		con		con		x	con	pro				con		con
Dover, 1 d (Queensberry)	+	pro												
Dundonald, 4 e														pro
Dunmore, 2 e														pro
Eglinton, 9 e					pro							pro		pro
Exeter, 6 e		pro									+	pro		pro
Ferrers, 1 e		pro		+			pro	con	+		+	pro		pro
Findlater, 4 e														pro
Fitzwalter, 18 b		pro		con		x	pro	a	+		+	con		con
Foley, 1 b												pro	+	con
Gainsborough, 3 e		con					con				+	con		
Godolphin, 1 e		con				x	con[q]	a						
Godolphin, 2 e												con		con
Grafton, 2 d		con		+		I	con	pro				con		con
Grantham, 1 e		d	+[q]	+			pro[q]	pro	+		+	con		con
Greenwich, 1 e (Argyll)		pro		pro								con	+	con
Guernsey, 1 b		pro		pro		x	con	con				con		con
Guilford, 2 b		pro	+		pro		pro	pro				pro		pro
Halifax, 1 b		con				x	con	con				con		con
Hamilton, 4 d	+			pro										
Harcourt, 1 b			+				pro	pro				pro		pro
Hatton, 2 v			+	+			con[q]	con				d	+	
Haversham, 1 b	+	pro												
Haversham, 2 b				+		x	pro[q]	con			+	con		con
Hay, b												pro		pro

	1710		Dec. 1711							1712	1713			1714
	1.	2.	3.	4.	5.	6.	7.	8.	9.	10.	11.	12.	13.	14.
Herbert of Chirbury, 2 b		con		+		I	con	con		+	+	pro[q]		d
Hereford, 9 v			+								+	pro		pro
Hervey, 1 b		con				x	con	con				con		con
Holderness, 3 e		d		+			con	con				con		con
Home, 7 e							pro	pro				pro		
Howard of Effingham, 6 b		d	+	+	con	x	con					con		con
Howard of Escrick, 4 b		pro	+	+	pro	x	pro	pro	+	+		pro		pro
Hunsdon, 8 b		pro					pro	pro		+	+	pro		
Ilay, 1 e				pro			pro	pro				con	+	
Jersey, 1 e	+	pro												
Jersey, 2 e			+	+			b	pro				pro		pro
Kent, 1 d		con	+		con	I	pro	pro		+		con		con
Kilsyth, 3 v							pro	pro				pro		pro
Kinnoull, 7 e												pro		pro
Lansdowne, 1 b												pro		pro
Leeds, 1 d		pro		+			pro							
Leeds, 2 d		pro[1]					pro	pro	+			pro		pro
Leicester, 6 e		con			?con[2]	x	con	con				con		con
Leigh, 2 b		pro												
Leigh, 3 b			+					con	+					pro
Leominster, 1 b		pro		+										
Lexinton, 2 b	+	pro	+[q]		pro[q]	I	pro	pro			+	pro		pro
Lincoln, 7 e		d	+	+	con	x	con	con			+	con		con
Lindsey, 1 m		d					pro	con			+	con		con
Longueville, 2 v				+						+		con[q]		con
Loudoun, 3 e							pro	pro				pro		pro
Manchester, 4 e		d		+	con	x	pro[q]					con		con
Mansel, 1 b												pro		pro
Mar, 23 e							pro	pro				pro		pro

	1710		Dec. 1711							1712	1713		1714	
	1.	2.	3.	4.	5.	6.	7.	8.	9.	10.	11.	12.	13.	14.
Marischal, 8 e			+											
Marlborough, 1 d		con			con	x	con	a	+					
Masham, 1 b										+		pro		pro
Maynard, 3 b		con	+	+[q]							+	pro		pro
Middleton, 1 b												pro[q]	+	
Mohun, 4 b		con[q]				x	con	con						
Montagu, 2 d					con	x	con	con				con		con
Mountjoy, 1 b										+		con[q]	+	pro
Newcastle, 1 d	d													
North and Grey, 6 b		pro		pro		pro	con		+	+		pro		pro
Northampton, 4 e	+	pro	+	+	pro	I	con[q]	con				pro		pro
Northesk, 4 e							pro					pro		pro
Northumberland, 1 d		pro		+		pro	pro		+			pro		pro
Nottingham, 2 e		pro				x	con	con				con		con
Orford, 1 e		con				x	con	con				con		con
Orkney, 1 e				+			pro	pro				pro		pro
Ormond, 2 d		pro			pro		pro	pro	+			pro		pro
Osborne, b												pro		pro
Ossulston, 2 b		con[q]		+		I	con	pro			+	con		con
Oxford, 1 e							pro	pro				pro		pro
Paget, 7 b		con				x	con[q]							
Paget, 8 b												pro		d
Pelham, 1 b		con				x	con	con						
Pembroke, 8 e		pro		+	con	I	pro[q]	con				con		con
Peterborough, 3 e	+	pro			pro						+	pro		
Plymouth, 2 e		pro		+		pro	pro	con			+	pro		pro
Portland, 2 e		con				x	con	a				con		con
Portmore, 1 e														pro
Poulett, 1 e		pro					pro	pro	+?[3]			pro		pro
Radnor, 2 e	d			+	con		pro[q]		+			con		con

	1710		Dec. 1711							1712	1713			1714
	1.	2.	3.	4.	5.	6.	7.	8.	9.	10.	11.	12.	13.	14.
Richmond, 1 d				+				con		+	+	pro		
Rivers, 4 e		pro		+	pro		pro	pro			+			
Rochester, 1 e	+	pro												
Rochester, 2 e								pro						pro
Rochford, 3 e		d	+^{q}	+										
Rockingham, 3 b		con				x	con	con				con		con
Rosebery, 1 e			+				pro	pro				pro		pro
Rutland, 2 d						x	con	con			+	con		con
St Albans, 1 d		d	+	+	con	x	con			+	+	con		con
St John of Bletso, 9 b														pro
Salisbury, 5 e											+	pro		pro
Saye and Sele, 5 v		pro					pro	pro			+	pro		pro
Scarbrough, 1 e		d				x	con	con				con		con
Scarsdale, 4 e		pro	+	+	pro		pro	con	+			pro		pro
Schomberg, 3 d		pro		+	con	I	pro	a		+		con		con
Shaftesbury, 3 e		con												
Shrewsbury, 1 d		pro					pro	pro				pro		
Somers, 1 b		con				x	con	con				con		con
Somerset, 6 d		d			con	x	con					con		con
Stamford, 2 e		con^q		+			con					con		con
Stawell, 3 b		pro		+	pro		pro	con		+		pro		
Strafford, 1 e	+											pro		
Suffolk, 6 e		pro^q					pro					con^q		con
Sunderland, 3 e		con				x	con	con						con
Sussex, 1 e		pro		+		I		pro	+			pro		pro
Thanet, 6 e		pro		+		Ix	con^q	con	+			pro		pro
Torrington, 1 e		d			pro	x	con	con			+	pro^q		d
Townshend, 2 v					con	x	con	con				con		con
Trevor, 1 b												pro		pro
Vaughan, 2 b		con				x	con	con						

	1710		Dec. 1711							1712	1713		1714	
	1.	2.	3.	4.	5.	6.	7.	8.	9.	10.	11.	12.	13.	14.
Warrington, 2 e		con	+									pro[q]		con
Westmorland, 6 e		d	+	con		con	con					con		con
Weston, 1 b		pro	+			pro	pro					pro		pro
Weymouth, 1 v		pro	+	pro	x	con				+		d	+	pro
Wharton, 1 e		con		con	x	con	con							con
Willoughby de Broke, 11 b		pro												
Willoughby de Broke, 12 b						pro	pro					pro		pro
Willoughby of Parham, 14 b														con
Winchilsea, 4 e	+	pro		pro		pro	pro							
Winchilsea, 5 e											+			
Yarmouth, 2 e		pro	+	pro		pro	pro			+		pro		pro

Bishops

	1710		Dec. 1711							1712	1713		1714	
	1.	2.	3.	4.	5.	6.	7.	8.	9.	10.	11.	12.	13.	14.
Atterbury (Rochester)														pro
Bisse (St David's & Hereford)		pro				pro	pro					pro		pro
Blackall (Exeter)		pro	+									pro		pro
Burnet (Salisbury)		con			I	con	a					con		con
Compton (London)		pro				pro						pro		.
Crew (Durham)		pro	+									pro		pro
Cumberland (Peterborough)		con			x	con						con		con
Dawes (Chester & York)						pro	pro					con	+	pro
Evans (Bangor)		con			x	con	con					con		con
Fleetwood (St Asaph)		con			x	con	pro					con		con
Fowler (Gloucester)		con			x	con						con		
Hooper (Bath & Wells)		pro	+							+		pro		pro

	1710		Dec. 1711							1712	1713		1714	
	1.	2.	3.	4.	5.	6.	7.	8.	9.	10.	11.	12.	13.	14.
Hough (Coventry & Lichfield)		con				x	con	con				con		con
Humphries (Hereford)		con												
Lloyd (Worcester)		con										con		
Manningham (Chichester)		d					pro	con		+		pro		pro
Moore (Ely)		con				x	con	con				con		con
Nicolson (Carlisle)						x	con	con		+		con		con [pro][4]
Ottley (St David's)												pro		pro
Robinson (Bristol & London)		pro					pro	pro				pro		pro
Sharp (York)		pro	+							+		pro		
Smalridge (Bristol)														pro
Sprat (Rochester)		pro		+			pro	pro			+			
Talbot (Oxford)		con		con		x	con	con				con		con
Tenison (Canterbury)		con					con					con		
Trelawney (Winchester)		con	+		con		con[q]	con			+	pro		d [pro][4]
Trimnell (Norwich)		con				x	con	con				con		con
Tyler (Llandaff)		con	+											con
Wake (Lincoln)		con				x	con	con				con		con

NOTES

1. Sat in his father's barony of Osborne until he succeeded as 2nd Duke of Leeds in 1712.
2. Erased by Oxford from the list of those who voted against the ministry.
3. 'Ld Steward' (i.e. Poulett) a questionable reading of the MS.
4. Bishops Nicolson and Trelawney are recorded as voting pro in Bodl. MS Fol θ 666, f. 68v in the division on the third reading of the bill on 15 June 1714. Nicolson's proxy vote was cast by Wake who opposed the bill; see *The London Diaries of Bishop Nicolson of Carlisle, 1702–1718*, ed. C. Jones and G. Holmes (1984), 606–7.

Appendix 2   Queen's servants and pensioners in the House of Lords, November 1710

C   Member of the Cabinet
I   Ireland
P.C.   Privy Councillor
S   Scotland

Italics indicate Whigs or Court Whigs

Abingdon, 2 e	P.C.; bounty of £1500 in March 1710
Anglesey, 5 e	P.C.; joint vice-treasurer & paymaster general [I]
Balmerino, 4 b	Governor of the Mint [S]
Beaufort, 2 d	Lord lieut. of Hampshire
Bedford, 2 d	Lord lieut. of Bedfordshire, Cambridgeshire & Middlesex
Berkeley, 3 e	Lord lieut. of Gloucestershire; warden of the Forest of Dean; constable of St Briavel's Castle; *custos rotulorum* of Surrey
Berkeley of Stratton, 4 b	Chancellor of the Duchy of Lancaster; P.C.; master of the Rolls [I] (for life)
Bolton, 2 d	Lord lieut. of Dorset
Bradford, 2 e	P.C.; lord lieut. of Shropshire
Bridgwater, 4 e	Lord lieut. of Buckinghamshire
Buckinghamshire, 1 d	Lord steward (C)
Carlisle, 3 e	Lord lieut. of Cumberland & Westmorland; governor of Carlisle
Cholmondeley, 1 e	Treasurer of the Household; P.C.; lord lieut. of North Wales & Cheshire; governor of Chester
Cowper, 1 b	Lord lieut. of Hertfordshire
Craven, 2 b	Lord lieut. of Berkshire
Dartmouth, 2 b	Secretary of state, south (C); P.C.; joint keeper of the Signet [S]
Derby, 10 e	Chamberlain of Chester; vice-admiral of Lancashire
Devonshire, 2 d	Lord lieut. of Derbyshire
Dorchester, 1 m	P.C.
Dorset, 7 e	Lord warden of the Cinque Ports
Dover, 1 d	Secretary of state, Scotland (C); P.C.; pension of £3000 p.a.

Ferrers, 1 b	P.C.
Godolphin, 1 e	Pension of £4000 p.a. on dismissal as lord treasurer in Aug. 1710
Grafton, 2 d	Lord lieut. of Suffolk; pension of £4700 p.a.
Greenwich, 1 e	Col. of 4th Troop of Horse Guards; col. of 3rd Regiment of Foot
Halifax, 1 b	Auditor of the Receipt (for life); ranger of Bushey Park
Hamilton, 4 d	Lord lieut. of Lancashire
Holderness, 3 e	Constable of Middleton Castle
Ilay, 1 e	Lord justice general [S] ; extraordinary lord of Sessions [S]
Kent, 1 d	Lord lieut. of Herefordshire
Kinnoull, 7 e	Annuity of £1000
Leeds, 1 d	Pension of £3500 p.a.
Lindsey, 1 m	Hereditary lord great chamberlain; P.C.; lord lieut. of Lincolnshire
Loudoun, 3 e	Lord keeper [S] ; extraordinary lord of Sessions [S] ; P.C. ; pension of £1000 p.a.
Manchester, 4 e	Lord lieut. of Huntingdonshire
Mar, 23 e	Joint keeper of the Signet [S] ; P.C.
Marlborough, 1 d	Captain general & master of the Ordnance; lord lieut. of Oxfordshire; pension of £5000 p.a.
Montagu, 2 d	Hereditary master of the Great Wardrobe
Newcastle, 1 d	Lord privy seal (C); lord lieut. of Nottinghamshire, East and North Ridings of Yorkshire; chief justice in Eyre north of Trent; P.C.
Northampton, 4 e	Lord lieut. of Warwickshire
Northumberland, 1 d	Lord lieut. of Surrey; constable of Windsor Castle; pension of £4700 p.a.
Orkney, 1 e	Governor general of Virginia
Ormond, 2 d	Lord lieut. of Ireland (C); P.C.; lord lieut. of Somerset; high steward of Exeter
Paget, 7 b	Lord lieut. of Staffordshire
Pembroke, 8 e	Lord lieut. of Wiltshire & Monmouthshire; pension of £3000 p.a.
Peterborough, 3 e	Lord lieut. of Northamptonshire; ambassador to Vienna
Portland, 2 e	Col. of 1st Troop of Life Guards
Poulett, 1 e	1st lord of Treasury (C); P.C.; lord lieut. of Devon
Raby, 3 b	Ambassador to Berlin; col. of Royal Regiment of Dragoons

Rivers, 4 e	Constable of the Tower; lord lieut. of Essex; recently returned envoy to Hanover; P.C.
Rochester, 1 e	Lord president of the Council (C); P.C.; lord lieut. of Cornwall; pension of £4000 p.a.
Rockingham, 3 b	Lord lieut. of Kent
Rosebery, 1 e	Chamberlain of Fife & Strathearn
Rutland, 1 d	Lord lieut. of Leicestershire
St Albans, 1 d	Master falconer (hereditary); captain of the Band of Gentlemen Pensioners; master of the Register Office; pension of £1000 p.a.
Scarbrough, 1 e	Lord lieut. of Durham & Northumberland
Schomberg, 3 d	P.C.; pension of £5000 p.a.
Shrewsbury, 1 d	Lord chamberlain (C); lord lieut. of Worcestershire; P.C.
Somerset, 6 d	Master of the Horse; P.C.
Stamford, 2 e	1st lord of Trade & Plantations
Suffolk, 6 e	Deputy earl marshal; P.C.
Townshend, 2 v	Ambassador to The Hague; lord lieut. of Norfolk
Weston, 1 b	Col. of 3rd Troop of Horse Guards
Wharton, 1 e	Chief justice in Eyre south of Trent
Burnet (Bishop of Salisbury)	Chancellor of the Order of the Garter
Sharp (Arch-bishop of York)	Lord almoner

Appendix 3   Pensions, annuities, royal bounties, and gifts to peers, 1710–14

	1710	*1711*	*1712*	*1713*	*1714*
Abingdon	1500	1500		arrears asked for Dec.	
Argyll (Greenwich)	3000	3000	3000 (750–1000 paid)	3000 (1500 paid)	3000
Atholl		500 or 600	700		1000
Balmerino					1000
Beaufort		1000		500	
Bridgwater		1000	1000	500	
Buckingham-shire		arrears asked for Dec.			5000
Byron			300	300	600
Clarendon	1000	1000 or 750	200	1000	2000 or 1500
Cleveland (Southampton)	3000	3000 (600 paid)			
Cornwallis		1000 (3000 lent)			
Dartmouth	3750				
Delawarr		1200	1200	600 (2400 arrears due Jan.)	arrears asked for July
Denbigh		500	arrears due	arrears due	arrears due
Derby			500		
Eglinton					1000
Findlater (Seafield) Scottish rep. peer 1712–15	3000	3000	3000 (750 paid)	3000 (pension cut to 1000; salary of 2000 as keeper of the Great Seal)	3000
Grafton	2000 or 4700	4700			
Grantham	2000	2000			

	1710	1711	1712	1713	1714
Herbert					500
Home Scottish rep. peer 1710–13				150	300
Howard of Effingham		600	600	300	600
Hunsdon		200 July, 1000 Dec.			
Ilay		? pension considered			
Jersey					175
Kilsyth		500			
Kinnoull	1000 (750)	1250 (1000 confirmed; 4000 paid on arrears)	1000	750	1250
Leeds, 1 d (d. 1712)	3500	3500	arrears asked for July		
Leeds, 2 d					200
Lincoln		600 (250)	600	300	
Loudoun	1000	1000 + 865	1000 (250)	1000 (not paid by 1715) + 500 arrears; (2000)	
Manchester	1000 (not paid by Dec. 1711)				
Mar	3000	3000	3000 (750 paid)		
Marischal		? pension considered			
Northesk				1000	1000
Northumber- land	3000 (4700)	4700			
Ormond					3000
Orrery (Boyle of Marston)			600	? 150	
Pembroke	3000	3000	3000 (750)	3000 (1500 paid)	

	1710	1711	1712	1713	1714
Queensberry (Dover) (d. 1711)	3000		3000 (750) paid to executors		
Radnor	1200 granted	1200 (500 paid)	arrears asked for Feb.		
Rivers			500 arrears asked for (300 paid)		
Rochester (d. 1711)	4000				
Rochester (suc. 1711)			260		
Rosebery			158		600 Apr. 1000 June
St Albans	1000 (750)	1000 (750)	1000	1000 (2500 paid on arrears of 2½ years' pension; 3431 paid on arrears of 2½ years' allowances as master of Hawks)	2500
Sandwich				2500, due since 1711	1000
Saye and Sele		250			
Schomberg	5000	4000	1000 (250)		
Stawell			1000		
Sussex			1200 granted (500 paid)	arrears asked for Aug. (Sept. 200 paid), Dec.	arrears asked for March, May
Warrington				1000 on arrears of father's pension	arrears asked for
Westmorland		600	600	300	
Willoughby of Parham (d. Apr. 1713)				400 March (100 paid)	
Windsor (Mountjoy)				40	
Yarmouth				400	

SOURCES

The main sources for this table are the *Calendars of Treasury Books*, 1710–14; the accounts compiled for the Committee of Secrecy of Bounties, etc., issued between 1707 and 1720, to be found in the papers of Robert Walpole in the Cambridge University Library, Cholmondeley (Houghton) Papers 53, items 3/1–3, 3a, 11/1–4; the papers of Robert Harley on pensions to be found in BL, Loan 29/45A/2,4,7–10. Information about individual peers can be found in the following papers:

Abingdon (Loan 29/307), Atholl (29/222/1765), Balmerino (Atholl MS 45/11/97), Delawarr (29/307), Denbigh (29/307), Eglinton (Atholl MS 45/11/97), Grantham (Cambridge UL, C (II) 53/39), Herbert (29/204), Howard of Effingham (29/307), Kilsyth (Nottingham UL, PW 2Hy 971), Leeds (29/161/3/Misc. 6; 29/152/5; 29/204), Loudoun (Huntington Library, LO 11102), Manchester (29/451/2/23, 29/151), Northesk (Atholl MS 45/11/97), Radnor (29/155/2–3), Rivers (29/204), St Albans (29/307–8), Sussex (29/155/6; 29/204), Warrington (29/127/1). General information is also to be found in PRO, Treasury Papers T. 52/25–27, T. 53/22–23, T. 61/22.

Some of these sources give conflicting evidence; where possible this has been reconciled and different figures have been indicated in brackets.

6 Constituents' instructions to Members of Parliament in the eighteenth century

Paul Kelly

In 1784 a pamphleteer attacked the view that Members of Parliament were bound by the instructions of their constituents: 'The prevailing idea, that all constituents have a right to instruct their delegates, and consequently that these are under the obligation of submitting their own opinions to those of their electors, need only to be fairly considered to appear deficient, impracticable and unjust.'[1] This was the conservative view of instructions. By contrast, in a pamphlet published in 1785 the Kentish attorney John Burnby declared that M.P.s were 'sent to Parliament to speak the sense of their constituents; whenever they receive instructions, it is their duty to pay an implicit obedience to them, even though their constituents' opinion should not coincide with their own'.[2] This was the radical view of instructions.

These conflicting views of the constitutional relationship between representatives and constituents are closely related to the contemporary debate about parliamentary reform. For the most radical[3] reformers preached the supremacy of public opinion. The House of Commons was simply the means through which the voice of the people could be expressed. Radicals demanded that there should be a dependence of the elected on the electors, and that public opinion must be the final arbiter in national political disputes. Parliamentary reform, which would achieve more frequent elections and an extension of the popular basis of representation, was the means to this end, as was also the practice of issuing instructions to M.P.s. The question of instructions has been examined by Dame Lucy Sutherland in an article which focuses on Edmund Burke and William Baker in their conflict with the City of London radicals at the general election of 1774.[4] This paper is concerned with a wider perspective, in an attempt to discover the source of radical ideas about instructions and the significance of instructions as an issue in late-eighteenth-century British politics.

The view that M.P.s were always bound by the instructions of their constituents was something new and at variance with the accepted constitutional theory and practice of the eighteenth century. John Hatsell, the leading authority of his time on the law and customs of Parliament, quotes Coke, Blackstone and Algernon Sydney in support of the conservative view of instructions, as well as Speaker Onslow's judgment that they 'are not absolutely binding upon votes and actings, and conscience, in Parliament'.[5] David Hume, writing at the beginning of the 1740s, observed that, if instructions were to be binding on M.P.s, this would 'introduce a total alteration in our government, and would soon reduce it to a pure republic'. Since such a notion was so alien to the accepted constitutional ideas and practice of the time, Hume goes on to remark that 'it is needless to reason any further concerning a form of government, which is never likely to have place in Great Britain, and which seems not to be the aim of any party amongst us'.[6] Thus the view of instructions put forward by Edmund Burke in 1774 in his famous speech to the electors of Bristol — that 'your representative owes you, not his industry only, but his judgment; and he betrays instead of serving you, if he sacrifices it to your opinion'[7] — was simply a statement of constitutional orthodoxy.

Yet the radicals did not claim to be innovatory in their views on this issue, and based their arguments on ancient precedent and usage. Thomas Day boldly claimed that the Burkeian position of parliamentary independence ' is a position as new as it is already proved pernicious; it was unknown to our plainer ancestors, who thought themselves obliged to consult their constituents in dubious points, and to be the oracles of the people's will'.[8] Similarly, James Burgh claimed that it was the conservative view of instructions which was 'mere innovation', and quotes in support of the radical view a number of examples in England, especially in the late seventeenth and early eighteenth centuries, as well as the practices in the old representative institutions of Castile, Switzerland, France, Germany and New England.[9] So what sort of precedents were there in English practice for the radical view of instructions?

The practice of instructing was certainly not new. It had a history as old as that of Parliament itself. Originally M.P.s were no more than attorneys for their constituents, and accordingly came up to Parliament with instructions.[10] But ideas of representation had changed, and by the end of the fifteenth century the medieval delegate of a locality was already being transformed into a representative of all the interests of the nation.[11] Even so, the representative obviously still retained his local connections, and was consequently obliged to see to the particular needs of his constituents. Hence, the practice of instructing on local issues persisted; the City of London representatives, for example, were instructed on local issues in the late fifteenth century.[12] But the principle was not readily projected from parochial to national concerns. By the time of James I, instructions from constituencies to representatives were generally taken for granted, but they nearly always concerned local issues.[13] In the years

1640 to 1649 constituents communicated their grievances to Parliament
in the form of instructions as an alternative to petitions. But M.P.s were
not instructed to vote in a particular way — they were simply to com-
municate the grievances to Parliament.[14] Subsequently, instructions were
issued on national concerns; but these were contrived by the representatives themselves as a propaganda device. Such instructions were a feature
of the 1681 general election, when they were used by Shaftesbury's
followers.[15] They were used again in the 1701 and 1715 general elections,
but were rarely resorted to in the reign of Anne.[16]

   In 1733, however, instructions were used on a massive scale when 54
constituencies issued them against Walpole's proposed excise scheme; and
there can be little doubt but that on this occasion instructions were an
authentic manifestation of a spontaneous public opinion.[17] Yet, despite
the support and publicity given to this movement by the parliamentary
opposition and by the press, no radical view of instructions emerged. It is
noticeable that *The Craftsman*, for example, propounded very orthodox
ideas concerning representation. It argued that, though 'a representative
is chosen by some one county, city or town, and is particularly obliged to
consult the interest of it; yet it must be admitted that he is a representative of the people in general'. This was of course the essence of what was
to become the conservative case against instructions. *The Craftsman* goes
on to argue that

> tho' the instructions of a particular county, city or town ought not
> to prevail against the instructions of all the rest of the Kingdom,
> or against the *common good of the Kingdom*; yet when the nation in
> general concurs in one and the same thing, as they have done against
> any *further extension of the excise laws*, this voice of the whole
> people, by whom all the *House of Commons* are elected, from whom
> the *whole House* derives its authority, may and ought to be con-
> sidered as of very great weight.[18]

Thus the argument is that the instructions should be obeyed in this particular case because they do signify the general wish and good of the whole
kingdom. The argument clearly does not assert the dependence of M.P.s
on the wishes of their constituents on all issues; nor does it propound any
new view of the relationship between an M.P. and his constituents.
   It is, therefore, a very different position from that of the late-eighteenth-
century radicals. Similarly, on the question of the excise, in the House
of Commons William Pulteney merely argued that M.P.s should have 'some
little regard to their constituents. It is well known that it was the custom
among our ancestors, when any new device was proposed, to desire time
to have a conference with their countries.' All that Pulteney asks for is
that M.P.s should be given time to consult their constituents, since the
interests of the latter would be affected by the proposed excise. He quotes
Coke's *Institutes* as his authority: 'It is also the law and custom of the

Parliament, that when any device is moved on the King's behalf, in Parliament, for his aid, or the like, the Commons may answer, that they tendered the King's estate, and are ready to aid the same, only in this new device, they dare not agree without conference with their countries.'[19] The application of this old constitutional principle scarcely had radical implications. The younger Pitt, for example, applied virtually the same principle in 1785, when he introduced his policy to regulate the trading relationship between Britain and Ireland. The policy was introduced first into the British House of Commons in the form of eleven propositions. Pitt went out of his way to insist that enough time would be given for consultation with various interests before a bill was prepared — though admittedly he was proceeding on the false assumption that his policy was acceptable 'without-doors'. The opinion of M.P.s' constituents was obtained through a deluge of petitions against the scheme. The House of Commons duly considered these petitions, and heard evidence, before formulating resolutions on which a bill was to be based.[20]

Thus the history of instructions to the time of Walpole scarcely affords much precedent for the late-eighteenth-century radical view of them. It is evident that the radicals read too much into the practice of instructing on purely local issues, and conveniently neglected to take account of the development of English constitutional theory. Further, though there was a constant radical challenge to the 'Whig constitution' throughout the eighteenth century, no assertion that the votes and opinions of M.P.s should be subjected to the directing force of public opinion appears to have been made in the first half of the century.

It is revealing to turn to the ideas of John Trenchard, a rugged exponent of the 'commonwealthman' tradition in the 1720s, to see how far radical ideas had advanced some two generations later. 'The first principles of power,' argues Trenchard, 'are the people; and all the projects of men in power ought to refer to the people, to aim solely at their good and end in it: and whoever will pretend to govern them without regarding them will soon repent it.' But for Trenchard the polarization of political conflict is still the seventeenth-century one of the Crown and its ministers on the one hand, and the people and their representatives on the other — that is Court versus Country. He does indeed consider the situation where the interests of the representatives and the people may diverge. M.P.s might be 'awed by force' or 'corrupted by places and pensions . . . as to be ready to give up publick liberty'. But this is to be resolved by the people asserting their right 'humbly to represent their publick grievances, and to petition for redress to those whose duty is to right them, or to see them righted'. This is not at all the same thing as authoritative instructions, which Trenchard does not advocate. He does argue that the public should be fully involved in political activity; for 'the people, when they are not misled or corrupted, generally make a sound judgment of things. They have natural qualifications equal to those of their superiors; and there is oftener found a great genius carrying a pitch fork than carrying a white staff.' Paraphrasing Coke's dictum, Trenchard observes that 'our records afford instances, where the House of Commons have declined entering upon a question of importance, till they had gone into the country, and consulted their principals, the people'. But Trenchard here asserts no more than the principle which was applied by Pitt in 1785 in the conduct of the Irish policy through the British House of Commons. In his emphasis on the right of petitioning rather than instructing, Trenchard clearly allows for considerable parliamentary independence. Although for him the interests of the people are paramount, and the opinion of ordinary men is to be valued in the conduct of national affairs, he does not develop the notion of an infallible public opinion which should dictate the decisions of M.P.s.[21] It is as though Trenchard's ideas have all the ingredients of late-eighteenth-century radicalism – to which indeed his ideas and polemics contributed not a little[22] – without the final conclusion.

Even when the specific issue of the relationship between M.P.s and their constituents was raised in the first half of the eighteenth century, and the conservative orthodox view propounded, the radical rejoinder was not made. There was in fact no constitutional debate on this point. The 'Country' opposition campaigns of instructions, and proposals for more frequent elections, were designed to curb the supposedly corrupting influence of the Court over the House of Commons, not to establish the dependence of M.P.s on electors. That instructions and more frequent elections would increase the power of electors at the expense of representatives was an unforeseen consequence.[23] Thus, on Bromley's motion for repealing the Septennial Act on 13 March 1734, John Willes, the attorney-general, approached the question of whether M.P.s were dependent on their constituents:

> That we have all a dependence on the people for our election is what, Sir, I shall readily grant; but after we are chosen, and have taken our seats in the House, we have no longer any dependence upon our electors, at least in so far as regards our behaviour here. Their whole power is then devolved upon us and we are in every question that comes before this House, to regard only the public good in general, and to determine according to our judgments; if we do not, if we are to depend upon our constituents, and to follow blindly the instructions they send us, we cannot be said to act freely, nor can such Parliaments be called free Parliaments.

However, Willes went on to suggest that it was better for M.P.s to be dependent on the influence of the Crown than on the caprice of electors; and it was this suggestion, rather than his remarks concerning instructions, that roused the fury of the 'Country' members of the opposition. 'I shall always look upon a dependence on the people of England, or even upon those I represent [the City of London], to be less dangerous and more honourable than a dependence on the Crown,' declared Sir John Barnard. Sir William Wyndham attacked Willes's argument as

> the most monstrous, the most slavish doctrine that was ever heard
> . . . though the people of a county, city or borough may be misled,
> and may be induced to give instructions which are contrary to
> the true interest of their country, yet I hope he will allow, that
> in times past the Crown has been oftener misled; and consequently
> we must conclude, that it is more apt to be misled in time to come,
> than we can suppose the people to be.

But Willes's main assertion, that the people delegate all their power to their representatives, was not questioned. The issue being discussed was the influence of the Crown, not parliamentary independence versus a radical view of instructions. Moreover, the idea of dependence on the people in this case was taken simply to mean the excessive preoccupation of an M.P. with the particular local concerns of his constituency, rather than the directing force of public opinion in national affairs. The point was fully brought out in the speech of Sir William Yonge, who sought to mitigate the provocativeness of Willes's argument. Yonge took that argument to mean

> that after we have taken our seats in this House we ought, every one
> of us, to look upon ourselves as one of the representatives of the
> whole body of the Commons of England, and ought not to have
> any particular bias for the county, city or borough we represent.
> This, Sir, is so far from being a doctrine very extraordinary, or
> altogether new, that I wish every gentleman in this House would
> make it a standing rule for his conduct; for I cannot help observing
> that here are some gentlemen in the House who on many occasions
> confine their thoughts too much to the particular county, city or
> borough they represent.[24]

Eleven years later Sir William Yonge again put forward the accepted conservative view of instructions in the debate of 23 January 1745 on the motion for annual Parliaments. To the statement of Thomas Carew that M.P.s 'are properly speaking the attornies of the people', Yonge replied;

> . . . the word attorney has been artfully brought into the debate,
> as if the members of this House were nothing more than the
> attornies of the particular county, city or borough they respectively
> represent; but every one knows, that by our constitution, after a
> gentleman is chosen, he is the representative, or, if you please, the
> attorney of the people of England, and as such is at full freedom
> to act as he thinks best for the people of England in general. He may
> receive, he may ask, he may even follow the advice of his particular

constituents; but he is not obliged, nor ought he to follow their advice, if he thinks it inconsistent with the general interest of his country.

Carew in fact was not putting forward any new notion of representation. He had used the term 'attornies of the people' loosely, and had consequently opened the way for Yonge to score debating points by articulating the unquestioned constitutional orthodoxy. The main point of Carew's argument was directed towards asserting the need for the Parliament to combat through more frequent elections, the corrupting influence of ministerial power. No one in the debate questioned Yonge's definition of the proper relationship between an M.P. and his constituents.[25]

In the 1740s, however, a periodical, *The Champion*, made much more than was usual of the instructions of major cities, and suggested that, if the weight of the people was exerted fully, the defects in the constitution caused by ministerial corruption could be remedied.[26] And one historian has detected in these signs of the radicalism-to-come the first indication of the possibility of a campaign for parliamentary reform not limited to the old proposals of simply excluding placemen and holding more frequent Parliaments.[27] But perhaps such a development was to be expected after twenty years of Walpolean rule; and, if John Trenchard had been writing in the 1740s instead of the 1720s, it is doubtful whether he would have been so moderate in his statements concerning the kind of pressure which might be brought to bear on representatives.

Walpole's fall in 1742 was followed by an impressive campaign of instructions. More than forty constituencies, mostly counties and cities, adopted instructions to M.P.s recommending a strict inquiry into Walpole's administration, and urging the restoration of triennial Parliaments and the enactment of a place and pension bill.[28] The instructions seem to have been largely contrived for propaganda purposes, and did not in fact lead to a campaign for parliamentary reform based on a more radical view of the relationship between M.P.s and their constituents. According to the Earl of Egmont, the 'faction' responsible for contriving these instructions:

> published a pamphlet to convince them [the people] that it was the duty of every Member of Parliament to vote in every instance as his constituents should direct him in the House of Commons — a thing in the highest degree absurd, *for it is the constant and allowed principle of our constitution that no man, after he is chosen, is to consider himself as a member for any particular place, but as a representative for the whole nation.*[29]

For our purposes, the important point made here by Egmont is implicit in his italics. He states the principle of representation as though it was an axiom — as indeed it was in the 1740s. Though instructions were 'got up' by interested politicians, and though they were interpreted as an exertion of the people, there was no challenge to the established representative principle. Thus instructions were simply a part of the opposition polemics, not part of any reasoned argument concerning constitutional principles. This was a very different situation from that of the late eighteenth century, when instructions were used by the radicals to assert the dependence of M.P.s on the opinion of their constituents as a primary constitutional principle. Perhaps the potential political radicalism of the 1740s was not realized because Walpole's fall made little impact on the structure of politics. Though Walpole departed, his system remained to be administered by the Pelhams; and it has been suggested that the ideological consequences of this were disillusionment, cynicism and scepticism,[30] which would have been scarcely conducive to the development of a positive radical reform programme.

And yet there was one occasion at the very beginning of the eighteenth century when the relationship between the people and their representatives was brought into question, and when the arguments of the late-eighteenth-century radicals on this point seem to have been anticipated. That occasion was the Kentish petition of 1701. A Tory majority in the House of Commons considered as offensive a petition from the county of Kent, which expressed support for the king's foreign policy against the inclinations of that majority, and imprisoned five of the organizers. The controversy gave rise to arguments which went beyond the issue of the right to petition, to the point of asserting that the House of Commons must be subject to the people.

The most prominent contributor to the literature was Daniel Defoe with his famous 'Legion' letter, *The History of the Kentish Petition*, and *The Original Power of the Collective Body of the People of England, Examined and Asserted*. Defoe argues that, though the people delegate their executive power to the king, their legislative power to the king, Lords and Commons, and the sovereign judicature to the Lords, the people retain the power of acting in the last resort in defence of their liberties. For 'there must always remain a supreme power in the original to supply, in case of the dissolution of the delegated power'. The outstanding example that Defoe sees as the practical application of this principle was the Glorious Revolution of 1688. Moreover, the people must retain their power of acting in the last resort because Parliaments can and do make mistakes. It is only in the power of the people to act on their own account through petitions to the king and Parliament, or, if need be, through the formation of associations of defence, that the general safety of the people can be guaranteed. To the House of Commons 'all needful powers and privileges are committed to make them capable of acting for the people they represent; and, extremities excepted, they are our last resort. But if they employ those privileges and powers against the people, the reason of those powers is destroyed, the end is inverted, and the power ceases

of course.' Hence, it is reasonable to give M.P.s instructions: 'Instructions
to Members are like the power given to an arbitrator, in which, though
he is left fully and freely to act, yet 'tis in confidence of his honour that
he will think himself bound by the directions he receives from the person
for whom he acts.'[31]

One must be wary, however, of attributing too much radicalism to
Defoe. He does not go deep into constitutional theory. He does not consider, for example, principles of representation; and it is not clear to what
extent in his view M.P.s are to be allowed independence of judgment.
On the one hand, he argues that instructions should be regarded as binding. But, on the other hand, it may be inferred from his argument that,
since the people would only take action on their own in the last resort,
he allows for considerable parliamentary independence in normal con-
ditions. And in his remarks concerning instructions Defoe clearly says
that M.P.s have political free will. Moreover, the view that the people
retain the power to act in the last resort was one to which any Walpolean
Whig could have subscribed in theory. In practice, however, once the
Hanoverian settlement had been secured, Walpolean Whigs preferred to
emphasize that, through the process of election, the people had delegated
all their legislative power to their representatives.[32]

But in the different circumstances of 1701, when the Whigs did not
have a majority in the House of Commons and before the Hanoverian
settlement had been secured, Defoe put the emphasis on the final determining power of the people as evidenced in the Glorious Revolution. And
this emphasis is expressed rhetorically rather than through a rigorous
analysis of the constitutional relationship between the people and the
House of Commons: 'the power of the people has a kind of eternity with
respect to politick duration. Parliaments may cease, but the people remain;
for them they were originally made, by them they are continued and
renewed; from them they receive their power, and to them in reason
they ought to be accountable.'[33] Nor does Defoe go deep into history.
His examples are the recent topical ones of the reign of James II and the
Glorious Revolution. His arguments, indeed, are more theological in tone
than legal or historical. He adapts for his purpose the Protestant principle
that general councils of the Church have erred, and that God, who alone
is infallible, has vested His truth in all his people. In the same way, Parliaments can and do err – *humanum est errare* – and *Vox Dei* is only to be
found in the people.[34] In short, Defoe's tracts were tracts for the times.
He was a Whig propagandist, deeply immersed in party controversy at a
time when the Whigs had stage-managed the Kentish petition and were
'getting up' public opinion on the 1681 pattern.[35]

Even so, it does seem surprising that the issue of the respective rights
of the House of Commons and the people, raised by the controversy of
1701, was not seriously debated again until the late eighteenth century.
Perhaps this can be explained at least in part by the remarkable readiness

of the Whig oligarchy, from the time of Walpole, to surrender to the
force of public feeling on particular issues in order to preserve its power
— as was shown in the case of the Excise Bill of 1733, the Jew Bill of
1753, and perhaps also in the campaign of 'gold boxes' in support of the
elder Pitt in 1757.[36]

It is clear, therefore, that, whereas instructions themselves were not a
constitutional novelty, the meaning injected into them by the late-
eighteenth-century radicals certainly was. The inspiration for the
'doctrine of instructions' cannot be discovered in English constitutional
theory and practice as it had developed since the fifteenth century, nor
in the 'Court versus Country' conflicts of the first half of the eighteenth
century.

It should be noted at this point that, though binding instructions were
alien to the English constitution, the same cannot be said of that of
Scotland, which survived the Union of 1707 until the Reform Act of
1832. Unlike his English counterpart, the Scottish M.P. was bound to
serve the interests and obey the instructions of his constituents. It seems
that the medieval idea of attorneyship in representation, which in England
was transformed into the principle that an M.P. represented the whole
nation, survived unchanged in Scotland.[37] Thus in 1760 Alexander Hume
Campbell, lord clerk register and M.P. for Berwickshire, who was certainly
no radical, was instructed by his constituents on the Scottish militia issue,
and a committee was appointed to correspond with him on the subject of
those instructions. Hume Campbell observed: 'This I apprehend to have
been the regular way of communicating to me the sentiments of my constituents, and to such I shall be particularly attentive.'[38] The observation
is not indicative of any radicalism, but merely acknowledges the peculiarly
Scottish constitutional proprieties.

Nor, in the years following the Union, were Scottish instructions
restricted to purely local or Scottish issues. In 1734 the Duke of Hamilton
and James Erskine of Grange were active in promoting instructions in
support of the bill for restoring triennial elections.[39] In 1739 the freeholders and heritors of Fife instructed Sir John Anstruther of Anstruther
over the whole range of domestic and foreign policy.[40] However, it is very
unlikely that the Scottish political system, which involved only a minute
electorate and which was even more oligarchical in nature than that of
England, made any contribution at all to the development of English
radical ideas — especially in view of Wilkes's xenophobic propaganda
against the Scots in the 1760s. Moreover, Scotsmen themselves seem to
have accepted that their constitution was peculiar to Scotland, and not
relevant to the English 'imperial' system to which all were subject by the
Union. Thus, in his observations on instructions, David Hume makes no
reference to the practices in his native Scotland, with which he must have
been familiar.[41] And the Scot James Burgh was willing to point to the constitutional practices of representative assemblies in Castile, France,

Germany, Switzerland and New England in support of the radical view
of instructions, but not to those of Scotland.[42]

America, on the other hand, was a more likely source of radical inspiration. G. S. Veitch, who pioneered the study of English parliamentary
reform movements in the early years of this century, argued that it was
'the dispute with America which had first led some of them [the radicals]
to examine the doctrine of representation upon which that dispute ultimately turned, and which had converted them, almost insensibly, into
advocates of a reform of Parliament'.[43] In a more recent book on politics
in the 1760s, Professor John Brewer documents the fact that there were
significant ideological exchanges across the Atlantic — the personal connections between English radicals and American patriots, and the exchange
of English and colonial printed propaganda — and suggests that the issue
of representation, which was new in the debate about parliamentary
reform, came into English politics as a consequence of 'ideological contamination' from the colonial debate on taxation and representation in
the 1760s. The cry of 'no taxation without representation', argues Brewer,
could scarcely fail in the English context to raise questions about the
franchise.[44] Could it have been, therefore, that the late-eighteenth-century
English radical view of instructions was a consequence of the same ideological contamination? For in America authoritative instructions were
accepted constitutional practice. It has been shown that colonial assemblies were reproductions of the English House of Commons, but had
diverged from English development. They had begun with seventeenth-
century assumptions, but then had reverted back to medieval forms of
attorneyship in representation. The regular practice of issuing instructions
was a logical progression from this, and was one of the ties which bound
representatives to largely autonomous local communities.[45]

However, though there undoubtedly was a close connection between
English and American radicalism, and though it can be safely assumed that
English radicals were familiar with colonial constitutional practices, there
is no clinching evidence to show that the English radicals simply took the
colonial theory of instructions and applied it to the English context. There
were, on the other hand, specifically English reasons for the emergence of
the 'doctrine of instructions' — as perhaps there were also specifically
English reasons for the emergence of the broader issue of representation[46]
— foremost of which was the controversy surrounding John Wilkes in the
late 1760s. The Middlesex election was different from earlier outbursts of
public feeling — such as the Excise Bill of 1733 or the Jew Bill of 1753 —
in that it provoked a head-on clash between the House of Commons and
the rights of electors. Ultimately the force of public opinion triumphed,
as it had done previously, but not before it had become apparent that a
Commons majority could thwart the wishes of the people. Five times
Wilkes was elected for Middlesex, and each time a Commons majority
denied him his seat. In such circumstances it was but a short though

momentous step for the radicals, who had always held that 'the first principles of power are the people',[47] to insist that here should be a dependence of the elected on the electors.

Thus it was at the beginning of 1769, when Middlesex, Westminster and the City of London instructed their M.P.s to protest against the expulsion of Wilkes from the House of Commons and to press for parliamentary reform, that the new type of campaign of instructions began to develop.[48] This type of campaign included the use of the election pledge, a novel device and part of the 'doctrine of instruction', by which a promise was usually exacted from the candidate, as a condition of his election, to follow the instructions of his constituents and to press for parliamentary reform.[49]

Despite their rhetorical appeals to antique precedents, the radicals could scarcely have been unaware of the novelty of the 'doctrine of instructions'. It seems, however, that they believed such a doctrine to be necessary when a majority of the House of Commons had attempted to override the wishes of electors. The doctrine was regarded by at least one leading radical thinker not so much as a permanent constitutional arrangement, but as an emergency measure by which the House of Commons might be brought back to a position of right-relatedness to the people. Such was the view of Catherine Macaulay, who is credited with having invented the tactic of the election pledge,[50] and who wrote in a pamphlet published in 1775:

> though the obeying every mandate of constituents may, in some very extraordinary conjunction of opinions and circumstances, be wrong, yet at a time when the representatives had affected an entire independency, or rather an absolute sovereignty, over their constituents, this might be a worthy sufficient reason for many worthy men, as a far lesser evil, to submit to an indefinite obligation of obedience.[51]

The new type of campaign characterized the exertions of the radicals at the 1774 general election.[52] Ten years later, the issuing of instructions was widespread enough for a pamphleteer to refer exaggeratedly to 'the prevailing idea that all constituents have a right to instruct their delegates'.[53] Instructions and pledges were a prominent feature at the 1784 general election in constituencies in and around London, where radicalism was strongest. In Middlesex the successful Pittite candidate, William Mainwaring, who received one thousand pounds from the government for his election expenses,[54] pledged 'that the sense of my constituents at all times will be the rule of my conduct, it being my decided opinion that the only meaning of representation is the declaring and supporting the voice of the people in the great council of the nation'.[55] At a meeting of the freeholders on 21 January 1784, which met to vote an address to the throne on the state of public affairs, the substance of John Wilkes's argument was that M.P.s should always obey the will of their constituents.[56] In April, probably at the instigation of either Mainwaring or Wilkes, the nomination meeting adopted a test specifically directed against the Foxite candidate, George Byng. According to one report, Byng refused to subscribe to it, referring to it as an 'ignominious bond'.[57] But Byng later issued a statement complaining that he had been misrepresented.[58] It appears that he was prepared to subscribe to some test, but not one which affected his allegiance in national politics. At the by-election for Southwark in June 1784, the nomination meeting decided unanimously that each candidate should pledge himself to support parliamentary reform, and always to obey the instructions of his constituents or resign his seat.[59] On 19 June, Paul Le Mesurier, a newly elected director of the East India Company, suddenly announced his candidature and his willingness to subscribe to the test. On the 21st he issued his election address, in which he declared his support both for Pitt's administration and for parliamentary reform. Polling began on the 22nd, and Le Mesurier was returned three days later, defeating his Foxite opponent, Sir Richard Hotham, by 935 votes to 924.[60]

Instructions and pledges were also an issue in constituencies outside London in 1784. Radicalism was much in evidence in East Anglia. In the constituencies of the county of Suffolk and the borough of Ipswich, seats were won by men who had made the cause of parliamentary reform an essential part of their election campaigns.[61] Joshua Grigby 'offered his services to the independent freeholders of the county, professing those principles which he had publicly declared, and of his determination on all occasions to abide by their decisions and to act conformable to their wishes'.[62] Charles Alexander Crickitt, who was victorious in Ipswich, pledged 'that I will at all times be ready to receive your instructions and make them rule my conduct in Parliament'.[63] Thomas Coke's refusal to give any pledge, combined with his professed support for the Fox–North coalition, caused him to lose his seat for the county of Norfolk.[64] Instructions and tests were also an issue in Berwick, Cambridgeshire, Canterbury, Essex, Hertfordshire, Northumberland and Oxfordshire, and even in some Welsh constituencies.[65]

The emergence of the 'doctrine of instructions' at the 1784 general election owed much to the activity of the radical reformers, who mostly supported Pitt rather than Fox in national politics. Though Pitt was only a moderate reformer, and never a radical, he had become the leading spokesman in the House of Commons for parliamentary reform, whereas Fox had struck up a political alliance with Lord North, the arch-enemy of reform who had presided over the American War. Further, as in 1769, so in 1784 public opinion was seen to be in conflict with a majority of the House of Commons. Though the king's dismissal of the Fox–North coalition and the appointment of Pitt to office were evidently popular 'without-doors', Pitt's ministry was opposed by a Foxite majority in the

House of Commons between January and the beginning of March 1784. There was, therefore, a coalescence of popular support for Pitt and radical causes.

Instructions, however, were not only used on occasions of acute consti- tutional crisis. Nor, though they were the favourite device of the radicals, were all instructions radical-inspired. In fact, they were most commonly used in the late eighteenth century against unpopular taxes; and there is a more mundane explanation for the issuing of instructions against taxes than the exigence of constitutional crisis or the inspiration of radical ideas. In the early decades of the eighteenth century, the House of Commons had evolved a rule whereby no petition from 'without-doors' should be received against money bills imposing taxes, except from the City of London.[66] This meant that the issuing of instructions was virtually the only means by which public opinion on fiscal measures, outside of the City of London, could be formally expressed. Radical activity apart, it seems that instructions were rarely used when other means of registering opinion were available. The campaign for 'economical' reform in 1780 largely consisted of petitions to the House of Commons. Public support for Pitt's ministry in the first three months of 1784, and again in the winter of 1788–9, was largely expressed through loyal addresses to the throne. Disapproval of Pitt's Irish commercial policy in 1785 was ex- pressed through petitions to the House of Commons. Hence, it is reason- able to suppose that most of those who issued instructions on fiscal matters were chiefly concerned with opposing a particular tax — not neces- sarily with the broader issue of public opinion. Further, though the radicals made a distinctive contribution to the general election of 1784, and though the question of instructions and pledges was one that they had made very much their own, instructions as an election issue would have had a strong appeal to those electors in urban constituencies[67] who sought protection against the ever-increasing number of taxes on goods and services that were being imposed in the 1770s and 1780s.

It is noticeable that, in the case of the receipt tax of 1783, the con- stitutional issue was raised — not in the fact that instructions had been issued against the tax but in the interpretation which some radical M.P.s chose to put upon their instructions. On 11 and 12 June 1783 nine M.P.s opposed the receipt tax on the grounds that their constituents had in- structed them to do so. These were Benjamin Hammet (Taunton), Sir Richard Hotham (Surrey), Sir George Howard (Stamford), James Martin (Tewkesbury), Sir Joseph Mawbey (Surrey), George Onslow (Guildford), John Smyth (Pontefract), Henry Thornton (Southwark) and Sir Cecil Wray (Westminster).[68] Apart from Howard and Onslow, these are recog- nizable as parliamentary reformers, and several of them used the occasion to enunciate radical principles. The constitutional issue of dependence on electors featured prominently in the debate. James Martin gave the instructions that he had received so much weight that he read out to the

House the letter he had received from his constituents 'rather than trouble them with any trifling discourse of his own'. Sir Joseph Mawbey 'contended that every representative was bound to obey his constituents and that the word itself imported as much'. The tone of the debate prompted William Baker to speak. A veteran opponent of the 'doctrine of instructions', he vigorously asserted the principle of parliamentary independence, and declared that he would support the receipt tax despite instructions to the contrary from his constituents in Hertford.[69]

The issue of instructions seems to have dominated the debates on the receipt tax in 1783, and, in at least one constituency, spilled over into the general election. In 1784 Lord John Cavendish lost his seat at York largely because, as chancellor of the Exchequer in the Fox–North coalition ministry, he had been responsible for the introduction of the receipt tax.[70] But it was only a vociferous minority of radical reformers on the one hand, and Burkeian conservatives on the other, who were concerned with the constitutional implications of the issue. Otherwise, it appears that most constituents who issued instructions were concerned simply with the effects of a particular tax; and it is to be strongly suspected that most M.P.s who obeyed instructions were chiefly concerned to be seen to be doing the right thing by their constituents in the press reports of parliamentary proceedings, rather than with any basic constitutional principle. Thus Sir George Howard, a notable courtier who was certainly no radical,[71] was simply playing to an audience in his constituency of Stamford when he declared in one of the receipt tax debates that he 'always considered it as his duty to comply with the instructions of his constituents, and therefore he rose to declare his opposition to the clause of the bill relating to the particular tax'.[72] The same is surely true of the two M.P.s for the borough of Leicester, Charles Loraine Smith and John Macnamara, who were not at all radical reformers, who had been elected with the full support of the traditionally Tory corporation of Leicester in 1784, and who declared their opposition to the receipt tax in June 1784 on the grounds that they had been instructed to do so;[73] similarly, William Windham, who had publicly avowed his opposition to parliamentary reform,[74] but who opposed the shop tax on 30 May 1785 because his constituents had instructed him to do so.[75]

If an M.P. could harmonize his views with those of his constituents on a particular issue, without subscribing to radical notions, then it seems that this was enough. Sir George Yonge, M.P. for Honiton and son of Sir William Yonge who had articulated the orthodox constitutional position on instructions some fifty years earlier,[76] was no radical — albeit an old Chathamite. He was a former office-holder, who held office again in the younger Pitt's ministry. He opposed the receipt tax in 1783 because he was instructed to do so, but made it clear that he was making an exception in this case. He 'declared it was with reluctance that he found himself under the necessity of opposing any tax whatsoever, but he had that day [12 June 1783] received such positive instructions from the whole body of his constituents, that he must vote in favour of the motion for omitting the clause concerning the receipt tax'.[77]

Since instructions were rarely used on party issues in national politics, it was not difficult for an M.P. to obey occasional instructions without formally subscribing to the radical view of the supremacy of public opinion over parliamentary proceedings. Nathaniel Newnham, one of the M.P.s for the City of London and its lord mayor in 1783, laid down his own guideline:

> upon all local questions, upon all oppressive internal taxes, and in every case that related to them in particular, the constituents' instructions ought in his mind to be implicitly obeyed; but where the characters, talents and views of Ministers were the matters under consideration, where measures affecting the general interests of the nation at large were to be discussed and decided upon, then he thought the representative ought to be left to himself.[78]

Newnham was a Foxite, and he was speaking in the Commons after the Pittite popular victory in 1784. Hence, he needed to reconcile his own partisan preferences with the constitutional implications of instructions, It seems likely, however, that this guideline would have satisfied most of those electors who were in the habit of instructing. On the face of it, such a guideline seems close to constitutional orthodoxy, in that M.P.s are to be left to make up their own minds on national issues. But Newnham, rather misleadingly, links 'oppressive internal taxes' with 'local questions'.

Yet taxes proposed in a national budget, though they might affect some localities more than others, could not avoid being national issues. Hence, though instructions against a particular tax might be prompted more by a dislike for the tax than by any predilection for radical ideas — and even without the radical 'doctrine of instructions' being brought into the discussion — the practice of instructing still touched upon a sensitive constitutional area. It had become, after all, the historic right and duty of the House of Commons to vote supplies. If instructions from constituents on fiscal matters were binding on M.P.s, then it followed that M.P.s no longer had the exclusive power of the purse. Hence, as it was unheard of in the eighteenth-century House of Commons to oppose the principle of granting supplies — such opposition would have savoured too much of the disastrous constitutional conflicts of the seventeenth century, and no one wanted a recurrence of that[79] — and as there was consequently a notable reluctance among some M.P.s to oppose taxes proposed by the government, so there was a similar reluctance on the part of others to oppose a tax on the instructions of constituents. Indeed, it almost seems that instructions against a tax sometimes perversely determined M.P.s to vote for it. The respected independent, Thomas Powys, was instructed in 1783 by the towns of Wellingborough and Peterborough in his county constituency of Northamptonshire to oppose the receipt tax. Powys, however, was determined to support the receipt tax on the grounds that the national interest should override the particular wishes of his constituents: 'He was there to vote according to the best of his judgment for the good of the whole community, and not as the local interests of any description of the represented might urge them to instruct him to vote.'[80]

There were, therefore, two new elements in the debate about instructions in the late eighteenth century, both of which raised controversial constitutional points: the radical 'doctrine of instructions' and the increasing use of instructions as a means of registering public hostility to particular taxes. And it was as much the link between instructions and taxes, as an aversion to radical ideas, that ensured that no politician who was a candidate for high office would subscribe to the view that instructions should always be obeyed. The younger Pitt, though a fervent advocate of parliamentary reform between 1781 and 1785, explicitly refuted the doctrine, not only because he wished to disassociate himself from the radical wing of the reform movement but also, one suspects, because he was a minister of finance and well acquainted with the problem of raising new taxes. In an exchange in the House of Commons on 4 February 1785, Thomas Pelham attributed to Pitt the view that M.P.s were bound by the commands of their constituents. Pitt, while explaining that he was a sincere friend to parliamentary reform, went out of his way to refute Pelham's charge:

> the honourable member ascribed to him this doctrine, that representatives are bound to obey the instructions of their constituents; but he assured the honourable gentleman, he never laid down such a doctrine in that House, or elsewhere; nay, that he condemned and reprobated such a principle; he had always said, that though a member was bound to pay particular regard to the local interests of the place which chose him, yet he must consider himself as the representative of the whole kingdom.[81]

Charles James Fox, also a supporter of reform, likewise refuted the 'doctrine of instructions'. In Fox's case, however, it can be seen that he was being pulled in two directions. On the one hand, he was M.P. for Westminster — a populous constituency which was in the habit of instructing its representatives — where he had first been elected with radical support in 1780. And, as the leader in the Commons of the parliamentary opposition to the government, Fox might well have been tempted to follow the opposition practice of earlier times in 'getting up' instructions against Pitt's government.[82] On the other hand, Fox himself was a moderate, rather than a radical, reformer. And having held high office and hoping to do so again, he could scarcely have forgotten that a prominent member of the Fox–North coalition ministry of 1783, Lord John Cavendish, had lost his seat in 1784 because he had rejected the instructions of his constituents to withdraw the receipt tax.[83] In 1785 Fox opposed Pitt's tax on maidservants, not for party-political reasons but because the tax was unpopular in his constituency of Westminster. He sought to explain himself thus in the House of Commons on 10 May 1785, laying particular emphasis on the need for parliamentary independence in fiscal matters:

> [He] felt his own situation exceedingly awkward. He was not one of those who considered the sense of their constituents binding on their conduct in every political proceeding, and of all others he thought that a question of finance that in which an implicit conformity was least to be expected. From the peculiar obligation he owed his constituents, he should hold himself exceedingly ungrateful if he did not pay every deference to their known opinions; and yet, when he stated their opinions to be averse to this proposition, and gave it as one reason for opposing it, he begged it to be considered as only one.[84]

It was probably as much the fate of Lord John Cavendish at York in 1774 as the stand of Burke at Bristol in the same year that ensured that parliamentary independence would be an essential part of the Whiggism of Fox's party, and that henceforth campaigns of instructions would not be espoused by the parliamentary opposition.

In the 1790s, indeed, the question of instructions seems to have entirely disappeared as a political issue. Any kind of public opposition to the government became associated with sedition and Jacobinism, and that effectively eliminated 'non-radical' instructions against government measures. For the radicals themselves, the 'doctrine of instructions' gave way to the great issues of the French Revolution that transformed English radical ideology. With the revival of the debate about parliamentary reform in the first decade of the nineteenth century, there was no revival of the doctrine.[85] Nevertheless, though instructions fell into disuse at the end of the 1780s, the constitutional debate to which they gave rise in the late eighteenth century did not end. At the time of the Great Reform Bill in 1832, pledges once again became a favourite device of radical M.P.s.[86] And, in his *Considerations on Representative Government*, first published in 1861, John Stuart Mill devotes a chapter to the question of whether pledges should be required from M.P.s. In our own time there has been debate about whether it is right that Parliament should decide on issues like capital punishment and entry into the European Economic Community, independently of the wishes of public opinion. And, within the Labour Party, there has been a continuing debate between the radical left, who wish to subject the parliamentary party to some kind of extra-parliamentary party control, and those who argue for the independence of the parliamentary party. The question of the respective rights of electors and representatives, raised by Wilkes and the Middlesex election issue in the 1760s, has never been finally resolved. Perhaps it is in the interests of liberty that the tension should always remain.

NOTES

1. *A Letter to the Right Honourable William Pitt upon the Nature of Parliamentary Representation, its Use and Abuse* (1784), 19.
2. J. Burnby, *Thoughts on the Freedom of Election* (1785), 12.
3. This term 'radical' does not of course belong to eighteenth-century political vocabulary, and strictly speaking should only be used in its nineteenth-century context. However, in common with other historians of the late eighteenth century, I use it to describe those parliamentary reformers associated with Wilkes in the 1760s and who advocated fundamental changes in the electoral system in the 1770s and 1780s. These 'radicals' are to be distinguished from 'moderates', like Christopher Wyvill and the younger William Pitt, who advocated much less drastic schemes of parliamentary reform.
4. L. S. Sutherland, 'Edmund Burke and the relations between Members of Parliament and their constituents', *Studies in Burke and his Time*, x (1968), 1005–21.
5. J. Hatsell, *Precedents of Proceedings in the House of Commons* (1818), II, 76. Onslow's judgment is reproduced in W. C. Costin and J. S. Watson, *The Law and Working of the Constitution: Documents, 1660–1914* (2 vols, 1961), I, 392.
6. D. Hume, *Essays and Treatises on Several Subjects* (1777), 32–3.
7. Quoted in Sutherland, 'Edmund Burke', 1006.
8. *Two Speeches of Thomas Day, Esq., at the General Meetings of the Counties of Cambridge and Essex, Held March 25, and April 25, 1780* (1783), 15.
9. J. Burgh, *Political Disquisitions* (3 vols, 1774–5), I, 204–5.
10. T. F. T. Plucknett, *Taswell-Langmead's English Constitutional History* (1960), 151.
11. See S. B. Chrimes, *English Constitutional Ideas in the Fifteenth Century* (1936), 131; and B. Bailyn, *The Ideological Origins of the American Revolution* (Cambridge, Mass., 1967), 164.
12. M. McKisack, *The Parliamentary Representation of the English Boroughs during the Middle Ages* (1932), 137.
13. D. Hirst, *Representative of the People? Voters and Voting in England under the Early Stuarts* (1975), 161–6.
14. C. S. Emden, *The People and the Constitution* (1956), 12.
15. *Ibid.*, 13; J. R. Jones, *The First Whigs: The Politics of the Exclusion Crisis, 1678–1683* (1961), 166–73.
16. W. A. Speck, *Tory and Whig: The Struggle in the Constituencies, 1701–15* (1970), 29–30.
17. See P. Langford, *The Excise Crisis: Society and Politics in the Age of Walpole* (1975).
18. *The Craftsman* (14 vols, 1731–7), X, 186–7.
19. Cobbett, *Parl. Hist.*, VIII, 1300–1.
20. P. Kelly, 'British and Irish politics in 1785', *EHR*, xc (1975), 547–50.
21. *Cato's Letters: or, Essays on Liberty Civil and Religious and other Important Subjects* (5th edn, 4 vols, 1748), I, 177–82.
22. See *Pamphlets of the American Revolution*, I, ed. B. Bailyn (Cambridge, Mass., 1965), 29. Two of Trenchard's pamphlets were reprinted in *Tracts Published and Distributed Gratis by the Society for Constitutional Information* (1783).
23. See H. T. Dickinson, *Liberty and Property: Political Ideology in Eighteenth-Century Britain* (1977), 188–90.
24. Cobbett, *Parl. Hist.*, IX, 434–5, 444–6, 450–1.
25. *Ibid.*, XIII, 1059–78.
26. C. Robbins, *The Eighteenth-Century Commonwealthman* (New York, 1968), 287.
27. M. M. Goldsmith, 'Faction detected: ideological consequences of Robert Walpole's decline and fall', *History*, lxiv (1979), 7.

28. E. and A. G. Porritt, *The Unreformed House of Commons: Parliamentary Representation before 1832* (2 vols, 1903), I, 268.
29. John Perceval, 2nd Earl of Egmont, *Faction Detected by the Evidence of Facts* (Dublin, 1743), 101.
30. Goldsmith, 'Faction detected', 19.
31. *The Works of Daniel Defoe*, ed. W. Hazlitt (3 vols, 1840–3), III: 'The Original Power of the Collective Body of the People of England Examined and Asserted', 5–15. Each tract in this edition is separately paginated.
32. See John Willes's speech in 1834, quoted above, p. 173.
33. Hazlitt, *Works of Defoe*, III: 'The Original Power . . .', 5–15.
34. *Ibid.*
35. See Sir K. Feiling, *A History of the Tory Party, 1640–1714* (1950), 350–1.
36. See Langford, *The Excise Crisis*; T. W. Perry, *Public Opinion, Propaganda, and Politics in Eighteenth-Century England: A Study of the Jew Bill of 1753* (Harvard, 1962); and P. Langford, 'William Pitt and public opinion, 1757', *EHR, lxxxviii* (1973), 54–80.
37. See the first chapter of W. Ferguson, 'Electoral law and procedure in eighteenth and early nineteenth century Scotland' (Ph.D. thesis, University of Glasgow, 1957).
38. NLS, MS 16713 (Fletcher of Saltoun MSS), f. 135: Alexander Hume Campbell to Lord Milton, 20 Feb. 1760.
39. NLS, MS 7044 (Yester papers), fos 64–5, 73: Duke of Hamilton to the Marquess of Tweeddale, 5 March 1734, and James Erskine to Tweeddale, 11 March 1734.
40. NLS, MS 14522 (Yester Papers), f. 94: copy of a letter from the freeholders and heritors of Fife to Sir John Anstruther, 1739.
41. See above, p. 170.
42. *Ibid.*
43. G. S. Veitch, *The Genesis of Parliamentary Reform* (1913), 43.
44. J. Brewer, *Party, Ideology and Popular Politics at the Accession of George III* (1976), 206–7.
45. See Bailyn, *Ideological Origins*, 164–5; and J. R. Pole, *Political Representation in England and the Origins of the American Republic* (1966), 70–2.
46. It has been suggested that Professor Brewer did not take sufficient account of the indigenous Commonwealthman tradition in the debate concerning representation. See C. H. Hay, 'The making of a radical: the case of James Burgh', *J. of British Studies, xviii* (1979), 100–1.
47. See above, p. 172.
48. Sutherland, 'Edmund Burke', 1010.
49. See G. Rudé, *Wilkes and Liberty* (1962), 194–5; and I. R. Christie, 'The Wilkites and the general election of 1774', in *Myth and Reality in Late-Eighteenth-Century British Politics and Other Papers* (1970), 247–8.
50. See Sutherland, 'Edmund Burke', 1011 n. 20.
51. Catherine Macaulay, *An Address to the People of England, Scotland, and Ireland on the Present Crisis of Affairs* (1775), 18–19. Mrs Macaulay was at this time the leading theoretician of the radicals. See B. B. Schnorrenberg, 'The brood hen of faction: Mrs Macaulay and radical politics, 1765–1775', *Albion, xi* (1979), 44.
52. See above, n. 49.
53. See above, p. 169.
54. *The House of Commons, 1754–90*, ed. Sir L. B. Namier and J. Brooke (3 vols, 1964), I, 335.
55. *Morning Chronicle*, 31 March 1784.
56. *English Chronicle*, 20–2 Jan. 1784.
57. *Morning Herald*, 5 April 1784.
58. *Morning Chronicle*, 12 April 1784.

59. *Ibid.*, 18 June 1784.
60. *Ibid.*, 19 and 21 June 1784.
61. See P. Kelly, 'Radicalism and public opinion in the general election of 1784', *BIHR, xlv* (1972), 77–81.
62. *Bury Post*, 8 April, 1784.
63. *Ipswich Journal*, 3 April 1784.
64. Kelly, 'Radicalism and public opinion', 82–3.
65. *Ibid.*, 75–7, 85–8.
66. See P. D. G. Thomas, *The House of Commons in the Eighteenth Century* (1971), 69–71.
67. In the case of the receipt tax, for example, it seems that it was more difficult to enforce it in country areas than in the towns. An anonymous correspondent wrote to William Pitt in 1784: 'in the neighbourhood where I live, a stamp is not used to one receipt in a hundred. People in the country generally know each other and depend upon honor' (PRO, 30/8, Chatham MSS, 266, fos 152–3). It is noticeable that the parliamentary opposition to the receipt tax came almost entirely from M.P.s representing urban areas.
68. *The Parliamentary Register, 1780–96*, ed. J. Debrett (83 vols, 1775–1804), X, 138, 143, 150–1, 157–61.
69. *Ibid.*, 143, 159–161.
70. See Kelly, 'Radicalism and public opinion', 86–7; and N. C. Phillips, *Yorkshire and English National Politics, 1783–1784* (Christchurch, New Zealand, 1961), 34–6.
71. He was a general who held the office of governor of Chelsea Hospital.
72. *Parliamentary Register*, X, 143.
73. *Ibid.*, XV, 218–19.
74. Kelly, 'Radicalism and public opinion', 81–2.
75. *Parliamentary Register*, XVIII, 411–12: 'he was instructed by his constituents to oppose it, and that their instructions were perfectly consistent with his own private sentiments'.
76. See above, p. 174.
77. *Parliamentary Register*, X, 157.
78. *Ibid.*, XV, 216–17: debate of 18 June 1784.
79. See P. Kelly, 'British parliamentary politics, 1784–1786', *HJ, xvii*, 739–40.
80. *Parliamentary Register*, XII, 334.
81. *Ibid.*, XVII, 58–60.
82. See above, p. 171.
83. See above, n. 70.
84. *Parliamentary Register*, XVIII, 240–2.
85. See J. R. Dinwiddy, 'Parliamentary reform as an issue in English politics, 1800–1810' (Ph.D. thesis, University of London, 1971). There was, indeed, in these years a revival of the older pre-Wilkes brand of 'Patriotism' that had been identified with independence. See Dinwiddy's article, 'Sir Francis Burdett and Burdettite radicalism', *History, lxv* (1980), 25.
86. N. Gash, *Politics in the Age of Peel* (1953), 29.

Index

Abergavenny, George Nevill, 11th lord, 7, 28; George Nevill, 13th lord, 153; John Nevill, 10th lord, 26
Abernathy, G. R., 5
Abingdon, Berks., parliamentary borough of, disputed election, 111–13
Abingdon, Montagu Venables-Bertie, 2nd earl of, 88, 91, 104 n. 16, 135, 141, 146 n. 44, 150 nn. 107, 112, 151 n. 115, 153, 161, 164
Acts:
Confirming and Restraining Ministers (1660), 5; Conventicle (1664), 8; Conventicle (1670), 9, 11; Corporation (1661), 5; Election (1770), 119; Five-Mile (1665), 8; Habeas Corpus (1679), 101; Last Determinations (1729), 115, 118; Regulating Elections (1696), 89; Resumption (1700), 61, 62; Settlement (1701), 52; Test (1678), 3, 12; Uniformity (1662), 5
Addison, Joseph, M.P., 110
Ailesbury, Robert Bruce, 1st earl of, 15, 17, 28
Aislabie, John, M.P., 69 n. 46, 76, 80
Albemarle, George Monck, 1st duke of, 6, 28
Alston, Sir Thomas, M.P., 76
Amersham, Bucks., parliamentary borough of, controverted election, 109
Amsterdam, 59
Andover, viscount, see Berkshire, earl of
Anglesey, Arthur Annesley, 1st earl of, 8, 9, 12, 20, 25, 28; Arthur Annesley, 5th earl of, 135, 140–3, 146 nn. 43, 44, 150 nn. 107, 112, 151 n. 115, 153, 161
Annandale, William Johnston, 1st marquess [S] of, Scottish representative peer (1709–13), 131, 133, 136, 140, 148 n. 77, 153
Anne, Queen, xvi, 96, 99, 102, 103, 134, 136, 137, 139–43, 145 n. 21, 146 n. 36
Annesley, Francis, M.P., trustee to execute the Resumption Act, 63, 74 n. 127
Anstruther, Sir John, M.P., 178
Ardglass, Thomas Cromwell, 3rd earl [I] of, 3rd baron Cromwell, 29; Wingfield Cromwell, 2nd earl [I] of, 2nd baron Cromwell, 26
Argyll, John Campbell, 2nd duke [S] of,

1st earl of Greenwich, 127, 131–3, 137, 140, 141, 145 nn. 32, 33, 146 n. 43, 148 nn. 70–2, 149, n. 82, 150 n. 103, 162, 164
Arlington, Henry Bennet, earl of, baron, 9, 10, 28
army, 59, 60
Arran, Charles Butler, earl [I] of, baron Butler of Weston, 150 n. 103, 159, 163; Richard Butler, earl [I] of, baron Butler of Weston, 28
Arundel, Thomas Howard, 16th earl of, 26
Arundell of Trerice, Richard Arundell, 1st baron, 28
Arundell of Wardour, Henry Arundell, 3rd baron, 7, 14, 15, 26, 28
Ashburnham, John Ashburnham, 3rd baron, 141, 145 n. 30, 153
Ashby, Matthew, cobbler of Aylesbury, 88–90, 92, 94–6, 102
Ashby v. *White*, 87–103
Ashe, Edward, M.P., 76
Ashe, William, M.P., 76
Ashley, baron, see Shaftesbury, earl of
Ashley, Maurice, M.P., 43, 54, 71 n. 77, 80
Ashurst, Henry, M.P., 76
Ashurst, Sir Henry, M.P., 76
Assiento, 142, 143
Astley, Jacob Astley, 3rd baron, 28
Atholl, John Murray, 1st duke [S] of, Scottish representative peer (1710–15), 131, 133, 136, 140, 153, 164
Atterbury, Francis, bishop of Rochester, 125, 139, 159
Aubrey, Sir John, M.P., 80
Audley, baron, see Castlehaven, earl of
Austen, Robert, M.P., 42
Aylesbury, Bucks., 90, 92; Bedford Charity, and trustees of, 88; constables of, 88, 89, 90, 95, 97, 100, 101, 103; parliamentary borough of, 87, 90, 103; parliamentary by-election (1704), 97

Baggs, John, M.P., trustee to execute Resumption Act, 63, 74 n. 127
Baillie, George, M.P., 148 n. 71, 150 n. 96
Bailyn, Bernard, 39
Baker, William, M.P., 169, 183
Balch, George, M.P., 80
Balmerino, John Elphinstone, 4th lord

parliamentary borough of, 174, 180, Members, 170; Thavies Inn, 98; Tower of, 116
Longueville, Talbot Yelverton, viscount de, 127, 146 n. 37, 156
Loraine Smith, Charles, M.P., 183
Lords, House of, xv, xvi, 2, 4–13, 16, 18–20, 41, 47, 87, 90–103, 104 n. 19, 123–6, 128, 130, 132–7, 140–3, 176; Committee of the Whole House, 5, 14; committees, 12; 'Draft Journal' of, 10; *Journals* of, 17, 18, 91, 100
Lorraine, 139, 141
Loudoun, Hugh Campbell, 3rd earl [S] of, Scottish representative peer (1707–31), 131, 133, 136, 140, 145 n. 33, 146 n. 44, 148 nn. 70, 71, 149 n. 94, 150 n. 111, 151 n. 115, 156, 162, 165
Louis XIV, king of France, 60, 64; representatives in London, 64–5
Lovelace, John Lovelace, 2nd baron, 26, 31; John Lovelace, 3rd baron, 16, 18, 31
Lowndes, William, M.P., 41, 93
Lowther, James, M.P., 48, 69 n. 47, 84
Lowther, Robert, M.P., 81
Lucas, Charles Lucas, 2nd baron; 31, John Lucas, 1st baron, 9, 11, 16, 31
Lucy, William, bishop of St David's, 34
Ludlow, Edmund, *Memoirs*, 56, 58
Luttrell, Narcissus, M.P., 47
Lyttelton, George, M.P., 119

Macaulay, Catherine, Mrs, 180
Macclesfield, Charles Gerard, 1st earl of, 20, 31
Mackworth, Sir Humphrey, M.P., 93, 96, 97, 101
Macnamara, John, M.P., 183
Mainwaring, William, M.P., 180, 181
Manchester, Charles Montagu, 4th earl of, 156, 162, 165; Edward Montagu, 2nd earl of, 3, 6, 9, 31; Robert Montagu, 3rd earl of, 15, 18, 31
Manningham, Thomas, bishop of Chichester, 160
Mansel, Thomas Mansel, 1st baron (1712), M.P., 42, 125, 128, 132, 136, 146 n. 40, 151 n. 117, 156
Mar, John Erskine, 6th earl [S] of, Scottish representative peer (1707–15), 131–3, 136, 139, 140, 144, 145 n. 33, 149 n. 82, 156, 162, 165
Marischal, William Keith, 8th earl [S], Scottish representative peer (1710–12), 131, 133, 149 n. 82, 157, 165
Marlborough, Wilts., 115
Marlborough, John Churchill, 1st duke of, 47, 64, 87, 112, 126, 136, 157, 162; Sarah Churchill, duchess of, 109
Marlborough, James Ley, 3rd earl of,

26; William Ley, 4th earl of, 31
Martin, James, M.P., 182
Marvell, Andrew, 'Last Instructions to a Painter', 1
Masham, Mrs Abigail, 140
Masham, Samuel Masham, 1st baron (1712), 125, 128, 132, 136, 146, 157
Mawbey, Sir Joseph, M.P., 182, 183
Maxwell, Henry, M.P., 65
Maynard, Banastre Maynard, 3rd baron, 157; William Maynard, 2nd baron, 25, 31
Maynard, Sir John, M.P., 53
Mayne, Simon, M.P., nominee of earl of Wharton, 88, 89, 90, 103
Mead, Robert, 88, 97, 98
Medlycott, Thomas, M.P., 111
Mew, Peter, bishop of Bath and Wells, 34
Michell, John, M.P., 43
Middlesex, parliamentary shire of, 179, 180
Middlesex, Lionel Cranfield, 3rd earl of, 25
Middleton, Thomas Willoughby, 1st baron (1712), 125, 128, 132, 136, 146 nn. 40, 43, 157
Mill, John Stuart, *Considerations on Representative Government*, 186
Mitchell, Robert, M.P., 77
Mohun, Charles Mohun, 3rd baron, 15, 31; Charles Mohun, 4th baron, 129, 147 nn. 50, 56, 157; Warwick Mohun, 2nd baron, 26
Molesworth, Jack, 51
Molesworth, Robert, M.P., 38, 39, 51, 54, 56, 59, 62, 63, 65, 73 n. 121, 83 n. 26; *Account of Denmark . . . in . . . 1692*, 59; *Principles of a Real Whig*, 51
Mompesson, Charles, M.P., 77
Monmouth, Henry Carey, 2nd earl of, 26
Monmouth, James Crofts, duke of, 17, 20, 31
Monmouthshire, 48
Monoux, Sir Philip, M.P., 81, 83 nn. 16, 22
Montagu, Edward, M.P., 77
Montagu, Edward Montagu, 2nd baron, 7, 25, 31; John Montagu, 2nd duke of, 156, 162
Montagu, Francis Browne, 3rd viscount, 26, 31; Henry Browne, 5th viscount, 145 n. 24
Montagu, James, M.P., 98–100, 103
Montrose, James Graham, 1st duke [S] of, 132, 149 n. 81
Moore, Arthur, M.P., 62, 143
Moore, John, bishop of Ely, 160
Mordaunt, Charles Mordaunt, 2nd viscount, 31; John Mordaunt, 1st viscount, 10, 31

Morgan, Anthony, M.P., 83 n. 17
Morgan, John, M.P., 47, 48, 69 n. 47, 81, 83 n. 17
Morgan, Mr, 83 n. 17
Morice, Humphry, M.P., 43
Morice, John, M.P., 77
Morice, Sir Nicholas, M.P., 43, 44
Morley, George, bishop of Winchester, 34
Morley, Thomas Parker, 15th lord, 7, 14, 15, 26, 31
Mountjoy, Baron, *see* Windsor of Black-castle, viscount
Mowbray, Henry Howard, lord, 31
Moyle, Walter, M.P., 38, 39, 53, 56, 60-2; (with John Trenchard), *Argument showing that a Standing Army is inconsistent with Free Government*, 56, 58
Moyser, John, M.P., 81
Mulgrave, earl of,*see* Buckingham, duke of
Musgrave, Sir Christopher, M.P., 72 n. 105

Namier, Sir Lewis, 39, 42, 44
Naples, 54
navy, 59
Neville, Grey, M.P., 51, 81
Neville, Richard, M.P., 48, 69 n. 47
Newcastle, dukedom of, 145 n. 20
Newcastle, Henry Cavendish, 2nd duke of, 32; William Cavendish, 1st duke of, marquess of, 23 n. 65, 26, 31
Newcastle, John Holles (d. 1711), duke of, lord privy seal, 42, 111, 125-7, 144 nn. 9, 16, 17, 145 n. 29, 157, 162; daughter of, 140
New England, representative institutions, 170, 179
New Model Army, 58
Newnham, Nathaniel, M.P., 184
Newnham, Thomas, M.P., 115
Newport, Henry Blount, 4th earl of, 32; Mountjoy Blount, 1st earl of, 7, 26, 32
Newport, Francis Newport, viscount, 16, 19, 32; Richard Newport, *styled* lord, M.P., 53
Newtown, Isle of Wight, parliamentary borough of, disputed election (1727), 114, 120 n. 32
Nicolini, Signor, 111
Nicolson, William, bishop of Carlisle, 160, 160 n. 4
Nocton, Lincs., 42
Norfolk, parliamentary shire of, 181
Norreys, James Bertie, 5th lord, 26, 32
North, Dudley North, 3rd lord, 25; Dudley North, 4th lord, 15, 32; Frederick North, *styled* lord, M.P., 181

North and Grey, Charles North, 5th and 1st lord, Lord Grey of Rolleston, 15, 17, 32; William North, 6th and 2nd lord, 142, 157
Northampton, George Compton, 4th earl of, 91, 104 n. 16, 157, 162; James Compton, 3rd earl of, 20, 22 n. 46, 26, 32
Northamptonshire, parliamentary shire of, 184
Northesk, David Carnegie, 4th earl [S] of, Scottish representative peer (1708-15), 131, 133, 136, 140, 157, 165
Northumberland, parliamentary shire of, 181
Northumberland, Charles Fitzroy, duke of, 150 n. 103, 156, 162, 165
Northumberland, Algernon Percy, 4th earl of, 25
Norwich, Norf., parliamentary borough of, election petition (1702), 107
Norwich, Charles Goring, 2nd earl (1663) of, *styled* Lord Goring, 9, 26, 32
Norwich, Henry Howard, earl of, 15, 32
Nottingham, Daniel Finch, 2nd earl of, 90, 97, 127, 134, 135, 141, 142, 146 n. 44, 153, 157
Nottingham, Charles Howard, 3rd earl of, 25, 32
Nutley, Richard, 63

Oates, Titus, 98
October Club, 43, 65
Onslow family, 43
Onslow, Arthur, M.P., speaker of the House of Commons, 114, 170
Onslow, Foot, M.P., 77
Onslow, George, M.P., 182
Onslow, Sir Richard, M.P., 48, 50-2, 62, 68 n. 32, 69 nn. 46, 47, 77, 81
Onslow, Thomas, M.P., 51, 69 n. 47, 70 n. 64, 81
Orfeur, John, 113
Orford, Suff., parliamentary borough of, 49
Orford, Edward Russell, earl of, 87, 157
Orkney, Elizabeth Hamilton, countess of, 61; George Hamilton, earl [S] of, Scottish representative peer (1708-37), 131, 133, 136, 140, 149 n. 94, 150 n. 111, 157, 162; proxy of, 148 n. 71
Ormond, James Butler, 1st duke of, 32; James Butler, 2nd duke of, 137, 157, 162, 165
Orrery, Charles Boyle, 4th earl [I] of, Baron Boyle of Marston (1711), 125, 128, 141, 144 n. 18, 154, 165
Osborne, Peregrine Hyde, lord, 128, 157